PRIME TIME

EMERIL

PRIME TIME

EMERIL

MORE TV DINNERS
FROM AMERICA'S
FAVORITE CHEF
EMERIL LAGASSE

WM

WILLIAM MORROW
75 YEARS OF PUBLISHING
An Imprint of HarperCollins*Publishers*

Other books by Emeril Lagasse

Every Day's a Party
with Felicia Willett and Marcelle Bienvenu (1999)

Emeril's TV Dinners
with Felicia Willett and Marcelle Bienvenu (1998)

Emeril's Creole Christmas
with Marcelle Bienvenu (1997)

Louisiana Real & Rustic
with Marcelle Bienvenu (1996)

New New Orleans Cooking
with Jessie Tirsch (1993)

FIRST EDITION

Designed by Jill Armus

Photographs by Quentin Bacon

Printed on acid-free paper

Library of Congress Cataloging-in-Publication Data
Lagasse, Emeril.
Prime time emeril
: more TV dinners from America's favorite chef /
Emeril Lagasse—

1st ed.
p.   cm.
Includes index.
ISBN 0-06-018536-8 (hc.)
1. Cookery.   I. Title.

TX714 .L33524   2001
641.5—dc21
2001030851

01   02   03   04   05   10   9   8   7   6   5   4   3   2   1

DEDICATION

Here's to all the special people at Homebase, our restaurants, the Food Network, and *Good Morning America*, who had the dream and belief to make it what it is, but to be committed to where it's going.

To my wife, Alden, for her constant complete support.

And to the people, viewers, fans, supporters, who believe that a life surrounded by good food and wine is to be enjoyed by everyone.

Food of love!

CONTENTS

FIRST AND FOREMOST, I OFFER THANKS TO MY FAMILY—MY DARLING WIFE, ALDEN; MR. JOHN AND HILDA, MY PARENTS; JESSICA AND JILLIAN, MY DAUGHTERS, WHOM I ABSOLUTELY ADORE; AND MARK, MY BROTHER, AND DELORES, MY SISTER, WHO MEAN A GREAT DEAL TO ME.

Thanks very much to:

Marcelle Bienvenu

Rock-O-Daddy

Trevor Wisdom

David McCelvey

Charlotte Armstrong

Alain Joseph

Marti Dalton

Mara Warner

Quentin Bacon, for his incredible talents and extraordinary photographs

Tina Rupp

And to all the folks at William Morrow/HarperCollins:

Jane Friedman, my publisher

Harriet Bell, my patient editor and dear friend

Karen Ferries, editorial assistant

Jill Armus, book designer

Leah Carlson-Stanisic, design director

William Ruoto, interior designer

Roberto de Vicq de Cumptich, for the great jacket design

Ann Cahn, special projects production editor

Karen Lumley, production manager

Carrie Weinberg, super friend and super publicist

ACKNOWLEDGMENTS

And to my right hands and my consiglieri in all matters, Eric Linquest, Tony Cruz, and Mauricio Andrade

The managers and staffs at Emeril's, NOLA, Emeril's Delmonico Restaurant and Bar in New Orleans, Emeril's New Orleans Fish House and Delmonico's Steak House in Las Vegas, and Emeril's in Orlando

All of you who make it happen every day, chefs de cuisine Chris Wilson, Joel Morgan, Bernard Carmouche, Sean Roe, Neal Swidler, and Christian Czerwonka, and pastry chefs Lou Lynch and Joe Trull

All of our great sommeliers, and to all the folks whom I love at Homebase

Judy Girard, president of the Food Network; my family at Scripps-Howard; the incredible teams of *Emeril Live* and the new *Essence of Emeril*—you guys are great!

Karen Katz, my executive producer extraordinaire, and her brilliant husband, Dan, for all his support

Susan Stockton, a dear friend and a great chef to boot

Rochelle Brown

Our little dynamo in a small package, Jill Novatt

The awesome Food Network kitchen staff, Leslie Orlandini, Emily Rieger, Robert Bleifer, Sal Passalacqua, and Derek Flynn, who always make it happen

Michael Schear, director extraordinaire

Janet Arena, for always making me look good

Patricia LaMorte, for keeping it all together

And give it up for Doc Gibbs and Cliff, everybody!

Margo Baumgart, my producer at *Good Morning America* and everyone else at *Good Morning America*

THE FOOD OF LOVE

THIS LAST DECADE HAS BEEN AMAZING. FROM OPENING EMERIL'S, MY FIRST RESTAURANT, IN NEW ORLEANS BACK IN 1990 TO THE FILMING OF MY 1,000TH SHOW ON THE FOOD NETWORK, IT'S BEEN AN UNBELIEVABLE EVOLUTION.

Avenues for touching people's lives have opened wide for me, and I truly feel like a food ambassador. Nothing makes me happier than getting people involved with food, excited about food, and cooking food.

Evolution is really the key word for everybody I work with. It's what we've truly done these past ten years, and something we're all grateful for. We're grateful to our clientele, our fans, our families, and our friends. And, more than anything else, the members of the team are grateful to each other and committed to taking everything to higher levels and to keep kicking up things another notch.

A good illustration of this evolution is where my Food Network shows are now. For me, there's nothing like *Emeril Live*. Working with a live audience, a live band, and special musical and cooking guests, all while doing some serious cooking, is quite a challenge. We aim for a wide range of subjects, covering as much ground as possible within the time allotted. On the early episodes, our emphasis was on educating people, teaching folks how to prepare stocks, cook a roux, season dishes, and so on. But now, with 1,000 shows behind us, our audience has evolved and grown, and viewers are ready to explore new techniques and ingredients with us.

Even though we like to wow everybody on *Emeril Live*, the show is really all about the versatility of food, and the joy of making that food and sharing it with others. With a little imagination, everybody can kick up their food to notches unknown. Food is fun, and food is meant for sharing. It's okay to play with your food—be innovative, kick it up with spices, with sauces, with fillings, with toppings. Be imaginative. Go beyond the basics. Have fun.

Then there's the new *Essence of Emeril* show. It has evolved (there's that word again!) into something completely different from what it was originally planned to be. The show is shorter than *Emeril Live*, moves at a quicker pace, and offers an in-depth exploration of a single subject, such as cooking *en papillote* (in parchment paper), or making *pâte à choux*, or choux pastry, the puffy pastry used in savory and sweet profiteroles,

INTRODUCTION

gougères, and éclairs. I want you to be at ease with making homemade pâtés or consommés, pickling, and home smoking. I want you to be familiar with culinary terminology, with terms such as *gastrique*, or "equal parts sugar and vinegar reduced to a syrup consistency," and unfamiliar ingredients such as foie gras and duck confit. I want to inspire people to cook with unusual, perhaps expensive ingredients that might be intimidating, such as calves' sweetbreads, saffron, and caviar.

I want you to look beyond the usual fare you prepare day in, day out and challenge yourself to discover new ways to cook. Most of all, I want you to enjoy the process as much as the end result. As I was saying, evolution is a beautiful thing.

But if there's one message I hope you take from both shows, as well as my *Good Morning America* appearances each Friday and my cookbooks, it is that food is meant to be shared. I strongly believe that the more time families and friends spend together cooking and eating, the stronger those family ties and friendships will become. From day one, my goal has been to be a positive influence on the family table. With everybody in the family as busy as they are today, what with balancing schedules, work, car pools, soccer games, and all the other activities, there's nothing like sitting down together to a meal of interesting, satisfying food to catch up on the day's news. And sitting down to a meal that the whole gang has cooked together is even more gratifying.

I receive tons (literally) of mail from people who tune in to my television shows. I hear from people who became interested in cooking as a result of my shows—from firemen and police officers to grandmothers and kids, from all cultures and all walks of life. They've helped me realize that food is a universal connection. Just as I've inspired them, they have inspired me to discover and develop new dishes that they enjoy preparing and sharing at home. Whether it is a simple soup, a creative salad with a special dressing, or a perfect roast chicken, I want to keep you excited about food and all of its limitless possibilities.

The five-to-six-minute pieces on *Good Morning America*'s Friday segments are a prime example of spreading this excitement. The "Pie of Emeril's Eye" recipe contest featured on the show resulted in an overwhelming 500,000 letters and entries. Wow! And that was just for pies! We received entries from men, women, and children from every corner of the United States. Some recipes had been family favorites for generations; others were created just for the contest. This excitement is what really keeps me going and evolving, and keeps me excited about where we're going with food.

So where *are* we going?

When I went to Indiana for the *Emeril Live* "Kick Up Your School Cafeteria" program, it was unbelievable to see kids so excited about a chef and what he was cooking. Much of my inspiration now comes from young people who are eight, ten, fourteen years old. They tell me what they like to cook and eat, and I encourage them with new recipes.

Just imagine what this interest in food will do to our markets, our restaurants, and food shows ten years from now. My prediction is that the culinary arts will only improve, as people demand better produce at markets, unique restaurants with innovative menus, and more dynamic food shows.

As I continue honing my culinary craft, the beauty of simplicity becomes more and more apparent to me. There is nothing better than simple ingredients properly handled when they are at their seasonal best. To cook great food, you have to have great ingredients, but that doesn't mean you have to blow a week's salary on the most expensive cut of meat or the most exotic vegetables. It does mean taking a simple ingredient such as rice and elevating it to a tasty, seasoned dish that you can share, like the Portuguese Rice and Salt Cod Salad, adding salt cod, tomatoes, bell peppers, peas, green onions, and more, so that the ingredients marry so well together you have the ultimate rice dish. It means combining garden-fresh lettuce with hazelnuts and goat cheese for the perfect salad.

This is what I mean when I talk about the food of love. It's the extra attention you give a dish, not just kicking it up, but knowing when it's been kicked up enough. It means seasoning both sides of a sliced tomato. It means preparing homemade stocks, marinating meats before grilling them, taking the time to tie up some herbs for a bouquet garni to add to soup. It's a common-sense approach to making uncommonly tasty dishes.

It's important for me to tell you that as we enter a new decade, our team is doing what we love to do. The enthusiasm we bring to the kitchen is what keeps our thinking fresh. We don't have an old trunk in the attic that we just open up to pull out recipes. We go through a creative process to decide what we think the audience wants, and we brainstorm food ideas and topics. We take seasonal shows under consideration, and whether big events are coming up, such as Valentine's Day, the Super Bowl, or my favorite, Mardi Gras. The shows are written to be fun and informative. The recipes are tested and tasted so they're accurate and easy for you to prepare at home. And we use that very same process when creating a new cookbook.

I'm blessed to be surrounded by and working with an amazing group of creative, focused, passionate people. When you're part of such a talented team, it's so much fun to produce the food of love.

BASIC

the recipes

I've said it before, and I'll keep on saying it, you gotta have homemade stocks for making flavorful sauces and soups. So, once again, I'm telling you how to make them. Also included in this chapter are other basic recipes that you should have on hand. For instance, make some Basic Beans (white or black) for quick appetizers or as additions to soups. ■ Since Tomato Sauce is so versatile, go ahead and make a batch or two on a weekend, and store it in the freezer for pastas and sauces. I'm not kidding! You won't believe how many times I've been able to whip up impromptu meals for my family and friends with this sauce. ■ The other basics, Bouquet Garni, Mayonnaise, and the Roasted Garlic Purée, will make your food so much better. And, they're really all simple and easy once you give them a try.

CHICKEN STOCK

MAKES 3 QUARTS

On the first *Essence of Emeril* shows, every time I'd mention making stock at home, viewers thought I was asking them to build a rocket ship. But as people become more comfortable with cooking, I find that their attitudes about making home-made stock are changing. Here's a simple recipe for a primary staple that no kitchen should be without. Chicken stock is the basis for everything from the simplest soups to elegant sauces. Two secrets: Keep the stock at a simmer, and skim the foam as instructed.

4 pounds chicken parts, such as wings, backs, carcasses, and necks, rinsed in cool water
2 cups coarsely chopped yellow onions
1 cup coarsely chopped carrots
1 cup coarsely chopped celery
3 garlic cloves, smashed with the side of a heavy knife
4 bay leaves
1 teaspoon whole black peppercorns
2 teaspoons salt
1 teaspoon dried thyme
½ teaspoon dried rosemary
½ teaspoon dried oregano

1. PUT all the ingredients in a stockpot. Add enough cold water to cover the bones by 1 inch. Bring to a boil over high heat. Reduce the heat to medium-low and simmer, uncovered, for 2 to 3 hours, occasionally skimming off the foam that forms on the surface.

2. STRAIN through a fine-mesh strainer into a large bowl. Cool completely. Cover tightly and refrigerate. (The stock can be refrigerated for up to three days. Or freeze in airtight containers for up to two months.)

BROWN CHICKEN STOCK

MAKES 2 QUARTS

When I want a more intensely flavored stock to use for rich sauces, I make this one. Roasting the chicken parts and the vegetables before simmering them in the water results in a richer stock. Use this for the Pan-Seared Squab with Dried Cherry Reduction (page 192) and other recipes to add a more robust taste.

1. PREHEAT the oven to 375°F.

2. LAYER the chicken parts in the bottom of a very large roasting pan. Roast until browned, turning halfway through roasting, about 2 hours.

3. REMOVE the pan from the oven. Add the onions, carrots, celery, and garlic and stir to mix well. Continue roasting until the vegetables soften, about 45 minutes.

4. TRANSFER the contents of the pan to a large heavy stockpot. Place the roasting pan on two burners on the stove over medium-high heat. Pour the wine into the roasting pan and stir with a wooden spoon to deglaze and dislodge any browned bits on the bottom of the pan. Pour the hot wine mixture into the stockpot. Add the tomato paste, parsley, thyme, bay leaves, peppercorns, and enough cold water to cover by 1 inch.

5. BRING to a boil over medium-high heat. Reduce the heat to medium-low and simmer, uncovered, for 4 hours, skimming from time to time to remove the foam that forms on the surface.

6. STRAIN through a fine-mesh strainer into a large bowl. Cool completely. Cover and refrigerate. (The stock can be refrigerated for up to three days. Or freeze in airtight containers for up to two months.)

4 pounds chicken parts, such as wings, backs, carcasses, and necks, rinsed in cool water
1 cup coarsely chopped yellow onions
½ cup coarsely chopped carrots
½ cup coarsely chopped celery
5 garlic cloves, smashed with the side of a heavy knife
1 cup dry red wine
One 6-ounce can tomato paste
5 sprigs fresh parsley
5 sprigs fresh thyme or ½ teaspoon dried thyme
2 bay leaves
1 teaspoon whole black peppercorns

VEAL STOCK

Use this hearty stock in dishes like the Tuna of Love (page 97) to give them an added depth of flavor. Ask your butcher for a bag of veal bones.

4 pounds veal bones with some meat attached, sawed into 2-inch pieces (have the butcher do this)
2 cups coarsely chopped yellow onions
1 cup coarsely chopped carrots
1 cup coarsely chopped celery
5 garlic cloves, smashed with the side of a heavy knife
¼ cup tomato paste
2 cups dry red wine
4 bay leaves
1 teaspoon dried thyme
1 teaspoon whole black peppercorns
1 teaspoon salt

1. PREHEAT the oven to 375°F.

2. SPREAD the bones in a large roasting pan. Roast, turning occasionally, until golden brown, about 1 hour.

3. REMOVE the pan from the oven and spread the onions, carrots, celery, and garlic over the bones. Smear the tomato paste over the vegetables and return the pan to the oven. Roast for another 45 minutes and remove the pan. Pour off the fat from the pan.

4. PLACE the pan over medium heat on the stove and pour the wine over the vegetables and bones. Using a wooden spoon, deglaze, scraping the bottom of the pan for browned bits. Put everything into a large stockpot. Add the remaining ingredients. Bring to a boil over high heat, skimming off the foam that forms on the top. Reduce the heat to medium-low and simmer, uncovered, for 8 hours, skimming occasionally.

5. LADLE the stock through a fine mesh strainer into a large bowl, taking care not to stir the stock. Cool completely. Cover and refrigerate. (The stock can be refrigerated for up to three days. Or freeze in airtight containers for up to two months.)

FISH STOCK

MAKES 1 GALLON

The secret to a clear, flavorful fish stock is to use fresh bones from a variety of white-fleshed fish, such as cod, flounder, snapper, trout and/or sole. Most fish markets will be glad to give you a few pounds of bones and heads. Rinse them well before using to remove any blood or impurities. Do not use bones from oily fish, such as pompano, redfish, salmon, mackerel, or bluefish. I use this stock to enrich soups such as the Corn and Crab Bisque (page 49).

1. **RINSE** the fish bones and heads well in a large colander under cold running water.

2. **PUT** all of the ingredients in a stockpot. Add enough cold water to cover by 1 inch. Bring to a boil over high heat. Lower the heat to medium-low and simmer, uncovered, for 1 hour, skimming occasionally to remove the foam that forms on the surface.

3. **LADLE** through a fine-mesh strainer into a large bowl. Cool completely. Cover and refrigerate. (The stock can be refrigerated for up to three days. Or freeze in airtight containers for up to two months.)

2½ pounds fish bones and heads, from any white-fleshed fish
1 cup dry white wine
1 cup coarsely chopped yellow onions
½ cup coarsely chopped celery
½ cup coarsely chopped carrots
3 garlic cloves, smashed with the side of a heavy knife
1 lemon, quartered
3 tablespoons fresh lemon juice
2 teaspoons salt
3 bay leaves
1 teaspoon whole black peppercorns
1 teaspoon dried thyme

SHRIMP STOCK

Shrimp stock is used to enrich the barbecue sauce base for the Barbecued Oysters with Rosemary Biscuits (page 96) and the lobster sauce in the Lobster Domes (page 100). It also imparts a depth of flavor to seafood gumbo and some chowders. You're in luck if you live in Louisiana or on the Gulf of Mexico, where fresh shrimp are available with heads and shells. Elsewhere, most shrimp are sold frozen without the heads. When you peel shrimp, store the shells in a plastic bag in the freezer until you have enough to make this stock.

1 pound shrimp shells and/or heads
1 cup coarsely chopped yellow onions
½ cup coarsely chopped celery
½ cup coarsely chopped carrots
3 garlic cloves, smashed with the side of a heavy knife
3 bay leaves
2 teaspoons salt
1 teaspoon whole black peppercorns
1 teaspoon dried thyme

1. RINSE the shrimp shells and heads in a large colander under cold running water.

2. PUT all the ingredients in a heavy medium stockpot. Add enough water to cover by 1 inch. Bring to a boil over high heat, skimming from time to time to remove the foam that forms on the surface. Reduce the heat to medium-low. Simmer for 45 minutes.

3. STRAIN through a fine-mesh strainer into a large bowl. Cool completely. Cover and refrigerate. (The stock can be refrigerated for up to three days. Or freeze in airtight containers for up to two months.)

BOUQUET GARNI

MAKES 1 BOUQUET

This little bundle of herbs is just the ticket for flavoring soups and stews. Using cheesecloth to keep everything together means the bag, or bouquet, can easily be pulled out without having to strain the dish, or pick through it to remove the bay leaves and herb stems. I use a bouquet garni in the Portuguese Kale and Clam Soup (page 138). And depending on what you're cooking, you can vary the ingredients to include other herbs such as rosemary or sage.

PUT all the ingredients in the center of a 6-inch square of cheesecloth. Bring the corners together and tie securely with kitchen twine. Use as directed.

5 sprigs fresh thyme
2 bay leaves
10 whole black peppercorns
3 sprigs fresh parsley

TOMATO SAUCE

MAKES 2½ QUARTS

When making pizza, this is the way to go . . . with homemade tomato sauce! Prepare this when you have some time one weekend, and then freeze the sauce in 1- or 2-cup portions, or refrigerate up to 5 days. Use it on pizza or as a pasta topping, jazzing it up to suit your taste with some browned ground meat or sausage, or sautéed bell peppers and celery for a Creole kind of thing. You can also use this sauce on the Portuguese Chorizo Pizza (page 147).

3 tablespoons extra-virgin
  olive oil
2 cups chopped yellow onions
½ cup chopped carrots
½ cup chopped celery
½ teaspoon salt, plus more to
  taste
¼ teaspoon cayenne
¼ cup thinly sliced garlic
  (5 to 6 cloves)
1 cup dry red wine
Four 15-ounce cans tomato sauce
4 cups Chicken Stock (page 2)
  or canned low-sodium chicken
  broth
One 28-ounce can crushed,
  peeled tomatoes
One 15-ounce can whole
  tomatoes
One 6-ounce can tomato paste
1 tablespoon Emeril's Italian
  Essence
1 tablespoon sugar (optional)
½ teaspoon crushed red pepper
  flakes

1. HEAT the oil in a large heavy stockpot over medium-high heat. Add the onions, carrots, and celery and season with the salt and cayenne. Cook, stirring often, until the onions are soft and golden, about 5 minutes. Add the garlic and stir until fragrant, about 1 minute. Add the red wine and cook until reduced by half, about 5 minutes.

2. ADD the tomato sauce, stock, crushed tomatoes, whole tomatoes, tomato paste, Essence, sugar, and crushed red pepper flakes. Increase the heat to high and bring to a boil. Reduce the heat to medium-low. Simmer, uncovered, stirring occasionally, until reduced nearly by half, about 3 hours. Season with additional salt to taste.

CREOLE SEASONING

The secret to Louisiana cooking is seasoning, and every cook or chef prefers to create his or her own. Some like theirs with more heat; others prefer more herbs. Here's a recipe for making your own, which is based on my Emeril's Original Essence, now available in supermarkets and gourmet shops. If you make your own, be sure to use new herbs and spices. There's nothing worse than ingredients that have been sitting on your spice rack for years; they have no flavor. No matter which one you use—your version or mine—this is the secret ingredient that kicks everything up. Double or triple the recipe as you wish, because you'll find plenty of ways to use it.

COMBINE all the ingredients thoroughly in a bowl. Store in an airtight container away from light. Use within three months.

- 2½ tablespoons paprika
- 2 tablespoons salt
- 2 tablespoons garlic powder
- 1 tablespoon freshly ground black pepper
- 1 tablespoon onion powder
- 1 tablespoon cayenne
- 1 tablespoon dried oregano
- 1 tablespoon dried thyme

PIZZA DOUGH

As you might have noticed, I have an infectious love for kids and have done lots of kid shows on the network. Every kid likes pizzas, and making them sure is fun—even my wild pizza-making experience with my friend Elmo on *Sesame Street*! For a great pizza, it's all in the dough and the quality of the toppings. Just add whatever you like best!

1 cup warm (110°F) water
One ¼-ounce envelope active
  dry yeast
1 tablespoon plus 1½ teaspoons
  extra-virgin olive oil
3 cups bleached all-purpose flour
1 teaspoon salt

1. POUR the warm water into a large bowl. Add the yeast and let stand for 3 minutes, then whisk until the yeast is dissolved. Stir 1 tablespoon of the oil into the yeast mixture.

2. ADD 1½ cups of the flour and the salt, mixing by hand until it is all incorporated and the mixture is smooth. Continue adding the flour, ¼ cup at a time, working the dough after each addition, until all the flour is incorporated but the dough is still slightly sticky. Turn the dough out onto a lightly floured surface and knead for 3 minutes.

3. OIL a large mixing bowl with the remaining olive oil. Place the dough in the bowl and turn to oil all sides. Cover the bowl with plastic wrap and set in a warm, draft-free place until the dough nearly doubles in size, 1 to 1½ hours.

4. REMOVE the dough from the bowl and briefly knead, separating into two equal-size disks. Place the dough on a lightly oiled baking sheet, cover with plastic wrap, and set in a warm, draft-free place to rest for 15 minutes. Use as directed.

ROASTED GARLIC PURÉE

MAKES ABOUT 1 CUP

This can be used as a base for soups or spreads, or, instead of butter, spread on bread. Just keep it tightly covered in the refrigerator for up to 2 weeks. And, yes, I mean ten heads, not cloves, of garlic.

1. PREHEAT the oven to 325°F. Line a baking sheet with parchment paper or aluminum foil.

2. CUT the top quarter off each garlic head so the cloves are exposed. Place cut side up on the prepared baking sheet. Drizzle the oil over the garlic and season lightly with the salt and pepper. Turn the garlic cut side down. Roast until the cloves are soft and golden brown, 1 to 1¼ hours.

3. LET the garlic cool. Squeeze the soft garlic flesh from each head into a bowl. Mash the flesh with a fork to blend it into a purée. (The purée can be stored in an airtight container in the refrigerator for up to two weeks.)

10 heads garlic
  (about 1½ pounds)
¼ cup extra-virgin olive oil
½ teaspoon salt
¼ teaspoon freshly ground black
  pepper

MAYONNAISE

MAKES ABOUT 1¼ CUPS

There's nothing like a sandwich or salad that's been dressed with the fresh, bright, lemony flavor of homemade mayonnaise. If you like, kick this up with a bit of Original Essence or cayenne for a spicier sauce. Or add minced fresh garlic or some Roasted Garlic Purée (page 11) to make aïoli, a garlicky mayonnaise that often accompanies fish and vegetables such as steamed artichokes and asparagus. I use this mayonnaise in the Hot Corn Dip (page 30).

1 large egg, at room temperature
1 tablespoon fresh lemon juice
1 cup olive oil
½ teaspoon salt
⅛ teaspoon freshly ground black pepper
⅛ teaspoon cayenne (optional)

COMBINE the egg and lemon juice in a food processor or blender and process for 10 seconds. With the processor running, slowly pour in the oil. Stop once the mixture has thickened. Add the salt, black pepper, and the cayenne if using, and pulse once or twice to blend. Transfer to an airtight container and refrigerate for at least 30 minutes before using. (The mayonnaise can be stored in the refrigerator for up to 24 hours.)

MAKING MAYO

With a blender or food processor, you can make mayo in minutes. But since mayo contains raw eggs, there are some precautions to take so no one gets sick. First of all, always buy your eggs from a store or market with a fast turnover. Store eggs in the refrigerator on a shelf, where it's cooler, not on the door. Don't use eggs past the expiration date. And don't serve mayonnaise or anything with raw eggs to small children, the elderly, or those who have health problems.

BASIC BEANS

MAKES ABOUT 3½ CUPS

This basic procedure can be followed for either black or white beans. The black beans can be added to other dishes, such as the Black Bean and Roasted Pepper Salsa (page 200) or the Turkey Chili (page 189). Or to make a hearty black bean dish, cook a chopped medium onion and a chopped medium red or green bell pepper in a little oil, add some diced ham, the beans, a cup or two of chicken stock (depending on how moist you like it), some chopped fresh cilantro, and salt and cayenne to taste, and you've got a great dish to serve with rice and corn bread! Throw it all in the food processor, and you've got black bean dip. Or add more stock and a little dry sherry, and cook the beans longer, and you've got an easy black bean soup!

The white beans lend themselves to a variety of flavors, particularly white truffle oil, which is how I used them in the white bean purée with the Seared Scallops (page 158). Oh, and you'll love them in the Turkey Chili too. Just one last word of advice: Some beans cook more quickly than others, so you may have to adjust your cooking time to have perfect, tender beans.

1. PUT the beans in a large pot or mixing bowl, add enough cold water to cover by 2 inches, and soak the beans at room temperature, uncovered, for at least 8 hours. Or, for the quick-soak method, bring the pot of beans to a boil over high heat and boil for 2 minutes. Remove from the heat, cover tightly, and let stand for 1 hour.

2. DRAIN the beans. Place them in a medium saucepan with the bay leaves and enough cold water to cover by 1 inch. Bring to a boil over high heat. Reduce the heat to medium-low. Simmer, uncovered, until the beans are tender, about 50 minutes, skimming occasionally to remove the foam that forms on the surface.

3. DRAIN in a colander and rinse under cold running water to cool. Discard the bay leaves and season with the salt and pepper. Put the beans in a bowl, cover, and refrigerate until ready to use. (The beans can be stored in an airtight container in the refrigerator for up to three days or frozen for up to two months.)

---

1 pound dried black or navy
    beans, rinsed and picked over
2 bay leaves
Salt, to taste
Freshly ground black pepper,
    to taste

MASHED POTATOES

I recommend using those big Idaho potatoes for mashed potatoes because of their higher starch content. Do not rinse them at any time during the cooking process. While there are a lot of ways to cook potatoes, you can only achieve the texture that I'm aiming for here by peeling and boiling the potatoes, then mashing them over a low flame. And don't add the cream and butter until you're ready to serve. It's only by doing it this way that you get that great, light, fluffy texture and the real potato taste. If you don't have a potato masher, use a heavy wire whisk.

These are basic mashed potatoes that can be used in other recipes or served on their own. Feel free to add more butter or cream if you want, but remember, you gotta serve these right away!

4 large Idaho potatoes
  (about 3 pounds)
1¾ teaspoons salt
½ cup heavy cream
3 tablespoons unsalted butter
¼ teaspoon freshly ground black
  pepper

1. **PEEL** and quarter the potatoes lengthwise, then cut into 1-inch wedges. Put them in a heavy medium saucepan with 1 teaspoon of the salt and add enough cold water to cover by 1 inch. Bring to a boil over high heat. Reduce the heat to medium-low. Simmer until the potatoes are fork-tender, about 25 minutes.

2. **DRAIN** in a colander. Return the potatoes to the saucepan. Add the cream, butter, the remaining ¾ teaspoon salt, and the pepper. With the heat on medium-low, mash and stir the mixture until well blended, 4 to 5 minutes.

3. **SERVE** immediately.

DUCK CONFIT

Confit, a French preparation, is one of the oldest forms of preserving meat. Pork, goose, or duck is cooked in its own fat, then stored in the fat to preserve it. I'm a big fan of duck confit, and consider it an important basic in my cooking, although I add olive oil to mine to supplement the duck fat. You can make your own, or buy it in specialty shops. It makes a terrific addition to lots of dishes, from salads to stuffed baked potatoes.

1. AT least two days before serving, lay the duck legs skin side down on a platter and sprinkle with 1 tablespoon of the kosher salt and the ground pepper. Place the garlic cloves, bay leaves, and sprigs of thyme on two of the legs. Lay the remaining two legs skin side up on top. Put the reserved fat from the ducks in the bottom of a nonreactive container and top with the sandwiched duck pieces. Sprinkle with the remaining 1/8 teaspoon kosher salt. Cover tightly with plastic wrap. Refrigerate to cure for 12 hours.

2. PREHEAT the oven to 200°F.

3. REMOVE the duck from the container. Remove the garlic, bay leaves, thyme, and duck fat and reserve. Rinse the duck under cold running water, rubbing off some of the salt and pepper. Pat the duck dry with paper towels.

4. PUT the reserved garlic, bay leaves, thyme, and duck fat in an enameled cast-iron pot or deep glass baking dish, and sprinkle evenly with the peppercorns and the 1/2 teaspoon salt. Lay the duck pieces skin side down on top and add enough olive oil to cover.

5. COVER and bake until the meat pulls away from the bone, 12 to 14 hours.

6. REMOVE the duck from the fat. Strain the fat into a bowl and reserve. Remove the meat from the bones and place it in a 1-quart stoneware or glass container; discard the skin and bones. Add enough of the strained fat to cover the meat by 1/4 inch. Cover and store in the refrigerator for up to 1 month. If you wish, pour the remaining fat into an airtight container and refrigerate to use as cooking fat.

4 whole duck legs, with thighs attached (about 2 pounds) (see Source Guide, page 282), excess fat trimmed and reserved

1 tablespoon plus 1/8 teaspoon kosher salt

1/2 teaspoon freshly ground black pepper

10 garlic cloves

4 bay leaves

4 sprigs fresh thyme

1 1/2 teaspoons whole black peppercorns

1/2 teaspoon salt

4 cups olive oil, or as needed

PERFECT RICE

Cooking rice properly seems to intimidate a lot of people. On a recent *Emeril Live* show, we featured all kinds of rice and, during the show, I realized we had lost the attention of about half of the audience. I stopped and asked the audience members how many knew how to cook rice without using electric rice cookers. Fewer than half raised their hands. Here we go! Just remember the ratio is one (rice) to two (water), and you can double or triple the recipe.

2 cups water
1 tablespoon unsalted
    butter
1/2 teaspoon salt
1 cup medium- or long-
    grain white rice

1. **BRING** the water, butter, and salt to a boil in a medium saucepan over medium-high heat. Stir in the rice, reduce the heat to low, and cover the saucepan with a tight-fitting lid. Cook until the rice is tender and all the water has been absorbed, 15 to 20 minutes. Remove from the heat and let stand, covered, for 10 minutes.

2. **BEFORE** serving, fluff the rice with a fork.

PERFECT HARD-BOILED EGGS

It's important to peel the eggs as soon as they are cool enough to handle, while they are still warm. Once they cool, the shells tend to stick more. If the eggs are still warm after they are peeled, put them in an ice-water bath to prevent discoloration of the yolks, then drain, wrap in plastic, and refrigerate until needed.

6 large eggs

1. **PUT** the eggs in a saucepan that can accommodate them in one layer. Add enough cold water to cover by ½ inch and bring to a boil over high heat. Reduce the heat to a gentle boil and cook for 10 minutes.

2. **DRAIN** the eggs in a colander and rinse under cold running water until cool enough to handle. Peel the eggs while still warm.

HOMEMADE TASSO

MAKES 1 POUND

Oh, yeah, baby, tasso is it! Now that I've lived in Louisiana for almost twenty years, I find that I can't cook without it. The spiciness in this cured pork is pure magic, and it gives an amazing flavor to any long-simmered dishes, such as gumbos or stews. I add tasso to the Stewed Black-Eyed Peas (page 135), Oyster Dressing Soufflés with Oyster-Tasso Sauce (pages 126–128), and Drunken Hominy (page 240). You could add tasso to the Basic Beans (page 13) to give them some oomph, or even a bit to your Turkey Chili (page 189), or Rabbit, Andouille, and Wild Mushroom Gumbo (page 50). The tasso will keep, tightly wrapped and refrigerated, for about 1 week after the curing process is completed. But trust me, I think you'll use it all up before then!

1. **MIX** the paprika, salt, black pepper, granulated onions, cayenne, garlic powder, and onion powder well in a medium bowl. Dredge each pork slice in the mixture, pressing it into the meat. Wrap tightly in individual pieces of plastic wrap.

2. **REFRIGERATE** to cure for at least three days and up to one week before using.

- 2½ tablespoons paprika
- 1 tablespoon salt
- 2¼ teaspoons freshly ground black pepper
- 2¼ teaspoons granulated onions
- 2 teaspoons cayenne
- 1½ teaspoons garlic powder
- 1½ teaspoons onion powder
- 1 pound boneless lean pork butt, cut into three or four 1-inch-thick slices

STARTERS

Some people call them appetizers. I call them starters simply because they are the dishes I prepare to start off a meal when my friends gather together. The starters give my guests and me something to eat while we chill out, have a glass of wine or a cocktail, and visit. ■ Entertaining at home can be as elaborate or as simple as you want it to be. Prepare the Egg Rolls with Hot Mustard Sauce ahead, and when the doorbell rings announcing your guests' arrival, just fry them at the last minute. The Hot Corn Dip with Crispy Tortilla Chips is a perfect crowd-pleaser for kids of all ages.

SHRIMP SUMMER ROLLS

MAKES 8 SUMMER ROLLS

Mrs. Hay Nguyen, a prep cook, has been at NOLA, one of our New Orleans restaurants, since day one. The dishes she makes for staff meals sometimes find their way onto the restaurant's menu. One of our most popular dishes that has been on the menu for years is her stuffed chicken wings and these Vietnamese summer rolls. Sliced and passed with the dipping sauce, they make a refreshing appetizer. Rice paper wrappers come in various sizes, small to large, round or square. They are very delicate, so be prepared to tear a few the first time you use them. Mung bean noodles and rice paper wrappers can be found in most Asian markets. Serve the rolls with Asian Dipping Sauce, or pair them with the Hot Mustard Sauce (page 23).

Two 1-ounce skeins mung bean noodles or cellophane noodles
One 2-inch piece ginger, peeled and thinly sliced
1 lemon, halved
¼ cup soy sauce
¼ cup sugar
4 bay leaves
1 tablespoon chopped green onions (green and white parts)
1 teaspoon chopped garlic
1 teaspoon salt
1 teaspoon freshly ground black pepper
½ teaspoon cayenne
16 large shrimp, peeled and deveined
2 teaspoons Emeril's Original Essence or Creole Seasoning (page 9)

1. **PUT** 2 cups hot water in a large bowl and add the noodles. Soak them until softened but slightly resilient, 20 to 30 minutes. Drain them and pat dry on paper towels. Put in a bowl and cover.

2. **COMBINE** 4 cups water, the ginger, lemon, soy sauce, sugar, bay leaves, green onions, garlic, salt, black pepper, and cayenne in a large saucepan. Bring to a boil.

3. **SEASON** the shrimp with the Essence, then add to the boiling water. Boil for 2 minutes, then remove the pan from the heat and allow the shrimp to sit in the hot liquid for 2 minutes, or until cooked through.

Using tongs or a slotted spoon, remove the shrimp from the water and let cool. Reserve ¼ cup of the cooking liquid for the dipping sauce. When the shrimp are cool enough to handle, cut lengthwise in half.

4. FILL a large bowl with hot water. Place a clean kitchen towel next to the bowl. Submerge 1 rice paper wrapper in the water and soak it until softened, about 1 minute. Carefully remove the rice paper from the water and lay it flat on the towel.

5. IN the center of the sheet, layer 4 lettuce pieces, about 20 sprouts, 4 shrimp halves arranged side by side in a row, 4 mint leaves, 4 cilantro sprigs, and one-eighth of the carrots. Pull the bottom up over the filling, fold over the sides, and roll up like an egg roll. Place seam side down on a plate and repeat the process with the remaining rice papers and filling.

6. SERVE immediately, with the dipping sauce.

Eight 8½-inch round rice paper
   wrappers
8 small romaine lettuce leaves,
   rinsed, patted dry, ribs
   removed, and torn into bite-
   size pieces
1 ounce alfalfa or radish sprouts
32 fresh mint leaves
32 sprigs fresh cilantro
1 large carrot, peeled and
   shredded
Asian Dipping Sauce (recipe
   follows)
Hot Mustard Sauce (page 23)

Asian Dipping Sauce

MAKES 1 CUP

COMBINE all the ingredients in a bowl and whisk until well blended. Set aside until needed; stir well before serving. (The sauce can be covered and refrigerated for up to three days.)

¼ cup grated carrots
2 tablespoons Asian (dark)
   sesame oil
2 tablespoons rice vinegar
1 tablespoon Vietnamese or Thai
   fish sauce
1 tablespoon soy sauce
1 tablespoon crunchy peanut
   butter
1 teaspoon minced garlic
¼ cup cooking liquid from
   Shrimp Summer Rolls
   (preceding recipe)

EGG ROLLS WITH HOT MUSTARD SAUCE

MAKES 20 EGG ROLLS

Talk about party food! And talk about one of the best things to eat! Fresh hot egg rolls just can't be beat, especially when dipped into this easy-to-make sauce. I'm wild for egg rolls; I'll eat them for breakfast when I can! Traditionally the rolls are made with pork, but, hey, if you don't want pork, go ahead and use beef or chicken.

1 tablespoon cornstarch, plus extra for dusting
1 tablespoon soy sauce
3/4 pound bok choy, tough outer leaves removed and rinsed well
2 tablespoons vegetable oil, plus more for deep-frying
1 pound ground pork
1 teaspoon salt
1/2 teaspoon cayenne
1 cup finely chopped green onions (green and white parts)
1 cup grated carrots (2 large carrots)
2 teaspoons minced garlic
1/4 cup chopped fresh cilantro
1 tablespoon Asian (dark) sesame oil
Twenty 6-inch square egg roll wrappers (about 1 package)
2 ounces alfalfa or radish sprouts
Asian Dipping Sauce (page 21)
Hot Mustard Sauce (recipe follows)

1. **SPRINKLE** the cornstarch over the soy sauce in a small bowl and stir well to dissolve.

2. **STACK** the bok choy leaves on top of each other. Trim off and discard the bottom 3 inches of the leaves. Roll the leaves up tightly and slice into long thin strips. (This should yield about 4 loosely packed cups.)

3. **HEAT** the 2 tablespoons vegetable oil in a wok or deep skillet over medium-high heat. Add the pork, salt, and cayenne and stir-fry for 3 minutes, or until the meat loses its pink color. Add the bok choy and stir-fry until beginning to soften, about 2 minutes. Add the green onions, carrots, garlic, cilantro, and sesame oil and continue cooking until just slightly wilted, about 2 minutes. Add the cornstarch mixture and stir well to blend and thicken, bring to a boil, and boil for 1 minute. Transfer to a wide bowl and let cool completely.

4. **POUR** 1/2 cup water into a small bowl and place next to your work area.

5. **LAY** 1 egg roll wrapper on the work surface, with one of the points toward you. Dip a finger in the water and wet the edges of the wrapper. Put 1/4 cup of the pork filling just below the center of the wrapper, above the bottom point. Top with a pinch of sprouts. Pull the bottom point up over the filling, fold over the sides, and roll up to completely enclose the filling. Place seam side down on a cornstarch-dusted baking sheet. Continue with the remaining wrap-

pers and filling. (Note: If the egg rolls will not be cooked right away, lightly dust them with cornstarch to prevent them from sticking together, and cover tightly with plastic wrap. Refrigerate for up to 4 hours.)

6. PREHEAT the oven to 200°F. Pour enough oil to come halfway up the sides into a large deep heavy pot or electric deep fryer and heat to 360°F.

7. IN batches, without crowding, carefully add the egg rolls to the hot oil and fry, turning with a slotted spoon, until golden brown on all sides, about 3 minutes. Remove and drain on paper towels. Keep warm in the oven while you fry the remaining rolls.

8. SERVE hot with the dipping sauce.

Hot Mustard Sauce

MAKES ½ CUP

PUT the mustard in a small bowl and slowly drizzle in the water, whisking to make a thin paste. Add the vinegar and salt and whisk well to blend. Set aside until needed. (The sauce can be refrigerated in an airtight container for up to one week. Stir well before serving.)

⅓ cup dry Chinese hot mustard
¼ cup water
3 tablespoons rice vinegar
Pinch of salt

CRABMEAT TIMBALES

A timbale is a cooked, molded dish made with meat, fish, or vegetables. The word *timbale* also refers to the mold itself. The best ones to use look like miniature soufflé dishes; they're just the right size for individual servings. While these crab timbales are served warm here, they're also delicious chilled. Instead of unmolding them while they're warm, let them cool, then cover with plastic wrap and refrigerate for at least 3 hours, and up to 1 day. Unmold as directed below, and serve cold with Mayonnaise (page 12) and Croutons (page 66) or crackers.

1. PREHEAT the oven to 350°F. Grease eight 4-ounce ramekins or baking dishes with the butter and set aside.

2. WHISK the cream, egg yolks, green onions, parsley, garlic, salt, and cayenne in a mixing bowl.

3. PUT about 2 tablespoons of the crabmeat in each of the buttered ramekins. Pour a generous ⅓ cup of the custard into each one. Place the ramekins, being sure they don't touch each other, in a large roasting pan. Put the pan in the oven and pour enough hot water into the pan to come halfway up the sides of the ramekins. Bake until the custards are just set and lightly golden brown (a knife inserted in the center will come out almost clean), about 45 minutes.

4. REMOVE from the oven. Let the timbales stand in the hot water for 15 minutes.

5. RUN a knife around the inside of each timbale, dry the outside of the ramekin with a towel, and invert the ramekin onto the center of a plate; gently shake to release the timbale. Serve immediately.

2 teaspoons unsalted butter, at room temperature
2 cups heavy cream
6 large egg yolks
¼ cup chopped green onions (green and white parts)
1 tablespoon finely chopped fresh flat-leaf parsley
2 teaspoons minced garlic
1 teaspoon salt
½ teaspoon cayenne
½ pound lump crabmeat, picked over for shells and cartilage

CRABMEAT AND HEARTS OF PALM STRUDELS WITH CORN REMOULADE

MAKES 12 STRUDEL

Edible hearts of palm really do come from palm trees, specifically the cabbage palm tree. To take advantage of the fresh hearts of palm that are cultivated in Florida, we came up with this recipe for Emeril's Restaurant in Orlando. Oh, man, what a great combination of fresh Florida ingredients—hearts of palm, crabmeat, and that Southern favorite, sweet corn. If you can't get fresh hearts of palm, substitute the canned ones, but rinse them well before using. The corn remoulade also makes a great substitute sauce for the Crawfish and Corn Cakes (page 124) or the Linguiça-Crusted Redfish (page 109), or try it as an alternate dressing for the Fried Crawfish Salad (page 72).

½ pound lump crabmeat, picked over for shells and cartilage
¼ cup finely chopped yellow onions
2 tablespoons finely chopped celery
2 tablespoons finely chopped red bell peppers
2 tablespoons finely chopped yellow bell peppers
2 tablespoons fine dried bread crumbs
1 teaspoon minced garlic
1 tablespoon minced fresh flat-leaf parsley
1¼ teaspoons salt
1 teaspoon cayenne
1 tablespoon unsalted butter
1 cup corn kernels (from 1 large or 2 small ears of corn)
Corn Remoulade (recipe follows)
½ cup olive oil
18 sheets phyllo dough, defrosted according to package directions

1. PREHEAT the oven to 375°F.

2. COMBINE the crabmeat, onions, celery, red and yellow bell peppers, bread crumbs, garlic, parsley, 1 teaspoon of the salt, and the cayenne in a large mixing bowl. Stir to mix well.

3. MELT the butter in a large heavy skillet over medium-high heat. Add the corn and the remaining ¼ teaspoon salt and cook, stirring, until lightly browned, about 5 minutes. Add the corn to the crabmeat mixture. Add ½ cup of the remoulade and stir to mix.

4. HAVE the olive oil in a small bowl near your work area. Lay the phyllo dough out near the work surface and cover with a damp kitchen towel to prevent it from drying out.

5. STACK 3 sheets of phyllo dough on the work surface, with a long side facing you, and cut them in half down the middle. With a pastry brush, lightly coat the top sheet of both stacks with olive oil.

6. SPREAD 3 tablespoons of crab-corn filling ½ inch from the bottom of each top phyllo sheet, leaving a 1-inch border along both sides. Lay 1 heart of palm (or heart of palm slice) directly on each portion of filling. Roll the bottom edge of the phyllo over the filling, pushing it up against the heart of palm. Bring the left and right sides over toward the filling and fold over. Roll the phyllo up from the bottom over the filling, and then roll into a tight cylinder, like rolling a cigar. Place the strudels about 2 inches apart on an ungreased baking sheet and cover with a damp kitchen towel to prevent them from drying out. Continue with the remaining phyllo and filling.

7. LIGHTLY brush the strudels with the remaining olive oil. Bake until golden brown, about 30 minutes.

8. SERVE hot, with the remaining remoulade.

One 14.5-ounce can hearts of palm, rinsed, drained, and sliced lengthwise to make 12 pieces, each about ½ inch in diameter (or if using fresh, you will need about 12 ounces)

Corn Remoulade

MAKES 2¼ CUPS

To remove the corn kernels from the cobs, thinly slice down across the tops of the kernels and then slice a second time to release the "milk" from the corn. Scrape the cob once or twice to extract all the milk.

1 tablespoon unsalted butter
1 cup corn kernels (from 1 large or 2 small ears of corn)
¾ teaspoon salt, or more to taste
¼ cup chopped yellow onions
¼ cup chopped green onions (green and white parts)
¼ cup chopped celery
3 tablespoons Creole or other spicy whole-grain mustard
3 tablespoons Dijon mustard
3 tablespoons fresh lemon juice
3 tablespoons chopped fresh flat-leaf parsley
1 tablespoon plus 1 teaspoon ketchup
1 tablespoon prepared horseradish
¼ teaspoon cayenne, or more to taste
1 large egg
1 cup vegetable oil

1. MELT the butter in a large skillet over medium-high heat. Add the corn and ¼ teaspoon at the salt. Cook, stirring, until lightly browned, about 5 minutes. (The corn will make popping sounds as it cooks). Let cool completely.

2. COMBINE the onions, green onions, celery, Creole and Dijon mustards, lemon juice, parsley, ketchup, horseradish, cayenne, and the remaining ½ teaspoon salt in a food processor or blender and purée. With the machine running, add the egg, then slowly add the oil in a thin, steady stream until the mixture thickens, like a mayonnaise. Transfer to a bowl and fold in the corn. Season to taste if necessary and serve. (The remoulade can be covered, and refrigerated for up to 8 hours.)

GRILLED EGGPLANT ROULADES WITH BALSAMIC SYRUP

MAKES 4 SERVINGS

Roulade is a French term for a thin slice of meat rolled around a filling of some kind. I've given these roulades an Emeril twist by using eggplant rather than meat. These are a fun little summer starter when you're outside and the grill is already heated up for other things. Just make the balsamic syrup a couple of hours ahead of time, and you'll be set.

If you want to make these a little fancier, toss some greens with the balsamic syrup and some extra-virgin olive oil, and serve the roulades on top. Or grill a couple of quartered heads of radicchio (toss them with the syrup and olive oil and a little grated Parmesan cheese) to serve with the roulades. There's no way you can lose with this one! And if you don't feel like kicking up the grill, just make these in the oven.

1 large eggplant
   (about 1½ pounds)
¼ cup olive oil
½ teaspoon salt
¼ teaspoon freshly ground black
   pepper
12 thin slices prosciutto or ham
   (about ¼ pound)
8 ounces fresh mozzarella, cut
   into twelve ⅛-inch-thick
   slices
½ cup Balsamic Syrup
   (recipe follows)
1 tablespoon extra-virgin olive
   oil (optional)

1. PREHEAT a gas or charcoal grill. (Alternatively, preheat the broiler.)

2. CUT the eggplant crosswise into twelve ¼-inch-thick slices. Lightly brush on both sides with olive oil, then season with the salt and pepper. Grill until just golden and slightly soft, about 2 minutes on each side. (If broiling, cook for 1 minute per side, carefully watching so that it does not burn.) Let cool slightly.

3. TOP each eggplant slice with a slice of prosciutto, followed by a slice of mozzarella cheese. Roll up each slice and secure with a toothpick.

4. RETURN the roulades to the grill. Grill until the cheese starts to melt and the eggplant is warmed through, about 2 minutes. (Alternatively, roast the roulades on a baking sheet at 400°F for 6 to 8 minutes.)

5. ARRANGE the roulades on a serving platter, or place 3 roulades each on four individual plates. Discard the toothpicks. Drizzle with the balsamic syrup and the extra-virgin olive oil, if desired, or pass the syrup on the side as a dipping sauce.

Balsamic Syrup

MAKES ¾ CUP

BRING the vinegar to a boil in a medium heavy saucepan over high heat. Reduce the heat to medium-low and simmer until reduced by nearly three-quarters in volume and thickened to a syrup. Remove from the heat and cool completely before using. This keeps indefinitely.

3 cups balsamic vinegar

HOT CORN DIP WITH CRISPY TORTILLA CHIPS

MAKES 6 CUPS DIP; 12 TO 18 SERVINGS

We developed this dip for a Father's Day *Emeril Live* show, but it's also a great dip for the day of a big football game! This hot, cheesy dip is perfect for entertaining or just vegging out during the Sunday games on television.

2 tablespoons unsalted butter
3½ cups corn kernels (from 4 ears fresh white or yellow corn)
½ teaspoon salt
⅛ teaspoon freshly ground black pepper
1 cup finely chopped yellow onions
½ cup finely chopped red bell peppers
¼ cup chopped green onions (green and white parts)
1 jalapeño, seeded and minced
2 teaspoons minced garlic
1 cup Mayonnaise (page 12) or store-bought mayonnaise
8 ounces Monterey Jack cheese, shredded (about 2 cups)
¼ teaspoon cayenne
Crispy Tortilla Chips (recipe follows)

1. **MELT** 1 tablespoon of the butter in a large heavy skillet over medium-high heat. Add the corn, salt, and pepper. Cook, stirring occasionally, until the kernels turn deep golden brown, about 5 minutes. (The corn will make a popping sound as it cooks.) Pour the corn into a mixing bowl.

2. **MELT** the remaining 1 tablespoon butter in the skillet. Add the onions and bell peppers and cook, stirring often, until the onions are wilted, about 2 minutes. Add the green onions, jalapeño, and garlic and cook, stirring, for 2 minutes, or until the vegetables are softened. Pour the mixture into the bowl with the corn and let cool.

3. **PREHEAT** the oven to 350°F.

4. **ADD** the mayonnaise, 1 cup of the grated cheese, and the cayenne to the corn mixture and mix well. Pour into an 8-inch square baking dish and sprinkle the remaining cheese on top. Bake until bubbly and golden brown, 10 to 12 minutes.

5. **SERVE** hot with the chips.

Crispy Tortilla Chips

MAKES 48 CHIPS

You can double or triple the recipe. Bake or fry—your choice!

6 corn tortillas, cut into quarters
6 flour tortillas, cut into quarters
1 teaspoon salt
Vegetable oil if deep-frying

1. TO bake the chips, preheat the oven to 400°F. Spread the tortillas in a single layer on baking sheets and bake for 15 minutes, until crisp and golden, turning once. Sprinkle lightly with the salt.

2. TO fry the chips, add enough oil to come halfway up the sides into a large heavy pot or electric deep fryer and heat over high heat to 360°F. In batches, without crowding, deep-fry the tortillas until golden brown, turning once, 2 to 3 minutes. Using a slotted spoon, transfer to paper towels to drain. Sprinkle lightly with the salt.

3. SERVE immediately.

BAKED CRABMEAT, ARTICHOKE, AND SPINACH DIP

MAKES ABOUT 6 CUPS

Trust me, this is one dip that everyone will go crazy over! The combination of crab-meat, artichokes, spinach, and cheeses is out of sight! I serve this to my friends when we watch football games, but you can use it anytime, and I promise you it'll be a hit.

Two 10- to 12-ounce bunches spinach, trimmed and washed
2 slices bacon, preferably apple-smoked, chopped
2 tablespoons olive oil
1 cup finely chopped yellow onions
1 tablespoon chopped garlic
Two 8-ounce packages cream cheese, at room temperature
2½ tablespoons fresh lemon juice
1 tablespoon Creole or other spicy whole-grain mustard
1 teaspoon chopped fresh tarragon or ½ teaspoon dried tarragon
1 tablespoon Worcestershire sauce
1 pound lump crabmeat, picked over for shells and cartilage
One 14-ounce can artichoke hearts, drained and coarsely chopped
1 cup shredded Monterey Jack cheese (about 4 ounces)
¾ cup freshly grated Parmigiano-Reggiano (about 3 ounces)

1. **COOK** the spinach in a large pot of lightly salted boiling water until wilted, about 3 minutes. Drain and rinse under cold water to cool. Squeeze well to remove the excess water. Coarsely chop the spinach and transfer to a bowl.

2. **FRY** the bacon in 1 tablespoon of the olive oil in a large skillet over medium-high heat until crisp, about 5 minutes. Add the onions and garlic and cook, stirring, until the onions are softened, 2 to 3 minutes. Add to the spinach and let cool.

3. **PREHEAT** the oven to 350°F.

4. **BEAT** the cream cheese, lemon juice, mustard, tarragon, and Worcestershire sauce in the bowl of an electric mixer fitted with a paddle attachment or with a wooden spoon until smooth and creamy. Mix in the spinach and bacon mixture, then the crabmeat, artichoke hearts, Jack cheese, ½ cup of the Parmigiano-Reggiano, the egg yolks, 1 teaspoon of the salt, the white pepper, cayenne, and pepper sauce. Mix well.

5. **LIGHTLY** butter an 11 × 7-inch baking dish or shallow 2-quart baking dish. Pour the mixture into the dish.

6. COMBINE the remaining ¼ cup Parmigiano-Reggiano, the bread crumbs, and the remaining 1 tablespoon olive oil and ¼ teaspoon salt in a food processor or electric blender. Pulse two to three times to blend. Spread the mixture evenly over the crabmeat mixture. Bake until bubbly and lightly golden, 30 to 35 minutes.

7. SERVE hot with the crispy tortillas chips.

2 large egg yolks
1¼ teaspoons salt
½ teaspoon freshly ground white pepper
½ teaspoon cayenne
½ teaspoon Emeril's Red Pepper Sauce or hot pepper sauce
½ tablespoon unsalted butter, softened for the baking dish
1 cup fine dried bread crumbs
Crispy Tortilla Chips (page 31)

SPICY DUCK EMPANADAS
WITH CILANTRO CREAM

MAKES 12 EMPANADAS

Empanadas are fried or baked turnovers, usually stuffed with meats and vegetables. Sometimes they are filled with fruit and served as dessert. Spanish in origin, they are popular throughout the Caribbean and southwestern United States, and in Central and South American countries. If you want to serve these as snacks or hors d'oeuvres, cut the dough with a 3-inch cookie cutter rather than into the bigger 5-inch circles called for here. Instead of frying them, brush the empanadas lightly with egg wash, then place them on a baking sheet lined with parchment paper. Bake at 375°F until golden brown, about 30 minutes. No duck? Use shredded leftover chicken or beef.

DOUGH
3 cups bleached all-purpose flour
1 teaspoon salt
¼ cup vegetable shortening,
   chilled
4 tablespoons unsalted butter
   (½ stick), cut into small
   pieces and chilled
2 eggs, lightly beaten with
   ½ cup cold water

FILLING
2 tablespoons vegetable oil
1 cup finely chopped yellow
   onions
½ cup finely chopped green bell
   peppers
2 teaspoons minced garlic
2 cups Duck Confit (page 15) or
   shredded cooked duck breast
½ cup chopped pimiento-stuffed
   green olives
½ cup golden raisins
¼ cup store-bought tomato
   sauce

1. TO make the dough, combine the flour and salt in a large mixing bowl. Using a pastry blender, cut in the shortening and butter until the mixture is crumbly. (Or rub the mixture between your fingers.) Stir in the egg mixture and knead the dough in the bowl until smooth. Form into a ball, cover tightly with plastic wrap, and refrigerate for 1 hour.

2. MEANWHILE, make the filling: Heat the oil in a large skillet over medium-high heat. Add the onions and bell peppers. Cook, stirring often, until softened and caramelized around the edges, 5 to 6 minutes. Add the garlic and stir until fragrant, about 1 minute. Add the confit and cook until hot, about 2 minutes. Add the green olives, raisins, tomato sauce, pine nuts, vinegar, both Essences, the sugar, and salt and bring to a simmer. Lower the heat to medium-low. Simmer until the mixture thickens, 5 to 7 minutes. Remove from the heat and spread the filling on a plate to cool completely. Adjust the seasoning to taste.

3. ROLL the dough out on a floured surface about ⅛ inch thick. Using a bread plate or a coffee can as a guide and a sharp knife, cut out 5-inch rounds of dough. Put about ¼ cup of the filling just below the center of each round, fold it in half, and press the edges together to seal. Crimp the edges of the pastry with a fork. Gather up scraps of dough and roll out again as needed to make 12 rounds.

4. POUR enough oil to come halfway up the sides into a large deep skillet or electric deep fryer and heat over high heat to 360°F. Fry the empanadas, in batches, without crowding, until golden brown, about 2 minutes. Using a slotted spoon, transfer to paper towels to drain.

5. SERVE hot with the cilantro cream passed on the side.

¼ cup pine nuts, toasted
    (see page 227)
2 tablespoons red wine vinegar
1 tablespoon Emeril's Southwest
    Essence
1 teaspoon Emeril's Original
    Essence or Creole Seasoning
    (page 9)
2 teaspoons sugar
1½ teaspoons salt, or more to
    taste
Vegetable oil for deep-frying
Cilantro Cream (recipe follows)

Cilantro Cream

MAKES 1 CUP

PUT all the ingredients in a bowl and stir to combine. Refrigerate in an airtight container until ready to serve. This keeps for five days.

1 cup sour cream
2 teaspoons fresh lemon juice
2 tablespoons chopped fresh
    cilantro
⅛ teaspoon salt

SINGING SHRIMP

I first tasted Singing Shrimp many years ago when I was chef at Commander's Palace in New Orleans. Since then, I have made a few adjustments to the original recipe (adding mushrooms and a few other twists), and I now serve these in puff pastry shells for an elegant appetizer. And, with the ½ cup of Cognac added to the dish, you can bet these shrimp are singing!

6 frozen puff pastry shells (each 4 inches in diameter)
2 tablespoons olive oil
½ pound small shiitake mushrooms, stems removed and wiped clean (cut into quarters if large)
½ teaspoon salt
½ teaspoon freshly ground black pepper
¾ pound medium shrimp, peeled and deveined
½ cup green onions (green and white parts)
1 tablespoon minced shallots
1 teaspoon minced garlic
½ cup Cognac or other brandy
¾ cup heavy cream
1 tablespoon Dijon mustard
1 tablespoon minced fresh flat-leaf parsley

1. **PREHEAT** the oven to 400°F.

2. **PLACE** the pastry shells on a baking sheet and bake until golden brown, 20 to 25 minutes. Remove from the oven, and, with the tip of a thin sharp knife, carefully cut out the tops from each pastry; discard the moist insides. Let the pastry shells cool.

3. **HEAT** the olive oil in a large skillet over medium-high heat. Add the mushrooms, salt, and pepper. Cook, stirring occasionally, until the mushrooms soften, about 4 minutes. Add the shrimp, green onions, shallots, and garlic and stir-fry for 1 minute. Remove the pan from the heat and carefully add the Cognac. Have a large lid nearby. Return the pan to the heat, and very carefully ignite the brandy. Once the flames go out (you may need to cover with the lid to extinguish if the flames leap too dramatically), add the cream, mustard, and parsley and stir well. Reduce the heat to medium-low and simmer for 2 minutes.

4. **TO** serve, place a pastry shell on each of six plates. Spoon the shrimp mixture into each shell. Serve immediately.

ONION TART

Onions are so versatile, and when caramelized, they have such a sweet flavor. This onion tart comes in handy for parties, because you can cut it into thin slices for an hors d'oeuvre, medium slices for a first course, or big wedges as a main course, accompanied by a green salad and some fruit.

1. PREHEAT the oven to 375°F.

2. ON a floured surface, roll the pie crust dough into an 11-inch circle. Transfer to a 9-inch tart pan with a removable bottom. Press the dough onto the bottom and up the sides, trimming off any excess dough.

3. LINE the dough with a round of parchment paper or aluminum foil. Place a layer of pastry weights or dried beans in the bottom and up the sides. Bake until the pastry looks set, about 10 minutes. Remove the parchment and weights, and bake until the pastry is barely golden, 6 to 8 more minutes. Let cool completely.

4. MELT the butter in a skillet over medium-high heat. Add the onions, ½ teaspoon salt, nutmeg, and bay leaf. Cook, stirring often, until the onions are golden, 7 minutes. Add the shallots and cook, stirring often, until softened, 1 minute. Add the garlic and stir until fragrant, 30 seconds. Add the ham and cook, stirring often, for 3 minutes. Transfer to a bowl and let cool.

5. STIR 1 cup of the cheese into the cooled onion mixture. Spread the mixture in the cooled tart shell.

6. WHISK the eggs in a bowl. Whisk in the cream, thyme, parsley, the remaining ½ teaspoon salt, and the pepper. Pour into the tart shell and sprinkle the remaining ¼ cup of cheese over the top.

7. BAKE for 35 minutes, or until set. Increase the oven temperature to 400°F and bake until the filling is puffed and golden brown, 8 to 10 minutes. Remove from the oven and cool for at least 15 minutes before cutting.

8. SERVE warm or at room temperature.

Savory Pie Crust (recipe follows)
2 tablespoons unsalted butter
4 cups thinly sliced yellow onions
1 teaspoon salt
⅛ teaspoon freshly grated nutmeg
1 bay leaf
3 tablespoons minced shallots
1 teaspoon minced garlic
½ cup chopped ham (about 3 ounces)
1¼ packed cups shredded Jarlsberg or Swiss cheese (about 5 ounces)
3 large eggs
1 cup heavy cream
1 tablespoon minced fresh thyme
1 tablespoon minced fresh flat-leaf parsley
¼ teaspoon freshly ground black pepper

SAVORY PIECRUST

MAKES ONE 9- OR 10-INCH PIECRUST

8 ounces flour (about 1½ cups
 plus 2 tablespoons)
½ teaspoon salt
1 stick cold unsalted butter,
 cut into ¼-inch pieces
2 tablespoons solid vegetable
 shortening
3 tablespoons ice water

1. SIFT the flour and salt into a large mixing bowl. Incorporate the butter pieces and shortening by hand, working the fat into the flour with your fingertips until the dough starts to come together and form small pea-shaped pieces. Work the ice water into the dough with your fingers until it just comes together, being careful not to overmix.

2. FORM the crust into a disk, wrap tightly in plastic wrap, and place in the refrigerator to rest for at least 30 minutes before rolling out to fit into a pie pan.

TOMATO, MOZZARELLA, AND ROASTED GARLIC TART

MAKES 4 TO 6 SERVINGS

I'm a fan of Caprese salad, the simple southern Italian favorite of vine-ripened tomatoes, the freshest mozzarella, fresh basil leaves, and best-quality olive oil. Now, tell me, what could be better? Answer: this tart, with the same ingredients layered on a sheet of store-bought frozen puff pastry and then baked. Simple, and a new twist on a classic, it promises to be a summer favorite.

1. **CUT** the tomatoes into ½-inch slices. Arrange in a single layer on a rack set over a baking sheet. Season lightly with ¼ teaspoon salt and let drain for 30 to 45 minutes.

2. **PREHEAT** the oven to 400°F.

3. **PLACE** the pastry sheet on a lightly floured surface and roll it into a 10½-inch square. Transfer to a baking sheet. Brush evenly with the oil, then the garlic purée. Arrange the tomato slices over the pastry. Cover each with a basil leaf, then top with a slice of cheese. Sprinkle with ½ teaspoon salt and the pepper.

4. **BAKE** until the crust is golden brown and the cheese is bubbly, about 20 to 25 minutes. Serve warm or at room temperature, cut into squares.

2 to 3 tomatoes (about ¾ pound)
¾ teaspoon salt
1 sheet frozen puff pastry (half a 17.3-ounce package), defrosted
2 tablespoons extra-virgin olive oil
½ cup Roasted Garlic Purée (page 11)
12 to 15 fresh basil leaves
6 ounces fresh mozzarella, thinly sliced
¼ teaspoon freshly ground black pepper

SOUPS

GUMBOS & CHOWDERS

the recipes

Soup can be a hearty meal unto itself, such as the Sweet Potato and Duck Chowder or Mr. John's Seafood-Chorizo Gumbo, or it can be lighter for a first course, such as the Chicken, Vegetable, and Rice Soup, or the Cold Cucumber Soup with Smoked Salmon. ■ For a casual party, try serving soup in mugs, or serve it in dainty demitasse cups as a first course for a more formal dinner party. Hey, in New Orleans, some restaurants offer soups 1–1–1: three different kinds of soup in three demitasse cups per person. Now that would really kick up a dinner party!

CARAMELIZED ONION AND PARMESAN CHEESE SOUP WITH PARMESAN CHEESE TOASTS

MAKES 8 TO 12 SERVINGS

Nothing is more comforting than soup, and one of my favorites is this combination of caramelized onions and Parmesan cheese. It was a cold winter day when we taped the show featuring this soup, and I knew when I saw the guests arriving that the soup was going to be a hit. The interesting twist to this soup is the French bread that is used to thicken it to the perfect consistency. Enjoy!

2 tablespoons olive oil
2 cups chopped yellow onions
8 to 12 garlic cloves, smashed,
    plus 1 tablespoon minced
    garlic
2 bay leaves
1½ teaspoons salt, or more to
    taste
½ teaspoon freshly ground black
    pepper, or more to taste
2 quarts Chicken Stock (page 2)
    or canned low-sodium
    chicken broth
2 teaspoons minced fresh thyme
2 cups 1-inch cubes crusty
    French or Italian bread
½ cup heavy cream
½ cup freshly grated
    Parmigiano-Reggiano
1 tablespoon minced fresh
    flat-leaf parsley
Parmesan Cheese Toasts
    (recipe follows)

1. **HEAT** the oil in a large heavy pot or Dutch oven over medium-low heat. Add the onions, the smashed garlic cloves, bay leaves, salt, and pepper. Cook, stirring often, until the onions are softened and golden, 10 to 15 minutes. Add the minced garlic and stir until fragrant, about 1 minute. Stir in the stock and thyme and bring to a boil. Reduce the heat to medium-low. Simmer, stirring occasionally, for 1 hour.

2. **ADD** the bread cubes. Cook, whisking often, until the bread disintegrates and thickens the soup, about 10 minutes. Remove and discard the bay leaves. Purée the soup with an immersion blender or in batches in a food processor or blender. Return to the pot and whisk in the cream, cheese, and parsley. Season with additional salt and pepper if necessary.

3. **LADLE** into bowls. Serve with the hot cheese toasts.

Parmesan Cheese Toasts

MAKES 12 TOASTS

1. PREHEAT the oven to 400°F.

2. SPREAD the bread on a baking sheet. Mix the cheese, mayonnaise, parsley, garlic, salt, and cayenne in a small bowl. Spread a heaping tablespoon of the cheese mixture onto each slice of bread.

3. BAKE until golden brown and bubbly, 6 to 8 minutes. Serve hot.

Twelve ¼-inch-thick baguette slices (cut on the diagonal to make large slices)
1 cup freshly grated Parmigiano-Reggiano
⅓ cup Mayonnaise (page 12) or store-bought mayonnaise
1 tablespoon finely chopped fresh flat-leaf parsley
1 teaspoon minced garlic
¼ teaspoon salt
⅛ teaspoon cayenne

CHICKEN, BACON, AND WHITE BEAN SOUP PORTUGUESE-STYLE

MAKES 8 TO 12 SERVINGS

My mother, Hilda, always had a pot of soup simmering on the back of the stove. This stick-to-your-ribs soup remains one of my favorites.

1 pound dried white beans, such as white kidney (cannellini) or great Northern, rinsed and picked over
½ pound bacon, cut into ½-inch-wide pieces
2 cups chopped yellow onions
½ cup chopped celery
2 tablespoons minced shallots
1 tablespoon minced garlic
2 bay leaves
1 teaspoon salt
¼ teaspoon cayenne
2 quarts Chicken Stock (page 2) or canned low-sodium chicken broth
¾ pound diced cooked chicken
1 cup freshly grated pecorino Romano

1. PUT the beans into a large pot or bowl. Add water to cover by 2 inches and soak for at least 8 hours or overnight. Then drain. (For a quick soak, bring the beans and water to a boil over high heat and cook for 2 minutes, then remove from the heat and allow to stand for 1 hour. Drain.)

2. FRY the bacon in a heavy medium stockpot over medium-high heat until crisp, about 7 minutes. Use a slotted spoon to lift onto paper towels to drain. Pour off all but 2 tablespoons of the bacon fat from the pot. Add the onions and celery and cook, stirring occasionally, until tender, about 4 minutes. Add the shallots, garlic, bay leaves, salt, and cayenne. Cook, stirring occasionally, until the shallots soften, about 1 minute.

3. ADD the beans to the pot with the stock, and bring to a boil. Reduce the heat to medium-low. Simmer, uncovered, stirring occasionally, until the beans are tender, about 1½ hours.

4. STIR in the chicken and the reserved bacon and heat through. Remove and discard bay leaves.

5. LADLE into warm bowls and sprinkle with the grated cheese.

CHICKEN, VEGETABLE, AND RICE SOUP

MAKES 12 SERVINGS

Chicken and rice, oh, so nice. Ah, I loved this when I was a child and I still crave it. As a matter of fact, I made this soup for a show on "Comfort Foods." And when I need a little TLC, this is what really hits the spot.

1. **PUT** the beans into a bowl and add enough water to cover by 2 inches. Soak for 8 hours, then drain. (For a quick soak, bring the beans and water to a boil over high heat and cook for 2 minutes, then remove from heat and allow to stand for 1 hour. Drain.)

2. **HEAT** the oil in a large heavy pot or Dutch oven over medium-high heat. In batches, cook the chicken, seasoning with the salt and pepper and turning once, until evenly browned, about 10 minutes. Transfer the chicken to a platter. Pour off all but 2 tablespoons of the fat from the pot.

3. **ADD** the onions, carrots, and celery. Cook, stirring often, until softened, about 3 minutes. Add the garlic and stir until fragrant, about 1 minute. Stir in the zucchini and yellow squash and cook for 1 minute. Add the stock, drained beans, tomatoes, parsley, bay leaves, and cayenne. Return the chicken to the pot. Bring to a boil over high heat. Reduce the heat to medium-low and simmer, uncovered, until the beans are almost tender, about 1 hour.

4. **USING** a long-handled slotted spoon or tongs, carefully transfer the chicken pieces to a plate. Cool slightly, then remove the meat from the bones, discarding the skin and bones.

5. **RETURN** the chicken meat and any accumulated juices to the pot. Add the rice, green onions, thyme, parsley, and spinach and simmer until the rice and beans are tender, about 15 minutes. Discard the bay leaves.

6. **LADLE** into warmed bowls and serve hot.

½ cup dried navy beans
2 tablespoons olive oil
One 4- to 4½-pound chicken, cut into serving pieces
1 teaspoon salt
½ teaspoon freshly ground black pepper
1 cup chopped yellow onions
½ cup chopped carrots
½ cup chopped celery
1 tablespoon minced garlic
½ cup chopped zucchini
½ cup chopped yellow squash
2 quarts Chicken Stock (page 2) or canned low-sodium chicken broth
½ cup seeded and chopped plum tomatoes
4 sprigs fresh parsley
3 bay leaves
¼ teaspoon cayenne
⅓ cup uncooked long-grain white rice
½ cup chopped green onions (green and white parts)
1 tablespoon minced fresh thyme
¼ cup chopped fresh flat-leaf parsley
1 cup torn spinach leaves

COLD ASPARAGUS SOUP WITH LUMP CRABMEAT

MAKES 8 SERVINGS

When we did an *Emeril Live* show on asparagus, we prepared fried asparagus and truffled asparagus, but this soup was the star! There's nothing better than fresh spring asparagus coupled with sweet crabmeat. The combination makes this an elegant lunch or brunch soup to die for!

2 pounds asparagus

1½ teaspoons salt

4 tablespoons (½ stick) unsalted butter

1 cup minced yellow onions

1 cup minced leeks (white parts only)

½ teaspoon freshly ground white pepper

2 teaspoons minced garlic

¼ cup bleached all-purpose flour

1 cup heavy cream

½ pound lump crabmeat, picked over for shells and cartilage

½ cup sour cream or crème fraîche

2 ounces sevruga caviar (optional)

1 tablespoon snipped fresh chives

1. **TRIM** the tough woody ends from the asparagus and discard. Cut the asparagus into 2-inch pieces.

2. **BRING** 2 quarts water and ½ teaspoon of the salt to a boil in a large pot over high heat. Add the asparagus and cook until crisp-tender, about 3 minutes. Drain, reserving the cooking liquid.

3. **MELT** the butter in a large saucepan over medium-high heat. Add the onions, leeks, the remaining 1 teaspoon salt, and the white pepper. Cook, stirring often, until the leeks are wilted, about 3 minutes. Stir in the garlic, then the flour, and reduce the heat to medium-low. Stir to cook the flour, without browning, about 2 minutes. Add the asparagus and the reserved cooking liquid. Bring to a boil over high heat. Reduce the heat to medium-low. Simmer, uncovered, until the asparagus is very tender, about 30 minutes.

4. **PURÉE** the soup with an immersion blender or in batches in a food processor or blender. Strain the soup through a wire sieve into a large bowl. Discard the solids. Whisk in the cream. Cover and refrigerate until well chilled, at least 2 and up to 8 hours.

5. **LADLE** the soup into bowls and garnish each serving with a heaping tablespoon of crabmeat, a dollop of sour cream, a small spoonful of caviar, if using, and a sprinkling of chives.

COLD CUCUMBER SOUP WITH SMOKED SALMON

This delicious, very light soup makes an elegant first course for an outdoor spring or summer luncheon. Or you could serve the soup in small cups as a first course at a large party or buffet.

1. **HEAT** the oil in a large heavy saucepan over medium-high heat. Add the onions, salt, and white pepper. Cook, stirring occasionally, until the onions are softened, about 4 minutes. Add the garlic and stir until fragrant, about 1 minute. Add the cucumbers, green onions, and dill. Cook until the cucumbers are starting to soften, about 3 minutes. Add the stock and bring to a boil. Reduce the heat to medium-low and simmer, stirring occasionally, for 20 minutes.

2. **PURÉE** the soup with an immersion blender or in batches in a food processor or blender. Transfer the soup to a bowl. Cover and refrigerate until cold, at least 2 hours.

3. **STIR** the parsley and yogurt into the soup. Refrigerate for at least 2 more hours, or overnight, to chill thoroughly.

4. **TO** serve, season the chilled soup to taste with additional salt and white pepper if needed. Ladle the soup into bowls and garnish each serving with a spoonful of chopped smoked salmon.

1 tablespoon vegetable oil
1 cup finely chopped yellow onions
1½ teaspoons salt, or more to taste
¼ teaspoon freshly ground white pepper, or more to taste
1 tablespoon minced garlic
6 large cucumbers, peeled, seeded, and chopped (about 6 cups)
½ cup finely chopped green onions (green and white parts)
½ teaspoon dried dill
4 cups Chicken Stock (page 2) or canned low-sodium chicken broth
¼ cup minced fresh flat-leaf parsley
1 cup plain yogurt
½ pound smoked salmon, finely chopped

SWEET POTATO AND DUCK CHOWDER

I grew up eating creamy New England–style chowders made with seafood fished right out of the Atlantic near my hometown of Fall River, Massachusetts, but I've come to love any thick, chunky rich soup. Adding tasso kicks it up even more. The duck and sweet potatoes make this a dish to serve when the winter winds are blowing and you're in the mood for a hearty, flavorful, one-pot meal.

Three 8-ounce boneless duck breasts
1 tablespoon Emeril's Original Essence or Creole Seasoning (page 9)
¼ cup diced Homemade Tasso (page 17) or other spicy sausage or ham
1 cup finely chopped yellow onions
½ cup finely chopped carrots
¼ cup finely chopped celery
½ teaspoon salt
2 tablespoons minced shallots
1 tablespoon minced garlic
2 large sweet potatoes (about 2 pounds), peeled and cut into 1-inch cubes
4 cups Chicken Stock (page 2) or canned low-sodium chicken broth
2 bay leaves
¾ cup plus 2 tablespoons heavy cream
3 tablespoons bleached all-purpose flour

1. SEASON the duck on both sides with 1 teaspoon of the Essence. Heat a large heavy pot or Dutch oven over high heat. Add the duck, skin side down, and immediately lower the heat to medium. Sear until the skin is browned, 5 to 6 minutes. Turn the duck and cook for 3 minutes. Transfer the duck to a plate and let cool. Discard the duck skin and cut the meat into ½-inch cubes.

2. POUR off all but 2 tablespoons of the duck fat from the pot and return the pot to medium-high heat. Add the tasso, onions, carrots, celery, and salt, and cook, stirring often, until softened, about 5 minutes. Add the shallots and cook, stirring often, until softened, about 1 minute. Add the garlic and stir until fragrant, about 30 seconds. Add the sweet potatoes and cook, stirring constantly, until beginning to soften, about 5 minutes. Add the stock, bay leaves, and the remaining 2 teaspoons Essence and the duck and bring to a boil. Reduce the heat to medium-low and simmer, uncovered, for 15 minutes.

3. WHISK 6 tablespoons of the heavy cream and the flour in a small bowl until smooth, then whisk into the soup. Increase the heat to medium-high. Add the remaining ½ cup cream and cook at a brisk simmer, stirring often, until the sweet potatoes are tender, about 15 minutes. Discard the bay leaves.

4. SERVE hot ladled into bowls.

CORN AND CRAB BISQUE

MAKES 4 TO 6 SERVINGS

When we opened Emeril's in New Orleans, this soup was a favorite of Eric Linquest (then a manager and now one of my right-hand men), Mr. Lou (the pastry chef), and myself, so we decided to serve it every Friday at the restaurant. I like to add a few drops of liquid crab boil to give it a little extra kick, but, hey, you might not like it! Do whatever makes you happy. T.G.I.F.!

1. **HEAT** the oil in a large heavy pot or Dutch oven over medium heat. Add the flour a tablespoon at a time, stirring constantly with a wooden spoon until blended. Continue stirring to make a light brown roux, 5 to 10 minutes.

2. **ADD** the onions, corn, shallots, celery, garlic, salt, and cayenne and cook, stirring occasionally, until the onions soften, about 4 minutes. Slowly stir in the stock. Add the bay leaves and bring to a boil. Add the milk, cream, and the crab boil, if using. Reduce the heat to medium-low. Simmer, uncovered, for 30 minutes.

4. **STIR** in the crabmeat and green onions and simmer for 5 minutes. Remove and discard the bay leaves.

5. **SERVE** hot ladled into bowls.

3 tablespoons vegetable oil
3 tablespoons bleached all-purpose flour
½ cup minced yellow onions
1 cup corn kernels (from 2 ears corn)
2 tablespoons minced shallots
2 tablespoons minced celery
1 tablespoon minced garlic
1 teaspoon salt
½ teaspoon cayenne
1 cup Fish Stock (page 5) or water
2 bay leaves
2 cups milk
2 cups heavy cream
1 teaspoon Zatarain's Concentrated Crab and Shrimp Boil (see Source Guide, page 282) (optional)
½ pound lump crabmeat, picked over for shells and cartilage
¼ cup minced green onions (green part only)

RABBIT, ANDOUILLE, AND WILD MUSHROOM GUMBO

MAKES 12 SERVINGS

In Louisiana, everyone has a favorite gumbo, and this rustic one, Acadiana-style, is mine. Rabbits have always been popular in this part of the country. If you can't find them at the local butcher, just get him to special-order one for you.

One 2½-pound rabbit, cut into large pieces
2 tablespoons plus 1 teaspoon Emeril's Original Essence or Creole Seasoning (page 9)
1½ cups plus 1 tablespoon vegetable oil, or as needed
½ pound andouille or other spicy smoked sausage, removed from casings and chopped
½ pound assorted wild mushrooms, such as oysters, chanterelles, and shiitakes, wiped clean and stems removed, trimmed and thinly sliced (about 2 cups)
1½ cups bleached all-purpose flour
1 cup chopped yellow onions
½ cup chopped celery
½ cup chopped green bell peppers
1 tablespoon chopped garlic
3 tablespoons Worcestershire sauce
3 tablespoons Emeril's Red Pepper Sauce or other hot pepper sauce
One 12-ounce bottle lager beer

1 SEASON the rabbit with 1 teaspoon of the Essence. Heat 1 tablespoon of the oil in a heavy skillet over medium-high heat. Add the rabbit and cook until golden, about 3 minutes per side. Transfer the rabbit to a large platter.

2. ADD the andouille to the pan. Cook, stirring, until browned, about 10 minutes. Using a slotted spoon, transfer the andouille to the rabbit platter. Add more oil to the pan if needed, then add the mushrooms and cook, stirring until soft, about 5 minutes. Transfer to the platter.

3. WHISK the remaining 1½ cups oil and the flour in a large heavy pot or Dutch oven until smooth. Cook over medium-high heat, stirring constantly with a wooden spoon, to make a dark chocolate-colored roux, 25 to 30 minutes.

4. ADD the onions, celery, and bell peppers and cook, stirring often, until the vegetables soften, about 5 minutes. Add the garlic and stir until fragrant, about 1 minute. Add the Worcestershire and hot pepper sauces and stir well. Carefully add the beer (it will splatter), and stir well to blend. Stir in the stock and bay leaves. Add the rabbit, andouille, and mushrooms and bring to a boil. Reduce the heat to medium-low and simmer, uncovered, until the rabbit is tender, about 45 minutes.

5. WITH tongs or a long-handled spoon, transfer the rabbit pieces to a large platter and let cool slightly.

6. ADD the remaining 2 tablespoons Essence and the salt to the gumbo and simmer over medium-low heat, stirring occasionally, for another hour.

7. MEANWHILE, remove the rabbit meat from the bones, discarding the bones, and cut into bite-size pieces. During the last 5 minutes of cooking, stir the rabbit into the gumbo. Just before serving, remove the bay leaves.

8. TO serve, spoon the gumbo into soup bowls and add a big spoonful of the rice to each.

9 cups Chicken Stock (page 2) or canned low-sodium chicken broth
3 bay leaves
1 tablespoon salt
Perfect Rice (page 16), hot

CREAM OF PARSNIP SOUP

Parsnips are a personal favorite of mine. If you haven't tried them, you should. The sweetness of parsnips really gives this soup an amazing richness and will make it a great addition to your winter holiday table.

3 tablespoons unsalted butter
2 cups chopped yellow onions
1 cup chopped celery
2¼ teaspoons salt
¼ teaspoon freshly ground black pepper
1 teaspoon chopped garlic
2 bay leaves
2 quarts Chicken Stock (page 2) or canned low-sodium chicken broth
3 pounds parsnips, peeled and chopped
¾ cup heavy cream
2 teaspoons apple cider vinegar
8 strips bacon, chopped and fried until crisp, for garnish
1 tablespoon snipped fresh chives, for garnish

1. **MELT** the butter in a large heavy pot or Dutch oven over medium-high heat. Add the onions, celery, salt, and pepper. Cook, stirring often, until the onions are softened, 4 minutes. Add the garlic and bay leaves and stir until the garlic is fragrant, about 1 minute. Add the chicken stock and parsnips and bring to a boil. Reduce the heat to medium-low. Simmer, uncovered, stirring occasionally, for 1 hour.

2. **STIR** in the cream and vinegar. Remove and discard the bay leaves. Purée the soup with an immersion blender or in batches in a food processor or blender.

3. **SERVE** the soup hot in bowls, garnished with the bacon and chives.

MONKFISH CHOWDER

MAKES 4 TO 6 SERVINGS

Monkfish is so sweet and delicate. It also has a tender texture, so take care not to overcook it. It can be baked, steamed, or braised, but we used it in a chowder on an *Emeril Live* show devoted to monkfish.

1. **SEASON** the monkfish with the Essence and set aside.

2. **COOK** the bacon in a large deep pot or Dutch oven over medium-high heat until just crisp, about 5 minutes. Using a slotted spoon, remove the bacon and drain on paper towels, leaving the fat in the pot.

3. **ADD** the onions, celery, bell peppers, salt, and cayenne to the pot. Cook, stirring often, until the vegetables soften, about 5 minutes. Add the garlic and stir until fragrant, about 30 seconds. Add the stock and potatoes and bring to a boil. Reduce the heat to medium-low and simmer, uncovered, until the potatoes are almost fork-tender, about 15 minutes.

4. **ADD** the corn and half-and-half and bring to a boil over medium-high heat. Add the monkfish, lower the heat, and simmer until the fish flakes, 10 minutes. Stir in the parsley.

5. **SERVE** hot ladled into bowls.

1½ pounds boneless monkfish
   fillets, cut into 1-inch pieces
1 tablespoon Emeril's Original
   Essence or Creole Seasoning
   (page 9)
4 strips bacon, chopped
1½ cups chopped yellow onions
¾ cup chopped celery
¾ cup chopped red bell peppers
1 teaspoon salt
¼ teaspoon cayenne
1 tablespoon minced garlic
3 cups Fish Stock (page 5) or
   canned low-sodium chicken
   broth
1 pound Idaho potatoes (about
   2 large), peeled and cut into
   ½-inch dice
2 cups fresh or thawed frozen
   corn kernels
1½ cups half-and-half
3 tablespoons minced fresh
   flat-leaf parsley

MR. JOHN'S SEAFOOD-CHORIZO GUMBO

MAKES 8 TO 10 SERVINGS

Although my father, Mr. John, hails from Fall River, Massachusetts, he's adapted quite well to living in New Orleans. Perhaps it's because he's of French descent and this is a French city at heart. He sure makes gumbo like a native. To honor him, this is a dish I did for an *Emeril Live* Father's Day show.

Don't forget what I call the "roux theory." Open a beer when you're just getting started; a nice, dark brown roux requires the drinking time of two beers, 25 to 30 minutes.

1½ cups vegetable oil
1½ cups bleached all-purpose flour
2 cups chopped yellow onions
1 cup chopped green bell peppers
1 cup chopped celery
1 tablespoon Emeril's Original Essence or Creole Seasoning (page 9)
1 teaspoon salt
½ teaspoon freshly ground black pepper
2½ quarts Shrimp Stock (page 6) or canned low-sodium chicken stock
1 dozen blue gumbo crabs, cracked in half, lungs and intestines removed
1 pound smoked chorizo or andouille sausage, half finely chopped and half cut into ¼-inch-thick slices
2 pounds medium shrimp, peeled and deveined
2 pounds peeled crawfish tails (see Source Guide, page 282)
2 tablespoons chopped green onions (green parts only)
2 tablespoons minced fresh flat-leaf parsley
Perfect Rice (page 16), hot

1. **HEAT** the oil in a large heavy pot or Dutch oven over medium heat. Whisk in the flour and cook, stirring constantly, to make a fragrant, dark chocolate-colored roux, 25 to 30 minutes.

2. **ADD** the onions, bell peppers, celery, Essence, salt, and pepper. Cook, stirring often, until the vegetables soften, about 4 minutes. Stir in the stock and crabs. Bring to a boil. Reduce the heat to medium-low. Simmer, uncovered, stirring occasionally, for 1½ hours.

3. **MEANWHILE,** heat a large skillet over medium-high heat. Add the chopped and sliced sausage and cook, stirring often, until browned, about 5 minutes. Remove from the heat.

4. **STIR** the shrimp, crawfish, and cooked sausage into the gumbo. Cook over medium-low heat until the seafood is firm, about 10 minutes. Remove from the heat and let stand for a few minutes. Skim any fat from the surface.

5. **STIR** the green onions and parsley into the gumbo. Spoon the rice into soup bowls and ladle the gumbo on top. Serve hot.

BUTTERNUT SQUASH, SAUSAGE, AND WILD RICE SOUP

MAKES 8 TO 10 SERVINGS

Now here's a dish we made on an *Emeril Live* show about possible side dishes to accompany Thanksgiving dinner. But don't wait till November to make this soup; it'll warm you up anytime.

1. PREHEAT the oven to 400°F.

2. RUB the cut sides of the squash halves with 1 tablespoon of the olive oil. Place on a baking sheet flesh side down and roast until tender when pierced with the tip of a knife, 45 minutes to 1 hour.

3. LET the squash cool until easy to handle, then scoop the flesh from the skin with a large spoon. Purée the butternut flesh with 2 cups of the stock in a food processor or blender.

4. BRING 4 cups of the stock and ½ cup of the chopped onions to a simmer in a large saucepan over medium-high heat. Stir in the wild rice. Return to the simmer, cover, and cook until the rice is tender and most of the liquid is absorbed, 45 minutes to 1 hour. Set aside.

5. MEANWHILE, heat the remaining 1 tablespoon oil in a large saucepan over medium-high heat. Add the sausage and cook just until browned, about 4 minutes. Add the remaining 2 cups onions, the corn, salt, and pepper. Cook, stirring often, until the onions are softened, about 4 minutes. Add the remaining 6 cups stock and the squash purée and bring to a boil. Reduce the heat to medium-low, cover, and simmer for 20 minutes, stirring occasionally and skimming any fat that rises to the surface.

6. STIR in the rice and cook for 5 minutes. Stir in the half-and-half and parsley.

7. SERVE hot ladled into bowls.

One 1½- to 2-pound butternut squash, cut in half, seeds and strings removed

2 tablespoons olive oil

3 quarts Chicken Stock (page 2) or canned low-sodium chicken broth

2½ cups chopped yellow onions

1 cup wild rice

¾ pound kielbasa or other smoked sausage, cut into ½-inch slices

2 cups fresh or thawed frozen corn kernels (about 2 large fresh ears of corn)

1 teaspoon salt

½ teaspoon freshly ground black pepper

1½ cups half-and-half

2 tablespoons minced fresh flat-leaf parsley

VIDALIA ONION SOUP WITH FRIED CHEESE TORTELLINI

Vidalia onions hail from Vidalia, Georgia, and their peak season is from May to June. For a while, they were only available locally or by mail-order, but now they're shipped everywhere. Substitute any other sweet onions, like Walla Walla, Oso Sweet, Maui, or Texas Sweets. Frozen cheese tortellini are available in any supermarket.

¼ cup olive oil
6 cups thinly sliced Vidalia or
  other sweet onions
2 teaspoons Emeril's Original
  Essence or Creole Seasoning
  (page 9)
1 teaspoon salt, or more to taste
½ teaspoon freshly ground black
  pepper, or more to taste
2 bay leaves
10 garlic cloves
1 tablespoon chopped fresh
  tarragon
1 tablespoon chopped fresh
  oregano
1 tablespoon chopped fresh basil
2 quarts Chicken Stock (page 2)
  or canned low-sodium
  chicken broth
2 cups diced day-old French
  bread (crusts removed),
  1-inch cubes
½ cup heavy cream
½ cup freshly grated
  Parmigiano-Reggiano
Vegetable oil for deep-frying
16 cheese tortellini, completely
  thawed if frozen
2 tablespoons minced fresh
  flat-leaf parsley

1. **HEAT** the olive oil in a large heavy pot over medium-high heat. Add the onions, 1 teaspoon of the Essence, the salt, pepper, and bay leaves. Cook, stirring, until the onions are just golden, 15 minutes. Add the garlic and stir for 1 minute. Add the tarragon, oregano, basil, and stock and bring to a boil. Reduce the heat to medium-low. Simmer, uncovered, for 30 minutes.

2. **ADD** the bread and cream. Increase the heat to medium-high and cook, whisking often, until the bread dissolves and the soup is thickened, about 10 minutes. Remove and discard the bay leaves. Using an immersion blender, or in batches in a food processor or blender, purée the soup. Add the cheese and adjust the seasonings to taste. Cover and keep the soup warm over very low heat.

3. **POUR** enough oil into a deep heavy pot or electric deep fryer to come halfway up the sides and heat over medium-high heat to 360°F. In batches, carefully add the tortellini to the hot oil and deep-fry, turning frequently with a long-handled slotted spoon, until golden brown, 1 to 2 minutes. Remove with the slotted spoon and drain on paper towels. Season with the remaining 1 teaspoon of Essence.

4. **LADLE** the hot soup into bowls and garnish with the fried tortellini and parsley.

CHILLED ROASTED BEET AND FENNEL SOUP WITH APPLE-MINT CREMA AND TOASTED PISTACHIOS

MAKES 4 TO 6 SERVINGS

We decided to show how delicious and versatile cold soups are on the new *Essence of Emeril* because, as you can guess, it gets pretty hot down here in New Orleans from April through early October. Lucky for us, though, vegetables are abundant and in season, and it's easy to whip up cold soups as satisfying starters to either lunch or dinner. Oven-roasting the beets and fennel first really brings out their sweetness, which is accented by the Apple-Mint Crema.

1. PREHEAT the oven to 375°F.

2. PUT the beets, fennel, 2 tablespoons of the oil, salt, and pepper in a large bowl and toss to combine. Spread the vegetables on a baking sheet covered with aluminum foil and roast until caramelized, 45 minutes to 1 hour.

3. REMOVE from the oven and cool slightly. When cool enough to handle, cut into ½-inch cubes.

4. HEAT the remaining oil in a saucepan over medium-high heat. Add the onions and cook, stirring, until soft, 3 to 4 minutes. Add the carrots and celery and cook, stirring, until soft, 3 minutes. Add the garlic and cook, stirring, for 30 seconds. Add the fennel, beets, and stock, and bring to a boil. Reduce the heat to medium-low and simmer for 20 minutes. Remove from the heat and cool slightly.

5. WITH an immersion blender, or in batches in a food processor or blender, purée the soup. Refrigerate the purée until cool, at least 2 hours.

6. IN a small bowl combine the sour cream, applesauce, mint, and sage, and stir to combine.

7. LADLE the chilled soup into serving bowls, top with a dollop of Apple-Mint Crema and pistachios, and serve.

1 pound medium beets, peeled, stems removed, and halved

1 fennel bulb, about ¾ pound, cored, stem removed, and quartered

4 tablespoons olive oil

1 teaspoon salt

1 teaspoon freshly ground black pepper

1 cup thinly sliced yellow onions

¼ cup finely chopped carrots

¼ cup finely chopped celery

1 teaspoon minced garlic

6 cups Chicken Stock (page 2) or canned low-sodium chicken broth

½ cup sour cream

3 tablespoons applesauce

1 teaspoon minced fresh mint leaves

1 teaspoon minced fresh sage leaves

¼ cup toasted and crushed pistachios

the recipes

SALADS

Let's face it. Salads can be boring. Too many people just throw together the usual lettuce-and-tomato combo. I often go for the unusual. Who would've thought to pair grapefruit and salmon? But it works. I was concerned that a simple Romaine Salad with Creamy Garlic Dressing might be too humdrum for our viewers, but it turned out to be one of the most requested recipes. Choosing the best lettuces, oils, vinegars, and other ingredients is what make the difference.

CRABMEAT SALAD WITH ASPARAGUS AND ZUCCHINI BLOSSOMS

MAKES 4 SERVINGS

Zucchini blossoms can usually be found during the summer at farmers' markets, specialty food stores, or even special-ordered through your greengrocer. They have a delicate flavor and make a beautiful presentation on the plate. There are many other edible flowers that can be used instead, such as pansies, nasturtiums, or rose petals; just make sure they haven't been sprayed with pesticides. If you can't find lump crabmeat in your town, substitute boiled shrimp or sautéed baby scallops—just make sure they're fresh—although lump (and jumbo lump) will definitely be the sweetest.

1 cup Mayonnaise (page 12) or store-bought mayonnaise
2 tablespoons minced shallots
1 tablespoon minced fresh tarragon
1 tablespoon capers, drained and chopped
2 teaspoons Dijon mustard
1 teaspoon minced garlic
1 pound lump crabmeat, picked over for shells and cartilage
½ teaspoon salt
¼ teaspoon freshly ground black pepper
½ pound pencil-thin asparagus, trimmed and steamed until just tender
1 small red onion, thinly sliced
1 tablespoon extra-virgin olive oil
1 teaspoon balsamic vinegar
12 zucchini blossoms, rinsed well and patted dry
2 tablespoons chopped fresh flat-leaf parsley

1. MIX the mayonnaise, shallots, tarragon, capers, mustard, and garlic in a medium bowl. Fold in the crabmeat and season with ¼ teaspoon salt and ⅛ teaspoon pepper.

2. IN another bowl, toss the asparagus and onion with the olive oil and vinegar and season with the remaining ¼ teaspoon salt and ⅛ teaspoon pepper.

3. PLACE equal amounts of the asparagus in the centers of four salad plates. Arrange the crabmeat salad over the asparagus. Lay three zucchini blossoms over each portion of crabmeat and garnish with the parsley.

ROASTED VEGETABLE SALAD

Sometimes all you want is a plate of vegetables. Here you go. Or serve this as a side dish with grilled lamb chops, fish, or shrimp. Take it up another notch by tossing with a half cup of chopped black olives (like kalamatas) and some crumbled goat cheese and finish with a sprinkling of toasted pine nuts or walnuts.

1. **PREHEAT** the oven to 350°F.

2. **PUT** the vegetables in a large mixing bowl with the olive oil, salt, and pepper. Toss well to coat evenly.

3. **SPREAD** the vegetables in a single layer in a large roasting pan. Roast until soft and golden brown, about 45 minutes. Let cool for 15 minutes.

4. **TRANSFER** the vegetables to a large serving bowl and toss with the herbs, extra-virgin olive oil, and lemon juice. Add more salt and pepper if necessary. Serve warm or cold, or at room temperature.

1 large eggplant (about 1¼ pounds), peeled and cut into ½-inch dice

1 large zucchini (about ¾ pound), cut into ½-inch dice

1 medium yellow squash (about 6 ounces), cut into ½-inch dice

1 cup chopped yellow onions

¼ cup olive oil

2 teaspoons salt, or more to taste

1 teaspoon freshly ground black pepper, or more to taste

½ cup finely chopped mixed fresh herbs, such as chives, tarragon, dill, chervil, basil, cilantro, and/or flat-leaf parsley

2 tablespoons extra-virgin olive oil

1 tablespoon fresh lemon juice

CURED SALMON AND CARAMELIZED RUBY RED GRAPEFRUIT SALAD WITH BLOOD ORANGE GASTRIQUE

MAKES 4 SERVINGS

When we did a show called "Citrus Rules," we discovered that grapefruit isn't just for breakfast anymore; it can be part of a sophisticated first course. This grapefruit and fennel salad is just the right accompaniment for the Vodka-and-Citrus-Cured Salmon. The concentrated orange flavors in the *gastrique* (sugar and vinegar reduced to a syrupy consistency) set off everything beautifully. Blood oranges give the sauce a brilliant red color, but if you can't find them, substitute juice oranges. Serve this in the fall or winter, when grapefruit is in season.

1 fennel bulb
1 tablespoon olive oil
½ teaspoon salt
¼ teaspoon freshly ground black pepper
3 Ruby Red grapefruit
½ cup sugar
2 cups arugula, stemmed, washed, and patted dry
1 tablespoon extra-virgin olive oil
Vodka-and-Citrus-Cured Salmon (page 162), thinly sliced
Blood Orange Gastrique (recipe follows)
1 tablespoon minced fresh flat-leaf parsley

1. PREHEAT the oven to 400°F.

2. TRIM off the fennel stalks, cut the bulb in half, and remove the tough core. Toss the fennel with the olive oil, ¼ teaspoon of the salt, and ⅛ teaspoon of the pepper. Put the fennel in a roasting pan cut side down and roast until golden brown, 25 to 30 minutes. Cool completely.

3. PEEL the grapefruit and trim away all of the white pith. Working over a bowl, using a serrated knife, cut between the membranes to release the grapefruit segments. Pat the grapefruit segments dry with paper towels, then toss with the sugar.

4. HEAT a large nonstick skillet over medium-high heat. Add the grapefruit and cook, turning once, until each segment is caramelized, 3 to 4 minutes. Transfer to a bowl and let cool.

5. THINLY slice the fennel. Place in a mixing bowl and toss with the arugula, extra-virgin olive oil, and the remaining ¼ teaspoon salt and ⅛ teaspoon pepper. Add the grapefruit and toss well.

6. MOUND the fennel salad in the centers of four serving plates and arrange the sliced salmon around it. Drizzle the gastrique over the salads. Garnish with the parsley and serve.

Blood Orange Gastrique

MAKES 1 CUP

COMBINE the sugar, vinegar, and juice in a small nonreactive saucepan. Bring to a boil over high heat. Cook until the mixture has reduced to 1 cup and thickened into a syrup, about 10 minutes. Cool completely before using.

1 cup sugar
½ cup rice wine vinegar
1 cup blood orange juice (from 2 to 3 oranges) or regular orange juice

STIR-FRIED BOK CHOY AND SHRIMP SALAD WITH WONTON CHIPS

MAKES 4 SERVINGS

I love Asian flavors and it always makes me happy, happy, happy to introduce them to others, as I have done on some of the *Emeril Live* shows. This works as either a first course or a main course for two.

12 wonton skins
1¼ pounds bok choy
½ pound peeled rock shrimp or peeled and deveined medium shrimp (about 1 cup)
1¼ teaspoons Emeril's Original Essence or Creole Seasoning (page 9)
2 tablespoons vegetable oil
⅔ cup finely grated carrots (2 small carrots)
1 small red onion, finely sliced
½ teaspoon salt
¼ teaspoon cayenne
Hoisin Dressing (recipe follows)

1. PREHEAT the oven to 375°F.

2. STACK the wonton skins on a cutting board and cut into ⅛-inch-wide strips. Gently toss to separate the strips and spread on an ungreased baking sheet. Bake for 6 minutes. Remove from the oven and toss again to separate the strips. Return to the oven and continue baking until they are light brown and crisp, about 8 minutes more. Set aside to cool.

3. CUT off the bottom 3 inches of each bunch of bok choy and discard the bottom sections. Roll the bok choy leaves tightly together and cut into thin strips.

4. COMBINE the shrimp and Essence in a small bowl, tossing to coat the shrimp evenly.

5. HEAT a wok or deep skillet over high heat for 1 minute. Pour in the oil and heat until very hot. Add the shrimp and stir-fry until they turn pink, about 1 minute. Add the bok choy, carrots, and onion and stir-fry for 2 minutes. Remove from the heat and season with the salt and cayenne.

6. SPOON the stir-fry onto four dinner plates. Top each with some wonton strips. Drizzle each serving with 1 to 2 tablespoons of the dressing, and serve warm.

Hoisin Dressing

MAKES ½ CUP

There was a time when you had to travel to an Asian food store to buy hoisin sauce, rice wine vinegar, and dark sesame oil, but now most supermarkets carry these items. Be sure to buy Asian sesame oil, which is orange-red in color.

¼ cup hoisin sauce
2 tablespoons rice vinegar
1 tablespoon Asian (dark)
    sesame oil
1 teaspoon soy sauce
½ teaspoon minced garlic
¼ teaspoon cayenne

COMBINE all the ingredients in a small mixing bowl and whisk well to blend. This keeps for 5 days.

ROMAINE SALAD WITH CREAMY GARLIC DRESSING AND ROASTED GARLIC CROUTONS

MAKES 4 SERVINGS

This awesome salad was one we featured on an *Essence of Emeril* show and it's become one of our most requested recipes! People love garlicky dressings. While this may seem like it has a lot of garlic, the garlic is roasted first so the flavor is sweet and mellow, not at all pungent. This salad is a great starter or side dish for grilled or roasted chicken, or would make an enjoyable light dinner for two. And the dressing makes a fantastic dip for vegetables or chips.

CROUTONS

One loaf French bread, cut crosswise into ½-inch-thick slices
¼ cup olive oil
¼ teaspoon salt
⅛ teaspoon freshly ground black pepper
¼ cup Roasted Garlic Purée (page 11)

1 head romaine lettuce, separated into leaves, rinsed, and patted dry
Creamy Garlic Dressing (recipe follows)

1. **TO** make the croutons, preheat the oven to 400°F.

2. **ARRANGE** the slices of bread on a baking sheet. Brush one side of each with the olive oil. Sprinkle with the salt and pepper. Bake until golden brown, about 15 minutes. Remove from the oven and let cool a bit. Spread the croutons with the roasted garlic purée.

3. **WHILE** the croutons are baking, prepare the lettuce: Tear the larger leaves into bite-size pieces, and leave the smaller, tender leaves whole. Toss in a large salad bowl with the desired amount of dressing.

4. **DIVIDE** the greens among four salad plates and serve with the croutons on the side.

Creamy Garlic Dressing

MAKES ABOUT 1 CUP

MIX the mayonnaise, garlic purée, cheese, heavy cream, and lemon juice in a medium bowl with a rubber spatula. Season with the salt and pepper. Serve with salad, or as a dip. (The dressing will keep in an airtight container in the refrigerator for 24 hours.)

½ cup Mayonnaise (page 12) or store-bought mayonnaise
¼ cup Roasted Garlic Purée (page 11)
3 tablespoons freshly grated Parmigiano-Reggiano
2 tablespoons heavy cream
1 tablespoon fresh lemon juice
¼ teaspoon salt
¼ teaspoon freshly ground black pepper

HAZELNUT, GOAT CHEESE, AND BABY GREENS SALAD WITH HAZELNUT-CHARDONNAY DRESSING

MAKES 4 SERVINGS

This simple salad is ideal to serve before or after a big, elaborate meal. There are few ingredients, but the taste is really sophisticated. This was one of the recipes that came from a show called "Going Nuts," and you certainly can substitute walnut or olive oil, but that will, of course, change the flavor of the dressing.

1 cup hazelnuts
¼ cup Chardonnay or other dry white wine
½ cup hazelnut oil
½ teaspoon salt
¼ teaspoon freshly ground black pepper
12 ounces baby greens
8 ounces goat cheese, such as Montrachet, crumbled

1. **PREHEAT** the oven to 350°F.

2. **SPREAD** the hazelnuts on a baking sheet. Bake, stirring occasionally, until the skins are cracked and peeling, about 10 minutes. Wrap the nuts in a kitchen towel and let cool for 10 minutes. Rub the nuts in the towel to remove most of the skins. Let cool completely.

3. **CHOP** ¾ cup of the hazelnuts. Place the wine in a small bowl and gradually whisk in the oil. Add the chopped hazelnuts, season with the salt and pepper, and whisk well to combine. Place the greens in a bowl and toss with the dressing.

4. **DIVIDE** the greens among four salad plates. Crumble the goat cheese over the greens, sprinkle with the reserved ¼ cup whole hazelnuts, and serve.

GRAPE TOMATO, ARUGULA, AND RED ONION SALAD

MAKES 4 SERVINGS

Go ahead and kick this up to suit your tastes. A sweet blue cheese like Gorgonzola, or a nice creamy goat cheese or sheep's milk cheese like feta, would be great, and so would a couple of tablespoons or so of toasted walnuts. Man, what a way to start a meal! Note that this dressing will probably make more than you want to use, so just dress the salad according to your own preference, and keep the rest refrigerated in an airtight container for up to 1 week.

1. TO make the dressing, combine all of the ingredients in a small bowl and whisk to blend thoroughly.

2. COMBINE the salad ingredients in a salad bowl, add the dressing, and toss to coat evenly.

DRESSING
2 tablespoons balsamic vinegar
¼ cup extra-virgin olive oil
1 teaspoon minced garlic
½ teaspoon salt
½ teaspoon sugar

SALAD
8 cups arugula, washed and
    patted dry, tough stems
    removed
1 pint grape or cherry tomatoes,
    cut lengthwise in half
1 cup thinly sliced red onions

ARUG'EN'RAD SALAD

MAKES 6 SERVINGS

This was one of the first salads we created at the original Emeril's in New Orleans, and it is now a standard feature on the menu at Emeril's in Orlando. I featured this on an *Emeril Live* show about summer soups and salads because there's just something about this dressing combined with arugula, radicchio, and walnuts that makes it a great warm-weather salad.

4 ounces (1 cup) walnut halves
2 teaspoons vegetable oil
1 head radicchio, quartered
1½ teaspoons minced shallots
½ teaspoon minced garlic
½ teaspoon orange zest
¼ cup fresh orange juice
2 tablespoons rice wine vinegar
1 tablespoon apple cider vinegar
1 teaspoon honey
½ cup walnut oil
¼ teaspoon kosher salt
⅛ teaspoon freshly ground black pepper
8 cups baby arugula, washed and patted dry
1 head endive, washed, patted dry, and separated into spears
4 ounces Maytag or Danish blue cheese, crumbled (about 1 cup)

1. **PREHEAT** the oven to 300°F.

2. **SPREAD** the walnuts on a baking sheet and bake, stirring once, until fragrant and lightly toasted, 5 to 7 minutes. Remove from the oven and let cool.

3. **HEAT** 1 teaspoon of the oil in a large skillet over medium-high heat. Add the radicchio and cook until soft, about 2 minutes on each side. Remove from the pan and drain on paper towels. Cool, then remove and discard the cores. Cut into thin strips.

4. **ADD** the remaining teaspoon of oil to the skillet. Add the shallots and cook until soft, about 1 minute. Add the garlic and orange zest and cook for 30 seconds. Add the orange juice and reduce by half, about 1 minute. Remove from the heat and pour the mixture into a bowl.

5. **ADD** the rice wine and apple cider vinegars and honey, and whisk. Slowly drizzle in the walnut oil and whisk until blended and slightly thickened. Add ½ cup of the walnuts and the salt and pepper, and whisk well.

6. **COMBINE** the arugula, radicchio strips, and endive in a large salad bowl and toss with the walnut dressing. Divide the salad among six plates. Top with the remaining walnuts and the cheese and serve.

FRIED CRAWFISH SALAD WITH MIRLITON RELISH AND CREOLE REMOULADE

MAKES 4 SERVINGS

Mirlitons, also known as chayotes, vegetable pears, christophines, or cho-chos, grow on a vine and are very popular in the South, especially in Louisiana. They have a prickly outer skin and soft flesh surrounding a large flat seed. To get at the edible flesh and remove the tough skin and seed, they must be parboiled. But believe me, the little bit of effort required is definitely worth it.

1 mirliton (about ¾ pound)
3 Roma plum tomatoes (about ½ pound), seeded and cut into ½-inch dice
¼ cup finely chopped red onions
1 teaspoon minced garlic
2 tablespoons finely chopped fresh flat-leaf parsley
2 tablespoons extra-virgin olive oil
½ teaspoon salt
¼ teaspoon freshly ground black pepper
½ cup buttermilk
3 teaspoons Emeril's Original Essence or Creole Seasoning (page 9)
1 pound peeled crawfish tails
½ cup yellow cornmeal
½ cup masa harina
4 cups vegetable oil
4 cups assorted salad greens, cleaned and patted dry
1 cup Creole Remoulade Sauce (page 103)
½ cup freshly grated Pecorino Romano

1. **PUT** the mirliton in a heavy medium pot and cover with water. Bring to a boil and cook until the flesh is tender when pierced with a fork, about 40 minutes. Remove from the heat and drain. Cool, then peel and cut in half. Remove the seed and any stringy membranes surrounding it and cut the halves into ½-inch cubes.

2. **COMBINE** the mirliton, tomatoes, red onions, garlic, and parsley in a small bowl. Add the olive oil, salt, and pepper and toss to coat evenly.

3. **COMBINE** the buttermilk and 1 teaspoon of Essence in a large bowl. Add the crawfish tails and let stand for 10 minutes.

4. **COMBINE** the remaining 2 teaspoons of Essence with the cornmeal and masa harina in a shallow bowl.

5. **REMOVE** the crawfish from the buttermilk mixture and add to the cornmeal mixture. Toss to coat evenly, shaking to remove any excess.

6. **HEAT** the oil in a large, heavy pot or electric fryer to 360°F. Add the crawfish tails, in batches, and cook, turning with a slotted spoon, until golden brown, 1 to 2 minutes. Remove and drain on paper towels.

7. **DIVIDE** the salad greens into four equal portions and place on salad plates. Arrange equal amounts of the vegetable mixture on the greens. Top with equal amounts of the crawfish, then drizzle each portion with the remoulade, and sprinkle with cheese. Serve immediately.

ARUGULA WITH HAM AND BLUE CHEESE AND FIG VINAIGRETTE

MAKES 4 SERVINGS

The great thing about the dressing is that you can have a taste of summer anytime, since it's made with preserves instead of fresh figs. There's something about this flavor combination that's just magic in every bite—peppery arugula, salty ham, sharp and creamy cheese, and the slightly sweet fig dressing.

1. PREHEAT the oven to 350°F.

2. CUT the bread into ½-inch cubes. Toss with the olive oil, salt, and pepper. Place the croutons on a baking sheet and bake, stirring once, until golden, about 4 minutes. Remove and let cool.

3. HEAT a small skillet over medium-high heat. Add the ham and cook, stirring, until crispy, 3 to 4 minutes. Remove from the heat.

4. TO make the vinaigrette, whisk the fig preserves, vinegar, shallots, salt, and pepper in a small bowl. Slowly whisk in the vegetable oil. Set aside.

5. TOSS the arugula with the vinaigrette in a large bowl. Divide the greens among four salad plates. Arrange the quartered figs, ham, and croutons over the greens. Sprinkle with the blue cheese and serve.

Four ½-inch-thick slices brioche, challah, or white bread, crusts removed
¼ cup olive oil
⅛ teaspoon salt
Pinch of freshly ground black pepper
¼ pound thinly sliced Virginia ham or prosciutto
8 cups arugula, tough stems removed, washed, and patted dry
8 fresh figs, stems removed and quartered
6 ounces blue cheese, such as Maytag or Danish, crumbled

VINAIGRETTE
½ cup fig preserves
3 tablespoons apple cider vinegar
1 tablespoon minced shallots
3/8 teaspoon salt
Pinch of freshly ground black pepper
¼ cup vegetable oil

PASTA & RICE

Just when I think I've cooked pasta and rice about every way, I find new ways to give them an inspired twist. ■ Take for example, the Fettuccine with Bacon and Peas. It's a variation on fettuccine carbonara. And who doesn't like lasagna? The rich, hearty Meat Sauce is out of sight. Don't feel like making lasagna? Ladle the sauce over pasta, polenta, or rice. ■ And if you really want to walk on the wild side, try the Pasta "Rags" with kicked-up Vodka Sauce or the "Chairman of the Board" Linguine. ■ Risotto fans, try the Crawfish and Artichoke Risotto or the one with shrimp and saffron.

TRUFFLED CORN AND
WILD MUSHROOM FETTUCCINE

MAKES 3 TO 4 SERVINGS

Farmers' markets always intrigue me, and I love visiting them across the country. I'm finding that farmers now are selling exotic produce like wild mushrooms, in addition to favorite American staples like sweet corn. This fantastic pasta dish marries these ingredients. The crispiness of the pancetta and the flavor of truffle oil and sweet corn are fantastic!

½ pound pancetta or bacon, cut into 1-inch-wide strips

2 cups corn kernels (from 3 to 4 ears of corn)

2½ teaspoons salt

½ teaspoon freshly ground black pepper

1 pound mixed wild mushrooms, such as wood ear, chanterelle, and/or shiitake, stems wiped clean, and sliced

1 tablespoon minced garlic

1 pound fresh fettuccine

1 tablespoon white truffle oil, or more to taste

3 ounces Parmigiano-Reggiano, grated (about ¾ cup)

2 tablespoons minced fresh basil

1. HEAT a large skillet over medium-high heat. Add the pancetta and cook until crispy, about 5 minutes. Using a slotted spoon, transfer to paper towels and drain. Let cool and coarsely chop.

2. ADD the corn, ½ teaspoon of the salt, and the pepper to the skillet. Cook, stirring occasionally, until the corn is heated through, about 2 minutes. Add the mushrooms and cook, stirring occasionally, until they are tender and give off their juices, about 4 minutes. Add the garlic and stir until fragrant, about 1 minute. Remove from the heat, add the pancetta, and cover to keep warm.

3. MEANWHILE, bring 1 gallon water and the remaining 2 teaspoons salt to a boil in a large pot over high heat. Add the fettuccine and cook, stirring occasionally to separate the noodles, until al dente, 4 to 5 minutes for fresh, or about 10 minutes for dried. Drain the pasta and return to the pot.

4. ADD the corn mixture and truffle oil and toss to coat evenly. Add the cheese and basil and toss again. Serve hot.

FETTUCCINE WITH BACON AND PEAS

Pasta rocks my boat! On an *Essence* show, I came up with this new version of a classic favorite, fettuccine alla carbonara. I omitted the traditional eggs and added peas for some crunch and color.

½ cup fresh or defrosted frozen peas
¾ pound bacon, cut into 1-inch pieces
¾ cup finely chopped yellow onions
1 teaspoon minced garlic
1 cup heavy cream
1 cup freshly grated Parmigiano-Reggiano
1 teaspoon Emeril's Original Essence or Creole Seasoning (page 9)
2½ teaspoons salt
½ teaspoon freshly ground black pepper
12 ounces dried fettuccine or tagliatelle

1. **BRING** a small saucepan of lightly salted water to a boil. Add the peas and blanch for 2 minutes. Drain and set aside.

2. **COOK** the bacon in a large skillet over medium-high heat, stirring frequently, until browned and crispy, about 5 minutes. Using a slotted spoon, transfer to paper towels to drain.

3. **POUR** off all but 1 tablespoon of the fat from the pan. Add the onions and cook, stirring often, until softened, about 4 minutes. Add the garlic and stir until fragrant, about 1 minute. Whisk in the cream, then stir in ½ cup of the grated cheese, the Essence, ½ teaspoon of the salt, and the pepper. Bring to a boil and cook, stirring often, until slightly thickened, about 2 minutes. Remove from the heat and cover to keep warm.

4. **MEANWHILE,** bring 1 gallon water and the remaining 2 teaspoons salt to a boil in a large pot over high heat. Add the pasta. Cook, stirring frequently to keep the pasta from sticking together, until al dente, about 7 to 10 minutes. Drain, reserving ½ cup of the cooking liquid.

5. **RETURN** the pasta to the pot. Add the cream mixture, the reserved cooking liquid, peas, and bacon and toss over medium heat for 1 minute, or until the sauce is warmed through and coats the pasta.

6. **DIVIDE** the pasta among four dinner plates, and sprinkle with the remaining ½ cup cheese. Serve hot.

EMERIL'S LASAGNA

The worst part about making lasagna is fishing the slippery hot noodles out of the boiling water and layering them in the pan before they stick together. With this technique, you don't have to cook the noodles—just assemble the lasagna and bake it for a longer time at a lower temperature. The meat sauce that's used in the lasagna can also be spooned over penne or any favorite pasta of yours, served with a light dusting of Parmesan.

2 teaspoons unsalted butter for the baking dish
1 pound ricotta cheese
2 cups grated provolone (about 8 ounces)
2 cups grated mozzarella (about 8 ounces)
2 cups freshly grated Pecorino Romano (about 8 ounces)
¼ cup milk
1 large egg
1 tablespoon minced fresh basil
1 tablespoon minced garlic
1 teaspoon salt
½ teaspoon freshly ground black pepper
Meat Sauce (recipe follows)
1 package dried lasagna noodles (1 pound)
2 cups freshly grated Parmigiano-Reggiano (about 8 ounces)

1. PREHEAT the oven to 375°F. Butter a 15 × 10-inch baking dish or a roasting pan.

2. STIR the ricotta, provolone, mozzarella, Romano, milk, egg, basil, and garlic in a large mixing bowl. Add the salt and pepper and mix well.

3. SPOON ½ cup of the meat sauce over the bottom of the baking dish. Top with a layer of uncooked noodles. Cover the noodles with a layer of meat sauce, then a layer of the cheese mixture. Repeat layering the lasagna, sauce, and cheese until all have been used, ending with a topping of the cheese mixture. Top the lasagna with the grated Parmesan cheese.

4. COVER tightly with foil and bake for 1½ hours. Uncover and continue baking until golden and bubbly, about 15 minutes longer. Let stand for 10 minutes before serving.

Meat Sauce

MAKES ABOUT 1½ QUARTS

This sauce is one of my favorites for any kind of pasta, but especially the short, ridged shapes like penne or rigatoni, which hold the sauce well. You'll notice the optional addition of chicken livers, which we included for a recent *Essence* show. The livers add a unique flavor and texture to bring this up another notch.

1. **MELT** the butter in a large heavy stockpot over medium-high heat. Add the bacon and ham and cook, stirring often, until browned, 8 to 10 minutes. Add the ground meats and increase the heat to high. Cook, stirring occasionally, until the meat is well browned, about 20 minutes.

2. **ADD** the onions, carrots, celery, and mushrooms. Cook, stirring often, until the vegetables soften, about 5 minutes. Add the garlic, nutmeg, and cloves, and stir until the garlic is fragrant, about 1 minute. Stir in the tomato paste, salt, and pepper and cook for 2 minutes. Add the wine and cook until almost evaporated, about 5 minutes.

3. **STIR** in the stock and bring to a boil. Reduce the heat to medium-low. Simmer, stirring occasionally, until the sauce has thickened, 45 minutes to 1 hour.

4. **ADD** the chicken livers, if using, and cook until firm, about 5 minutes. Stir in the cream and parsley. Heat through and adjust the seasoning to taste. Use hot.

2 tablespoons unsalted butter
6 strips bacon, diced
¼ pound boiled ham, diced
1 pound ground beef
½ pound ground veal or ground pork (or ¼ pound of each)
1½ cups chopped onions
½ cup finely chopped carrots
½ cup finely chopped celery
¼ pound white button mushrooms, trimmed, wiped clean, and thinly sliced
3 garlic cloves, minced
¼ teaspoon freshly grated nutmeg
⅛ teaspoon ground cloves
3 tablespoons tomato paste
1½ teaspoons salt, or more to taste
¼ teaspoon freshly ground black pepper, or more to taste
1 cup dry white wine
3 cups Chicken Stock (page 2) or canned low-sodium chicken broth
4 chicken livers, finely chopped (optional)
½ cup heavy cream
¼ cup chopped fresh flat-leaf parsley

EMERILIZED PILAU

Pilau and pilaf are first cousins! This dish, which can be rice- or bulghur-based, originated in the Near East. You begin by first browning the rice in butter or oil before adding water or stock. The dish can be variously seasoned and usually contains cooked chopped vegetables, meats, seafood, or poultry. It's easily prepared and can accompany a variety of foods. You'll really be surprised at how versatile it is. Be creative and add whatever chopped vegetables—like yellow squash, zucchini, eggplant, green beans—you've got on hand, or whatever suits your fancy. The important thing is the proportion of liquid to rice.

1½ tablespoons unsalted butter
¼ pound boiled ham, diced
1½ cups finely chopped yellow onions
½ cup finely chopped celery
1 teaspoon salt
¼ teaspoon freshly ground black pepper
2 bay leaves
2 cups long-grain white rice
½ cup finely chopped green onions (green and white parts)
½ cup seeded and chopped tomatoes
2 teaspoons finely chopped garlic
½ cup frozen peas
3½ cups Chicken Stock (page 2) or canned low-sodium chicken broth

1. **PREHEAT** the oven to 325°F.

2. **MELT** the butter in a large ovenproof saucepan over medium-high heat. Add the ham and cook for 2 minutes. Add the onions, celery, salt, pepper, and bay leaves and cook, stirring often, until the vegetables soften, about 4 minutes. Add the rice and stir to coat. Add the green onions, tomatoes, and garlic and cook, stirring occasionally, for 2 minutes. Stir in the peas and chicken stock. Bring to a boil over high heat.

3. **REMOVE** the pan from the heat and cover tightly with aluminum foil. Bake until the rice is tender and the liquid is absorbed, about 30 minutes.

4. **REMOVE** from the oven and let stand, covered, for 10 to 15 minutes. Remove the bay leaves.

5. **BEFORE** serving, fluff the rice with a fork.

WILD PECAN RICE DRESSING

MAKES 6 SERVINGS

I came up with this dish to accompany roast goose for an *Emeril Live* Christmas show, but it's also good with roast chicken, duck, lamb, or veal. Don't wait until the holidays to make it. Wild Pecan Aromatic Rice is a Konriko Brand product and is available throughout the United States. The rice is grown in the moist soil of Iberia Parish in southern Louisiana, about a two-hour drive from New Orleans. The rice, a long-grain variety, is not grown anywhere else in America. When it cooks, there's a rich nutty aroma and flavor, but it does not contain wild rice or any pecan pieces. I tip my hat to Mike Davis, who introduced me to this wonderful product at the Konriko Company Store.

1. FRY the bacon in a large skillet over medium-high heat, stirring occasionally, until just crisp, about 5 minutes. Add the tasso and cook for 2 minutes. Using a slotted spoon, transfer the bacon and tasso to paper towels to drain.

2. MELT the butter in a large saucepan over medium-high heat. Add the onions and celery and cook, stirring, until softened, about 4 minutes. Stir in the garlic, salt, and pepper and cook until the garlic is fragrant, about 1 minute. Stir in the pecans and cook, stirring occasionally, until heated through, about 3 minutes. Add the rice and apples and cook, stirring to coat the rice with the juices, about 1 minute.

3. ADD 2 cups water and bring to a boil. Reduce the heat to medium-low, cover, and simmer until the water has been absorbed, about 20 minutes.

4. REMOVE from the heat and let stand, covered, for 5 minutes. Stir in the reserved bacon and tasso, green onions, and parsley. Serve hot.

½ pound bacon, chopped
1 cup chopped Homemade Tasso (page 17) or smoked ham
1 tablespoon unsalted butter
¼ cup chopped yellow onions
¼ cup chopped celery
2 teaspoons minced garlic
½ teaspoon salt
½ teaspoon freshly ground black pepper
½ cup chopped pecans
One 7-ounce package Konriko Wild Pecan Rice (see Source Guide, page 282)
1 Granny Smith apple, unpeeled, cored, and chopped (about 1 cup)
½ cup chopped green onions (green and white parts)
2 tablespoons minced fresh flat-leaf parsley

CRAWFISH AND ARTICHOKE RISOTTO

MAKES 4 SERVINGS

I'm amazed at the different cultures and cuisines that have rice as a staple. Louisianans eat rice at just about every meal; the same goes for Asians. And rice comes in all sorts of forms—take Arborio rice, for instance. The high-starch kernels of this Italian rice are shorter and fatter than other short-grain rice, which makes it ideal for one of my favorite dishes—risotto. It was a no-brainer to combine Louisiana crawfish and artichokes in a risotto!

5 to 6 cups Shrimp Stock (page 6), Chicken Stock (page 2), or canned low-sodium chicken broth, or more as needed
1 tablespoon olive oil
2 tablespoons unsalted butter
3/4 cup chopped yellow onions
1/4 cup chopped red bell peppers
2 teaspoons chopped garlic
2 cups Arborio rice
1 cup dry white wine
2 1/2 tablespoons fresh lemon juice
2 teaspoons salt
1/2 teaspoon freshly ground black pepper
1/2 cup chopped green onions (green and white parts)
2 cups cooked and chopped Artichoke Bottoms (recipe follows)
1/2 pound cooked and peeled crawfish tails (see Source Guide, page 282)
1/2 cup heavy cream
3/4 cup freshly grated Parmigiano-Reggiano
1/2 cup chopped fresh flat-leaf parsley

1. BRING the stock to a simmer in a medium saucepan over high heat. Reduce the heat to very low to keep the stock hot. Heat the olive oil in a large saucepan over medium-high heat. Add the butter and melt. Add the onions, bell peppers, and garlic, and cook, stirring, until the vegetables are just wilted, 3 minutes. Add the rice and cook, stirring constantly, until the grains are opaque, about 2 minutes. Add the wine and cook, stirring, until it evaporates, about 1 minute. Add 3/4 cup of the stock, the lemon juice, salt, and pepper and cook, stirring, until the liquid has been absorbed by the rice. Continue to cook and stir, adding 1/2 cup of the stock at a time as the rice absorbs the liquid.

2. AFTER the rice has cooked for 20 minutes, add the green onions and artichoke bottoms. Cook, stirring constantly, for 3 minutes. Add the crawfish tails, heavy cream, 1/2 cup of the Parmesan cheese, and parsley. Stir to combine. Remove from the heat and let stand for 5 minutes uncovered.

3. DIVIDE the risotto among four serving plates and top each portion with the remaining Parmesan cheese.

Artichoke Bottoms

MAKES 8 BOTTOMS

Artichoke bottoms make tasty additions to a lot of dishes—from casseroles and poached eggs to salads and pastas. If you're not going to use these right away, be sure to give them a light coating of olive oil, then cover them tightly and store in the refrigerator.

8 whole, raw artichokes
4 lemons, cut in half
1 tablespoon salt
4 bay leaves

1. WITH a sharp paring knife, cut the stem from each artichoke and trim the tough outer leaves to reach the inner core of soft, light green leaves.

2. BRING 2 gallons of water to the boil in a large, nonreactive pot. Add the artichokes, lemons, salt, and bay leaves. Cover, reduce the heat to low, and simmer until the artichokes are tender and the base can easily be pierced with the tip of a knife, about 25 minutes. Drain the artichokes in a colander and allow to cool before handling.

3. REMOVE the outer leaves of the artichokes, and with the tip of a spoon, scoop the fuzzy choke from the center of the artichoke bottoms.

4. USE the artichoke bottoms as needed.

SHRIMP AND SAFFRON RISOTTO

MAKES 8 APPETIZER OR 4 MAIN-COURSE SERVINGS

We've made a lot of risotto at the restaurants and on the shows, and it's definitely one of my favorite comfort foods. Risotto is very adaptable—you can add meat, seafood, or anything else that suits your fancy, depending on the time of year and what's fresh at your local market. One of my favorites is wild mushroom risotto with truffle oil. Once you learn the basics, you can make your own creations. The secrets of great risotto are to stir it constantly as it cooks and to make sure the broth or other liquid is kept at a simmer.

6 cups Shrimp Stock (page 6), Chicken Stock (page 2), or canned low-sodium chicken broth, or more as needed
2 tablespoons olive oil
1 cup finely chopped yellow onions
1¼ teaspoons minced garlic
2 cups Arborio rice
1 cup dry white wine or vermouth
¼ teaspoon saffron threads
½ pound medium shrimp, peeled and deveined
½ cup heavy cream
¼ cup minced green onions (green and white parts)
1 tablespoon unsalted butter
½ cup freshly grated Parmigiano-Reggiano
1¼ teaspoons salt
½ teaspoon freshly ground black pepper

1. **BRING** the stock to a simmer in a medium saucepan over high heat. Reduce the heat to very low to keep the stock hot.

2. **HEAT** the oil in a large heavy saucepan over medium-high heat. Add the onions and garlic. Cook, stirring often, until the onions soften, about 3 minutes. Add the rice and cook, stirring constantly, until the grains are opaque, about 2 minutes. Add the wine and stir until it evaporates, about 1 minute. Add the saffron. Add ¾ cup of the stock and cook, stirring, until it has been absorbed by the rice. Continue to cook and stir, adding ½ cup of the stock at a time as the liquid is absorbed by the rice.

3. **WHEN** the rice is almost tender, after about 20 minutes of stirring and adding stock, stir in the shrimp, cream, green onions, and butter. Continue cooking, adding more stock (or water) as needed, until the rice is just tender and creamy and the shrimp have turned pink, 3 to 4 more minutes.

4. **REMOVE** from the heat and stir in the cheese. Season with the salt and pepper. Serve immediately.

PASTA "RAGS" WITH VODKA SAUCE

MAKES 4 SERVINGS

If you have a shop that sells fresh pasta in your neighborhood, you can make this with sheets of pasta torn into rough-shaped "rags," which is a favorite of Italian cooks. Otherwise, just use fresh fettuccine. Vodka is integral to cocktails such as Bloody Marys, screwdrivers, and martinis, and it is the classic accompaniment to caviar and smoked salmon. Think of vodka as a flavoring to use in your cooking, as in this pasta dish.

1. **FRY** the bacon in a large skillet over medium heat just until crisp, about 4 minutes. Add the onions and crushed red pepper. Cook, stirring often, until the onions are deep golden, soft, and slightly caramelized, about 10 minutes. Add the garlic and stir for 1 minute. Stir in the tomatoes. Bring to a boil, stirring often, and cook for 2 minutes.

2. **ADD** the vodka and cook until the sauce is slightly reduced, about 4 minutes. Stir in the cream and peas. Cook until thickened, about 2 minutes. Remove from the heat and stir in the basil. Cover and keep warm.

3. **MEANWHILE**, bring a large pot of lightly salted water to a boil. Cook the pasta in the boiling water until just al dente, about 4 minutes. Drain in a colander. Return to the pot.

4. **ADD** the sauce to the pasta and mix well. Serve immediately in soup bowls, with the cheese passed on the side.

¼ pound bacon, cut into ½-inch pieces
2 cups finely chopped yellow onions
½ teaspoon crushed red pepper flakes
2 tablespoons minced garlic
One 14-ounce can crushed tomatoes
1 cup vodka
1 cup heavy cream
½ cup frozen green peas, thawed
⅓ cup chopped fresh basil
1 pound fresh pasta sheets, torn into 3 × 1-inch "rags," or fresh fettuccine
Freshly grated Parmigiano-Reggiano, for serving

"CHAIRMAN OF THE BOARD" LINGUINE WITH CLAM SAUCE AND VIVA LAS VEGAS TOMATO SAUCE

MAKES 6 TO 8 SERVINGS

In honor of Frank Sinatra, the "Chairman of the Board," we made this linguine dish, his way, when we taped *Emeril Live* in Las Vegas! I mean, after all, it was Frank and the Rat Pack who ruled the strip back in the '60s! Right?! There's nothing like taking a trip down memory lane!

2 teaspoons salt plus more to taste
1½ pounds dried linguine
½ cup extra-virgin olive oil
3 garlic cloves, thinly sliced
Pinch of crushed red pepper flakes
1 cup dry white wine
Viva Las Vegas Tomato Sauce (recipe follows)
2 pounds littleneck clams, scrubbed well (discard any that are open)
¼ cup chopped fresh flat-leaf parsley
2 tablespoons chopped fresh oregano
Freshly ground black pepper

1. **BRING** 1 gallon water and the salt to a boil in a large pot over high heat. Add the linguine and cook, stirring occasionally to keep the pasta from sticking together, until just al dente, about 9 minutes.

2. **MEANWHILE,** heat the olive oil in a large saucepan or Dutch oven over medium heat. Add the garlic and cook, stirring until fragrant, about 1 minute. Add the crushed red pepper, wine, and tomato sauce, and cook for 1 minute. Add the clams, stir well, cover, and cook until the clams open, 5 to 6 minutes. Stir in the parsley and oregano. Discard any unopened clams.

3. **DRAIN** the linguine. Add to the sauce and mix well. Season with salt and pepper. Transfer to a large pasta bowl and serve hot, with lots of crusty Italian bread.

Viva Las Vegas Tomato Sauce

MAKES ABOUT 3 CUPS

This tomato sauce is made in a jiffy and can be used in all sorts of dishes. Toss it with your favorite pasta, spread it on pizza, or spoon it on hot crusty French or Italian bread!

1 tablespoon olive oil
½ cup chopped yellow onions
2 tablespoons finely chopped garlic
2 teaspoons salt
½ teaspoon freshly ground white pepper
2½ cups peeled and chopped tomatoes, with their juice
¼ cup chopped fresh basil
½ cup Chicken Stock (page 2) or canned low-sodium chicken broth
¼ teaspoon freshly ground black pepper
Pinch of sugar (optional)

1. **HEAT** the oil in a large skillet over medium-high heat. Add the onions, garlic, salt, and white pepper. Cook, stirring often, until the onions are softened, about 4 minutes. Add the tomatoes and basil. Cook, stirring often, for 5 minutes. Add the stock and black pepper. Reduce the heat to medium-low and simmer for 2 minutes.

2. **ADD** the sugar to balance the acidity if needed, and cook for 1 minute. This keeps for five days, refrigerated in an airtight container.

GMA
Emeril Lagasse

BAKED ZITI WITH ITALIAN SAUSAGE AND FENNEL

MAKES 6 TO 8 SERVINGS

Wow—comfort food city, this! When you need some love in a bowl, go ahead and cook yourself up a heap of this; it'll definitely put you right in two minutes flat. We made this dish on a "Wholly Macaroni" show on *Emeril Live* where I was trying to show that there's more to baked pasta than simple mac and cheese. The secret? A white or béchamel sauce gives the baked pasta a nice creamy texture. Once you eat it, you'll know just what I mean. Trust me.

4 tablespoons (½ stick) unsalted butter

3 tablespoons bleached all-purpose flour

2½ cups milk

2½ teaspoons salt

¼ teaspoon freshly ground black pepper

⅛ teaspoon freshly grated nutmeg

1¼ cups freshly grated Parmigiano-Reggiano (about 5 ounces)

2 pounds sweet Italian fennel sausage, cut into ½-inch slices

1 large fennel bulb, trimmed, cored, and coarsely chopped

1 tablespoon minced garlic

1 pound dried ziti or penne

2 tablespoons extra-virgin olive oil

¼ cup thinly sliced fresh basil leaves

1. PREHEAT the oven to 375°F. Generously butter a 9 × 13-inch baking dish with 1 tablespoon of the butter.

2. MELT the remaining 3 tablespoons butter in a medium saucepan over medium-low heat. Add the flour and let foam, stirring constantly, without browning the flour, for about 2 minutes. Whisk in the milk ½ cup at a time, and season with ½ teaspoon of the salt, the pepper, and nutmeg. Bring to a simmer, whisking often, and cook until thick, about 5 minutes. Whisk in ½ cup of the grated cheese. Remove from the heat, cover, and keep warm.

3. HEAT a large nonstick skillet over medium-high heat. Add the sausage and cook until just browned, about 4 minutes. Add the fennel and cook, stirring, until wilted, about 3 minutes. Add the garlic and stir until fragrant, about 1 minute.

4. MEANWHILE, bring 1 gallon water and the remaining 2 teaspoons salt to a boil in a large pot over high heat. Add the ziti and cook, stirring occasionally to keep the pasta from sticking together, until just al dente, about 8 minutes. Drain, then return to the pot.

5. TOSS the pasta with the olive oil. Add the sausage mixture, the cream sauce, and basil and mix well.

6. SPREAD the pasta in the prepared dish and sprinkle with the remaining ¾ cup cheese. Bake until golden brown and bubbly, about 30 minutes. Serve immediately.

MARDI GRAS JAMBALAYA

MAKES 6 SERVINGS

I'm crazy about Mardi Gras parades and the best thing, well, one of the best things about them, is eating along the parade route. Everybody, I mean everybody, brings food. Some have fried chicken, others have sandwiches. Me, I tote this fantastic jambalaya in an ice chest so it stays nice and hot. You should see how quickly I make new friends with this stuff! If you don't have any parades to go to, serve this on Sunday night. Oh, you can substitute chicken if you don't have any duck.

1. SEASON the duck pieces with 2 tablespoons of the Essence.

2. HEAT the vegetable oil in a large heavy pot over medium-high heat. Add the duck, skin side down, and sear for 5 minutes. Turn and sear on the second side for 3 minutes. Remove from the pot and drain on paper towels.

3. ADD the sausage to the fat in the pot and cook, stirring, until browned, about 5 minutes. Add the onions, bell peppers, celery, salt, cayenne, and black pepper and cook, stirring often, until the vegetables are softened, about 5 minutes. Add the tomatoes, garlic, and bay leaves and cook, stirring, until the tomatoes give off some of their juices, about 2 minutes. Add the rice and cook, stirring, for 2 minutes.

4. ADD the thyme, stock, and duck. Bring to a boil. Reduce the heat to medium-low, cover, and simmer, stirring occasionally, until the rice is tender, about 30 minutes.

5. SEASON the shrimp with the remaining 1 tablespoon Essence. Add the shrimp to the pot and cook until they turn pink, about 5 minutes. Remove the pot from the heat and let sit, covered, for 15 minutes.

6. ADD the green onions and parsley to the jambalaya and stir gently. Remove and discard the bay leaves. Adjust the salt, pepper, and cayenne to taste. Serve directly from the pot. (Or, if desired, transfer the jambalaya to a small ice chest to transport to the outing.)

One 5-pound duck, trimmed of fat and cut into 8 pieces
3 tablespoons Emeril's Original Essence or Creole Seasoning (page 9)
2 tablespoons vegetable oil
1 pound andouille or other spicy smoked sausage, cut into ¼-inch slices
2 cups chopped yellow onions
½ cup chopped green bell peppers
½ cup chopped red bell peppers
½ cup chopped celery
1 teaspoon salt, or more to taste
½ teaspoon cayenne
½ teaspoon freshly ground black pepper
2 cups peeled, seeded, and chopped tomatoes
1 tablespoon chopped garlic
3 bay leaves
2 cups long-grain white rice
2 teaspoons minced fresh thyme
2 quarts Chicken Stock (page 2) or canned low-sodium chicken broth
1 pound medium shrimp, peeled and deveined
1 cup chopped green onions (green and white parts)
½ cup minced fresh flat-leaf parsley

LOBSTER RAVIOLI IN A FENNEL-
AND-CHERVIL-INFUSED NAGE

MAKES 6 SERVINGS

These ravioli were created for an *Emeril Live* "Year-End Blast," where we highlighted sophisticated dishes for kicking off the New Year at home. At first glance, you might wonder about the lengthy cooking time for the sauce, but all the reduction time really is necessary to achieve the full-flavored intensity we want. Just go about your business in the kitchen and make something else while this is cooking, and you'll find that it really doesn't seem so time-consuming after all. If you want, you can cook the sauce base up to the final reduction (when you get the 2 to 3 cups, before the cream and butter are added) a day in advance. Just let the sauce base and lobsters rest in the refrigerator until you're ready to finish the dish.

1 cup dry white wine
⅓ cup fresh orange juice
¼ cup fresh lemon juice
2 celery ribs, coarsely chopped
2 medium yellow onions,
    coarsely chopped
2 medium carrots, coarsely
    chopped
1 teaspoon salt, or more to taste
1 teaspoon whole black
    peppercorns
2 sprigs fresh thyme
2 sprigs fresh flat-leaf parsley
2 garlic cloves, smashed, plus
    1 teaspoon minced garlic
2 bay leaves
Two 1½- to 2-pound live lobsters
½ cup finely chopped fennel
    bulb, fronds and upper stalks
    reserved
½ cup heavy cream

1. **BRING** 1 gallon water and the wine, orange juice, 2 tablespoons of the lemon juice, the celery, onions, carrots, salt, peppercorns, thyme, parsley, smashed garlic, and bay leaves to a boil in a very large heavy pot over high heat. Reduce the heat to medium-low. Add the lobsters and cover. Poach until the lobster shells turn red, about 9 minutes.

2. **REMOVE** the lobsters from the water with tongs and drain in a colander. When cool enough to handle, remove the tail and claw meat from the shells, finely chop, and set aside; reserve the shells.

3. **STRAIN** the cooking liquid through a fine-mesh strainer into a clean pot. Add the lobster shells, bring to a boil, and cook until the liquid is reduced by half, about 30 minutes. Add the fennel fronds and upper stalks (you'll use the fennel bulb later) and boil until reduced to about 2 cups, about 1 hour.

4. **STRAIN** the liquid into a clean saucepan. Bring to a simmer over medium-high heat. Whisk the cream, 2 tablespoons of the butter, the chervil, and 1½ teaspoons of the lemon zest into the liquid and season to taste with salt and pepper. Remove the sauce from the heat and cover to keep warm.

5. MELT 2 tablespoons of the butter in a large skillet over medium heat. Add the fennel bulb, shallots, and minced garlic and cook, stirring, until the fennel softens, about 3 minutes. Add the chopped lobster meat. Cook, stirring often, until the lobster is heated through, about 2 minutes. Add the remaining 2 tablespoons lemon juice, 2 tablespoons butter, and 1½ teaspoons lemon zest and stir well. Pour onto a rimmed baking sheet or platter and let cool.

6. LAY out 18 of the wonton wrappers on a work surface. Spoon 1 tablespoon of the lobster filling into the center of each wrapper. One at a time, brush a little water on the edges of each filled wrapper and top with one of the remaining 18 wrappers. Press gently around the filling and the edges of the wrappers to seal. (The ravioli can be refrigerated for up to 2 hours at this point, covered tightly with plastic wrap.)

7. GENTLY reheat the sauce over low heat, stirring occasionally.

8. BRING a large pot of salted water to a boil. Drop the ravioli into the water, in batches, and cook until the ravioli are tender, about 30 seconds. Remove with a large skimmer or slotted spoon and drain well.

9. PLACE three ravioli on each of six serving plates. Spoon over the sauce and serve.

6 tablespoons (¾ cup) unsalted butter
3 tablespoons minced fresh chervil or parsley
1 tablespoon grated lemon zest
Freshly ground black pepper
½ cup minced shallots or onions
36 wonton or egg roll wrappers

the recipes

EMERILISMS

What are Emerilisms? They're my twists—they are where I really get my juices flowing, on dishes like the Tuna of Love, Lobster Domes, or Caramelized Onion and Foie Gras Bread Pudding. These new takes on classic preparations will make you happy, happy, happy. ■ And I always encourage cooks to be creative themselves! Don't be afraid to try something different! Of course, you'll make mistakes, but you'll learn from them. Believe me, that's how cooking works.

BARBECUED OYSTERS
WITH ROSEMARY BISCUITS

The barbecued shrimp that we serve at a couple of the restaurants is one of our most popular dishes. An adaptation of a New Orleans classic, the shrimp are baked with butter, olive oil, and spices. Gulf oysters are so flavorful that I just couldn't resist kicking them up with the barbecue sauce base, which really is a highly concentrated reduction of shrimp stock, Worcestershire sauce, spices, and aromatics.

24 large shucked oysters, with
   their liquor
1 teaspoon Emeril's Original
   Essence or Creole Seasoning
   (page 9)
2 teaspoons olive oil
1/4 cup finely chopped yellow
   onions
3/4 cup heavy cream
3 tablespoons Barbecue Sauce
   Base (recipe follows)
Rosemary Biscuits (page 96),
   warm

1. **TOSS** the oysters (reserve the liquor for later) with the Essence in a medium bowl.

2. **HEAT** the olive oil in a large heavy skillet over medium-high heat. Add the onions and cook until softened, about 3 minutes. Add the cream and barbecue sauce base and boil until reduced by half, about 2 minutes. Add the oysters and their liquor and cook until the edges of the oysters just begin to curl, about 1 1/2 minutes. Remove from the heat.

3. **TO** serve, put three of the warm biscuits on each plate. Top each with two oysters. Spoon a few tablespoons of the sauce over each serving. Serve hot.

Barbecue Sauce Base

MAKES ABOUT ½ CUP

The barbecue sauce base recipe makes much more than you need for the 4 servings of oysters, but you can refrigerate the leftovers for three days, or freeze for up to two months for another dish. Or just go ahead and kick it up, and make a double or triple batch of the oysters! Of course, you can always substitute a half pound of peeled and deveined shrimp for the oysters.

1 tablespoon olive oil
½ cup finely chopped yellow
   onions
1 teaspoon salt
1 teaspoon coarsely ground black
   pepper
3 bay leaves
½ cup dry white wine
1 tablespoon minced garlic
3 lemons, peeled, white pith
   removed, and quartered
2 cups Shrimp Stock (page 6) or
   Fish Stock (page 5)
1 cup Worcestershire sauce

1. **HEAT** the olive oil in a large heavy saucepan over medium-high heat. Add the onions, salt, pepper, and bay leaves. Cook, stirring often, until the onions are softened, about 4 minutes. Add the wine, garlic, and lemons. Cook until the wine is reduced by half, about 2 minutes. Add the shrimp stock and Worcestershire sauce and bring to a boil over high heat. Reduce the heat to medium-low and simmer until the sauce is reduced to ¹/₂ cup, about 1¹/₄ hours.

2. **STRAIN** the sauce base through a fine mesh strainer into a small bowl, pressing on the solids with the back of a spoon to release as much liquid as possible (The sauce base can be refrigerated in an airtight container for up to three days, or frozen for up to two months.)

Rosemary Biscuits

These savory biscuits go with the Barbecued Oysters on page 94, but they're so good you can make them anytime.

1 cup bleached all-purpose flour
1 teaspoon baking powder
1/8 teaspoon baking soda
1/2 teaspoon salt
3 tablespoons unsalted butter, diced and chilled
1 tablespoon minced fresh rosemary
1/2 cup buttermilk, or as needed

1. PREHEAT the oven to 425°F.

2. SIFT the flour, baking powder, baking soda, and salt into a mixing bowl. Cut the butter into the flour with a pastry blender or a fork, or rub between your fingers, until the mixture resembles coarse crumbs. Stir in the rosemary. Stir in the 1/2 cup buttermilk a few tablespoons at a time. Knead the dough in the bowl just until it holds together, adding additional buttermilk, a tablespoon at a time, if the dough is too dry. Take care not to overwork the dough, or the biscuits will be tough rather than light and airy.

3. ON a lightly floured surface, pat the dough into a circle about 7 inches in diameter and 1/2 inch thick. Using a 1-inch round cookie cutter, cut out 12 biscuits. You can gather up the scraps to roll out more biscuits, but these won't be quite as light.

4. PLACE the biscuits on a large baking sheet. Bake until golden on top and lightly browned on the bottom, about 12 minutes.

TUNA OF LOVE

When top-quality fresh tuna is available, go ahead and indulge, because this is what I'm talking about when I call something "the food of love!" Five years ago, when chefs Michael Jordan and Sean Roe and I were creating the menu for the Fish House in Las Vegas, I experimented and made this dish on an *Essence of Emeril* show. The combination of tuna and foie gras received so much attention that we put it on the menu. Watch the foie gras carefully; sear it for just fifteen seconds on each side. For this recipe especially, top-quality ingredients are a must. Use veal stock if you can, though brown chicken stock will do.

2 teaspoons olive oil
¼ cup minced shallots
1 teaspoon minced garlic
1½ cups dry red wine, such as Cabernet Sauvignon
2 cups Veal Stock (page 4) or Brown Chicken Stock (page 3)
2 tablespoons unsalted butter, cut into pieces and chilled
2 teaspoons salt
1 teaspoon freshly ground black pepper
Four 6-ounce fresh tuna steaks, about 1¼ inches thick
¼ pound fresh foie gras (see Source Guide, page 282), cut crosswise into four ¼-inch slices

1. HEAT the oil in a heavy skillet over medium-high heat. Add the shallots and cook, stirring constantly, until softened, about 2 minutes. Add the garlic and stir until fragrant, about 30 seconds. Add the red wine and bring to a boil over high heat. Boil until reduced to ¼ cup, about 8 minutes.

2. ADD the veal stock and return to a boil, then reduce to 1 cup, about 15 minutes. Remove from the heat, then whisk in the butter. Season with ½ teaspoon salt and ¼ teaspoon pepper. Cover to keep warm.

3. MEANWHILE, cut a deep pocket in the long side of each tuna steak with a sharp knife. Lightly season the foie gras slices with ½ teaspoon salt and ¼ teaspoon pepper.

4. HEAT a large nonstick skillet (the skillet must be large enough to hold the tuna steaks in one layer) over medium-high heat until very hot. Quickly cook the foie gras just until seared, about 15 seconds on each side. Immediately remove from the pan, and insert 1 piece of foie gras into each tuna pocket.

5. SEASON the tuna on both sides with 1 teaspoon salt and ½ teaspoon pepper. Reheat the skillet until very hot. Add the tuna to the skillet and cook, turning once, for about 6 minutes for rare.

6. TO serve, place each tuna steak on a plate, and spoon the wine sauce over the top.

KICKED-UP FRIED CALAMARI WITH CREOLE OLIVE SALAD

MAKES 4 TO 6 APPETIZER SERVINGS

When I'm craving something fried, calamari is just the thing. The olive salad, a personal favorite and a New Orleans classic, adds a salty, crunchy dimension to this dish. Squid (calamari in Italian) actually consist of dozens of species within the mollusk family, related to octopus and cuttlefish. When cleaning squid, it's necessary to remove the eyes and innards, particularly the clear, plastic-like quill inside the body, but many fish stores sell squid cleaned and ready to go to save you the trouble. Popular not only in Mediterranean cuisines but also in Asia, squid is sold fresh, frozen, canned, sun-dried, and pickled. It can be deep-fried, panfried, baked, boiled, and stir-fried, but no matter which way you do it, keep your cooking time short, as the flesh becomes rubbery and tough when overcooked.

1 pound cleaned squid (thawed if frozen)
2 cups buttermilk
¼ cup plus 2 tablespoons Emeril's Original Essence or Creole Seasoning (page 9)
1 cup masa harina (available in Latin markets and many supermarkets)
1 cup bleached all-purpose flour
Vegetable oil for deep-frying
1 teaspoon salt
½ teaspoon freshly ground black pepper
½ cup freshly grated Parmigiano-Reggiano
Creole Olive Salad (recipe follows)

1. **CUT** the body sacs of the squid into 1-inch rings. Trim the clusters of tentacles as desired (cut in half or quarters).

2. **MIX** the buttermilk with ¼ cup of the Essence in a mixing bowl. Add the squid and marinate for 30 minutes at room temperature.

3. **COMBINE** the masa harina and all-purpose flour with the remaining 2 tablespoons Essence in a shallow dish.

4. **POUR** enough oil into a large, deep heavy pot or electric deep fryer to come halfway up the sides and heat to 360°F. In batches, remove the squid from the buttermilk mixture and dredge in the flour mixture, shaking to remove any excess flour. Without crowding, carefully add the squid to the hot oil and deep-fry, turning occasionally to prevent the pieces from sticking together, until golden on all sides, 2 to 3 minutes. Using a slotted spoon, transfer to paper towels to drain. Season with salt and pepper.

5. **TO** serve, place the calamari on plates, sprinkle with the Parmesan cheese, and top with the olive salad.

Creole Olive Salad

MAKES ABOUT 2½ CUPS

Olive salad is used to dress those wonderful Italian sandwiches called muffalettas. But I like the salad so much I've found other uses for it!

COMBINE all the ingredients in a medium mixing bowl and mix well. Cover and refrigerate until ready to use. (The salad can be refrigerated for up to 1 week.)

1 cup pitted brine-cured black
  olives, such as Niçoise, sliced
1 cup large (queen) pimiento-
  stuffed olives, sliced
½ cup extra-virgin olive oil
2 tablespoons minced shallots
2 tablespoons finely chopped
  celery
2 tablespoons minced fresh
  flat-leaf parsley
2 teaspoons minced garlic
1½ teaspoons freshly ground
  black pepper

LOBSTER DOMES

I've made several kinds of "domes" on both *Emeril Live* and *Essence of Emeril* shows. I made this one on an *Essence* show with a delicious lobster mixture spooned into individual soufflé bowls, which I then covered with pastry crust. The pastry puffs up and looks like a dome. Voilà! While these entail a lot of preparation, the effort is definitely worth it. Make the lobster sauce a day ahead, or even two, to make the assembly quicker. Another idea? Top sliced beef tenderloin with the lobster sauce for a kicked-up surf-and-turf.

Salt
½ pound haricots verts or small, tender green beans
½ pound small new potatoes
Two 1½-pound live lobsters
½ cup seeded and finely chopped plum tomatoes
2 tablespoons finely chopped fresh flat-leaf parsley
1 tablespoon finely chopped fresh tarragon
½ teaspoon freshly ground white pepper
One 17.3-ounce package frozen puff pastry (2 sheets)
1½ teaspoons white truffle oil
Lobster Sauce (recipe follows)
1 large egg, lightly beaten, for glaze

1. **BRING** 1 gallon water and 1 teaspoon of the salt to a boil in a large stockpot.

2. **MEANWHILE,** cook the haricots verts in a large saucepan of lightly salted boiling water until tender, about 4 minutes. Drain the beans in a colander set over a large bowl, reserving the boiling water. Transfer the beans to a bowl of ice water to cool, then drain. Return the water to the stockpot and return to a boil over high heat.

3. **PUT** the potatoes in a large saucepan, add lightly salted water to cover, and bring to a boil over high heat. Cook until just fork-tender, about 6 minutes. Drain the potatoes in a colander and rinse under cold running water until cooled.

4. **ADD** the lobsters to the stockpot and cook over high heat until the shells turn bright red, about 7 minutes. Transfer the lobsters to a large bowl of ice water and let stand until cool enough to handle, about 5 minutes.

5. **REMOVE** the tail and claw meat from the shells. Finely chop the meat; cover and refrigerate. Reserve the shells for the lobster sauce.

6. **PREHEAT** the oven to 375°F.

7. **QUARTER** the potatoes. Cut the haricots verts crosswise in half. In a large mixing bowl, combine the lobster meat, potatoes, haricots verts, tomatoes, parsley, tarragon, the remaining ½ teaspoon salt, and the white pepper.

8. ON a lightly floured surface, gently roll out 1 puff pastry sheet just to remove the creases; it should be ¼ inch thick. Using an inverted 1-cup ramekin as a template, cut out 3 pastry rounds. Roll out each pastry round to make it about 1 inch larger than the ramekin. Repeat with the other pastry sheet.

9. STIR the truffle oil into the lobster sauce. Divide the lobster mixture equally among six ½-cup ramekins. Spoon ¼ cup of the lobster sauce over the lobster mixture in each dish. Fit a pastry round on top of each ramekin and press around the rim to seal. Brush the top of the pastry with the egg glaze. Place the ramekins on a baking sheet.

10. BAKE until the pastry has puffed and is golden brown, about 15 minutes. Serve immediately.

Lobster Sauce

MAKES ABOUT 3 CUPS

1. HEAT the oil and melt the butter in a medium heavy stockpot over medium-high heat. Add the onions, celery, and carrots and cook until soft, about 4 minutes. Add the shallots and garlic and cook until softened, about 2 minutes. Stir in the flour and continue to stir until the mixture is a light blond color, about 2 minutes. Add the brandy and stir for 30 seconds, scraping the bottom of the pot with a wooden spoon to release browned bits.

2. ADD the lobster shells, then stir in the shrimp stock. Bring to a boil over high heat. Reduce the heat to medium-low. Add the tomato paste, salt, paprika, and cayenne. Simmer uncovered, stirring often, until the sauce is lightly thickened, about 1 hour.

3. STRAIN the sauce through a fine-mesh strainer into a medium saucepan. Add the cream and bring to a boil over medium-high heat. Reduce the heat to medium and simmer briskly until reduced to about 3 cups, about 15 minutes. Use warm. (The sauce can be stored in an airtight container in the refrigerator for up to two days.)

1 tablespoon vegetable oil
4 tablespoons (½ stick) unsalted butter
½ cup finely chopped yellow onions
¼ cup finely chopped celery
¼ cup finely chopped carrots
2 tablespoons minced shallots
1 tablespoon minced garlic
2 tablespoons bleached all-purpose flour
¼ cup Cognac or other brandy
Reserved shells from two 1½-pound lobsters (preceding recipe)
4 cups Shrimp Stock (page 6), Chicken Stock (page 2), or canned low-sodium chicken broth
3 tablespoons tomato paste
1 teaspoon salt
¼ teaspoon paprika
⅛ teaspoon cayenne
1 cup heavy cream

ROCK SHRIMP CONES WITH CREOLE REMOULADE SAUCE

At Emeril's Delmonico in New Orleans, we have a beautiful bar where we serve elegant food that recalls New Orleans' culinary history. Shrimp accompanied by remoulade is a New Orleans classic and the perfect bar food. We also featured these cones on a television show about movie snacks! If you don't want to make paper cones, I've used regular ice cream cones from the store that weren't too sweet and layered the fried shrimp and remoulade sauce inside. Serve these in champagne flutes or large martini glasses with cocktail forks for guests who aren't into eating them right from the cones. If you can't find rock shrimp, by all means substitute 1 pound peeled regular shrimp.

2 cups buttermilk
¼ cup plus 2 tablespoons Emeril's Original Essence or Creole Seasoning (page 9)
1 pound peeled rock shrimp, shells and heads removed (thawed if frozen)
1 cup masa harina (available at Latin markets and many supermarkets)
1 cup bleached all-purpose flour
Vegetable oil for deep-frying
1 teaspoon salt
½ teaspoon freshly ground black pepper
½ cup Creole Remoulade Sauce (recipe follows)

1. **COMBINE** the buttermilk with ¼ cup of the Essence in a medium mixing bowl. Add the shrimp and marinate for 30 minutes. Refrigerate.

2. **COMBINE** the masa harina and all-purpose flour with the remaining 2 tablespoons of Essence in another bowl.

3. **POUR** enough oil to come halfway up the sides of a large deep heavy pot or electric deep fryer and heat over high heat to 360°F. Drain the shrimp.

4. **IN** batches, dredge the marinated shrimp in the flour mixture and shake to remove any excess. Using a slotted spoon, carefully place the shrimp, several at a time, into the hot oil. Deep-fry, turning occasionally, until golden brown, 2 to 3 minutes. Using a slotted spoon, transfer to paper towels to drain. Season with the salt and pepper.

5. **CUT** four 6-inch squares of parchment paper. Roll each one into a cone and tuck in the ends to secure. Fill the cones with the shrimp, top each with 2 tablespoons of the remoulade sauce, and serve immediately.

Creole Remoulade Sauce

MAKES 2 CUPS

Remoulade sauce can be used for a dip for garlic shrimp or spooned on cold lump crabmeat.

1. COMBINE all the ingredients in a blender or a food processor fitted with a steel blade and process until fairly smooth, about 30 seconds.

2. TRANSFER to an airtight container and refrigerate for at least 1 hour before using. (The sauce will keep for up to one week in the refrigerator.)

¾ cup vegetable oil
½ cup chopped green onions (green and white parts)
½ cup chopped yellow onions
¼ cup fresh lemon juice
¼ cup chopped celery
3 tablespoons Creole or other whole-grain mustard
3 tablespoons ketchup
3 tablespoons chopped fresh flat-leaf parsley
2 tablespoons chopped garlic
2 tablespoons prepared horseradish
1 teaspoon salt
¼ teaspoon cayenne
¼ teaspoon freshly ground black pepper

KICKED-UP CHICKEN DRUMMETTES
WITH BLUE CHEESE SAUCE

I like to go to baseball games and enjoy eating hot dogs and Cracker Jacks, but when I'm home watching the game, I prefer finger food that's kicked up a bit more! We made this fried chicken with the drummettes—the big pieces of the wings that are perfect for snacking—but you can substitute whole chicken wings or any parts you prefer. Just remember to adjust the cooking time if you use a different part, increasing the time for larger pieces, such as whole wings. The Blue Cheese Sauce is also good with crudités like baby carrots and celery.

2½ pounds chicken drummettes (about 20), rinsed and patted dry
½ cup Emeril's Red Pepper Sauce or other hot pepper sauce
½ teaspoon salt
1 teaspoon cracked black pepper
2 tablespoons plus 1 teaspoon Emeril's Original Essence or Creole Seasoning (page 9)
Vegetable oil for deep-frying
1½ cups bleached all-purpose flour
Blue Cheese Sauce (recipe follows)

1. **COMBINE** the chicken, pepper sauce, salt, and pepper and ½ teaspoon Essence in a large shallow nonreactive container. Toss to coat the chicken evenly. Cover with plastic wrap and refrigerate for at least 1 hour, or up to 3 hours.

2. **POUR** enough oil to come halfway up the sides of a large deep heavy pot or electric deep fryer and heat over high heat to 360°F.

3. **COMBINE** the flour and 2 tablespoons of the Essence in a large mixing bowl and stir to blend. In batches, add the chicken pieces and toss to coat evenly, then carefully add the chicken pieces to the hot oil and deep-fry, turning occasionally, until golden-brown, about 10 minutes. Using a slotted spoon, transfer to drain on paper towels.

4. **SPRINKLE** the chicken with the remaining ½ teaspoon Essence. Serve immediately, with Blue Cheese Sauce.

Blue Cheese Sauce

MAKES ABOUT 1 CUP

PUT all the ingredients in a food processor or a blender and process until well blended. Pour into a bowl, cover, and refrigerate until ready to use. This keeps for three days refrigerated.

½ cup sour cream
¼ cup heavy cream
4 ounces blue cheese, crumbled
1 teaspoon Emeril's Red Pepper Sauce or other hot pepper sauce
½ teaspoon Worcestershire sauce
½ teaspoon salt

CARAMELIZED ONION AND FOIE GRAS BREAD PUDDING

MAKES 8 TO 10 SERVINGS

If there's one thing people have learned from my television show, it's not to be intimidated by high-end ingredients. Foie gras is an expensive treat, but sometimes you just need to splurge and indulge your taste buds with something out of the ordinary. This savory bread pudding is for just such occasions. Try it with that Thanksgiving turkey or holiday roast. Some supermarkets sell foie gras; elsewhere, you can get your specialty food shop or butcher to order it for you (or see the Source Guide). If you're going to make this dish, you might think about making the Tuna of Love (page 97) that same week, in order to use the whole lobe that is usually a minimum foie gras order. (A lobe usually weighs about ½ pound to 1¼ pounds, depending on the grade.) Of course, foie gras is also delicious when simply seasoned and sliced, pan-seared very quickly, and served on top of toasted buttered brioche or Homestyle Rolls (page 254) with a dab of Dried Cherry Reduction (page 192). Or substitute a couple of pan-seared slices of foie gras for the goat cheese in the Hazelnut, Goat Cheese, and Baby Greens Salad (page 68).

6 ounces fresh foie gras (see Source Guide, page 282), prepared as described on following page
4 large eggs
3 cups heavy cream
1½ teaspoons salt
½ teaspoon freshly ground black pepper
⅛ teaspoon freshly grated nutmeg
4 cups 1-inch cubes day-old French bread (about half of a large loaf)
2 tablespoons plus 1 teaspoon unsalted butter
3 cups thinly sliced yellow onions
2 teaspoons minced garlic

1. **CUT** the foie gras into ½-inch cubes. Wrap in plastic wrap and refrigerate until ready to use.

2. **WHISK** the eggs and cream in a large mixing bowl. Add 1¼ teaspoons of the salt, the pepper, and nutmeg and whisk to blend. Add the bread cubes and press them down to submerge them in the mixture. Let stand until the bread absorbs most of the liquid, about 1 hour.

3. **PREHEAT** the oven to 350°F. Butter an 11 × 7 × 2-inch baking dish with 1 teaspoon of the butter and set aside.

4. **UNWRAP** the foie gras and season with ⅛ teaspoon of the salt. Heat a large skillet over medium-high heat. Add the foie gras and cook, turning often, until just seared, no more than 1½ to 2 minutes. Using a slotted spoon, transfer to a platter.

5. ADD the onions to the fat in the hot skillet and season with the remaining 1/8 teaspoon salt. Cook, stirring frequently, until deeply golden, about 10 minutes. Add the garlic and stir until fragrant, about 1 minute. Remove the pan from the heat and let cool until the onions are lukewarm, about 10 minutes.

6. STIR the foie gras and onions into the bread and cream mixture. Pour into the prepared baking dish. Cut the remaining 2 tablespoons butter into thin slivers and dot the top of the bread pudding with it.

7. BAKE, uncovered, until golden brown and a knife inserted into the center comes out clean, about 1 hour. Scoop onto plates to serve.

HOW TO PREPARE FOIE GRAS

Remove the foie gras from the refrigerator, rinse briefly under cold running water, and pat dry. Gently separate the lobes with your hands, and place one lobe smooth side down. With your fingers, carefully lift up the main vein running through the lobe and gently pull it up and out. Pull any small veins up and out, being careful to keep the liver as intact as possible. (Should the smaller veins break or not come out easily, simply leave them in the meat.) Peel off any loose membranes attached to the surface, and pick out any green spots with your fingertips. Discard the removed veins and membranes. Repeat with the remaining lobe.

BAMBURGERS

I think you probably know from watching the television show that I'm a real beef man. These are he-man burgers that I loved featuring on a Fourth of July show! You want to really kick these up and make them "Big Bamburgers?" Use homemade condiments, like Mayonnaise (page 12), or the Creole Remoulade Sauce (page 103). Or even drizzle a bit of Barbecue Sauce (page 229) over these before you add the cheese. Now you're cookin'!

1 pound ground sirloin beef
1 tablespoon prepared
   horseradish
1 tablespoon minced garlic
1 teaspoon salt
½ teaspoon freshly ground black
   pepper
4 slices Havarti cheese
   (about 2 ounces each)
4 onion or kaiser rolls,
   split in half
2 tablespoons unsalted butter,
   at room temperature
Your favorite burger condiments,
   such as mayonnaise, mustard,
   sliced red onions, and
   ketchup

1. **PREHEAT** a gas or charcoal grill or heat a large skillet over medium-high heat.

2. **COMBINE** the beef, horseradish, garlic, salt, and pepper in a medium mixing bowl. Mix gently but thoroughly. Divide the mixture into 4 equal portions, form into balls, and flatten slightly to form ¾-inch-thick patties.

3. **GRILL** the burgers or cook in the skillet for 2 minutes. Flip the patties over and place 1 slice of cheese on each patty. Cook for 2 minutes more for medium-rare burgers, or longer if you wish. Transfer to a platter.

4. **SPREAD** both cut sides of each roll with the butter. Toast them on the grill or in the skillet for about 30 seconds. Put the burgers on the buns and serve immediately, with the condiments.

LINGUIÇA-CRUSTED REDFISH WITH PORTUGUESE OLIVE-TOMATO SAUCE

MAKES 8 SERVINGS

Linguiça is a Portuguese sausage that's heavily flavored with garlic. It can be found in some Latin American markets and many supermarkets. I grew up in Fall River eating linguiça and chorizo and learned early on that both sausages give an incredible flavor to just about anything! Here we're crusting redfish with a linguiça crust, but you can try it on salmon as well. When we made this on an *Essence of Emeril* show, we kicked it up by adding fried calamari to the top. If you're in the mood, go ahead and use the recipe for Fried Calamari on page 98.

1. HEAT 2 tablespoons olive oil in a heavy saucepan over medium heat. Add the onions and garlic and cook, stirring, until the onions are golden, about 7 minutes. Add the tomatoes and olives and cook, stirring occasionally, until the sauce thickens, about 25 minutes. Add the salt and pepper. Keep warm until ready to serve.

2. PREHEAT the oven to 400°F.

3. COOK the linguiça in a large skillet over medium heat, stirring often, for 3 minutes. Add the bread crumbs and mix to bind the sausage.

4. SEASON the fish fillets with the Essence. Heat the remaining olive oil in a large ovenproof skillet or two smaller ones over high heat. Add the fish and sear until slightly golden, 1 to 2 minutes on each side. Carefully drain off any excess oil. Put an equal portion of the linguiça mixture on each fillet. Bake for 5 minutes.

5. TO serve, arrange the fillets on eight serving plates. Spoon the olive-tomato sauce over each and sprinkle with the feta cheese.

6 tablespoons olive oil
1½ cups coarsely chopped yellow onions
2 teaspoons chopped garlic
2 pounds Roma tomatoes, peeled, cored, and coarsely chopped
⅔ cup cured black olives (such as kalamata), pitted and halved
½ teaspoon salt
¼ teaspoon freshly ground black pepper
10 ounces linguiça sausage, finely chopped
⅔ cup fine dried bread crumbs
Eight 6-ounce redfish fillets
1 tablespoon Emeril's Original Essence
½ pound feta cheese, crumbled

MINI OPEN-FACED CORN CAKE AND SALMON SALAD SANDWICHES WITH BELUGA CAVIAR

MAKES 32 "SANDWICHES"

Did you know that Las Vegas is the marriage capital of the United States? Over 110,000 couples get married there every year! Wow! When we did an *Emeril Live* show in Las Vegas, we prepared a wedding party for Sally and Carl Groves from East Yorkshire, England, who actually got married on the show. The feast we prepared was awesome, if I do say so myself. These salmon salad sandwiches are wonderful to serve at cocktail parties, or as an appetizer for any meal.

CORN CAKES

2 tablespoons olive oil
1 cup corn kernels (from 1 to 2 ears corn)
2 tablespoons minced shallots
1 teaspoon salt
1/8 teaspoon freshly ground black pepper
1 cup heavy cream
2 large eggs
3/4 cup yellow cornmeal
1/2 cup bleached all-purpose flour
1/2 cup masa harina (available at Latin markets and many supermarkets)
2 teaspoons baking powder
1/8 teaspoon cayenne
2 teaspoons vegetable oil
1 teaspoon Emeril's Original Essence or Creole Seasoning (page 9)

1. **TO** make the corn cakes, heat the olive oil in a skillet over medium heat. Add the corn, shallots, 1/2 teaspoon of the salt, and the black pepper. Cook, stirring, until the corn and shallots are tender, about 5 minutes. Set aside to cool slightly.

2. **WHISK** the cream and eggs in a large bowl. Whisk in the cornmeal, flour, masa harina, baking powder, cayenne, the remaining 1/2 teaspoon salt, and 3/4 cup water. Fold in the corn mixture.

3. **HEAT** the vegetable oil in a large nonstick skillet over medium-high heat. Using 1 tablespoon of batter for each corn cake, drop the batter into the skillet. (You can cook about 8 at a time.) Cook until golden brown, about 1 1/2 minutes on each side, adding more oil as necessary. Drain on paper towels and sprinkle with the Essence.

4. **TO** make salad, toss the salmon in a mixing bowl with the eggs, capers, and caper juice. Mix well. Stir in the mayonnaise to taste. Season with salt and pepper and mix well.

5. **SPREAD** 1 tablespoon of the salad over each corn cake and garnish with the caviar and chives.

SALMON SALAD

½ pound smoked salmon, chopped
6 Perfect Hard-Boiled Eggs
    (page 16), finely chopped
1 tablespoon capers, finely
    minced, plus 1 teaspoon juice
    from the bottle
¼ to ½ cup Mayonnaise
    (page 12), or store-bought
    mayonnaise
Salt and pepper, to taste
4 ounces beluga caviar, or
    4 ounces sevruga
2 tablespoons snipped fresh
    chives

Y'ALL SOUTHERN?

When I moved to New Orleans, I immediately fell in love with the food and the flavors of the city. I started taking side trips to other parts of Louisiana and other areas of the South, including Mississippi, Arkansas, and Alabama. Do Southerners know how to cook and enjoy themselves! Simple ingredients, like ham hocks and beans, are turned into something heavenly. ■ Go ahead, give yourself a real Southern treat and try the Crab Cakes with Poached Eggs and Wild Mushroom Sauce, the Crawfish and Corn Cakes, or the Oyster Dressing Soufflés with Oyster-Tasso Sauce. For a taste of New Orleans, try the Oyster and Shrimp Po' Boy or the Red Beans and Rice. If you really want to be a little daring, I have just the thing for you—Alligator Sauce Piquante. Tastes just like chicken.

CHILE-SCRAMBLED EGGS WITH FRIED OYSTERS AND EMERIL'S PICO DE GALLO

MAKES 4 SERVINGS

What a kicked-up way to start your day! This terrific Tex-Mex—inspired brunch item will really get your engine going! If you're in the mood to eat with your hands, roll the eggs, oysters, and sauce up into the tortillas for breakfast burritos. Or, instead of serving the eggs with the tortillas, try freshly made tortilla chips, like we do with the Hot Corn Dip (page 30), or serve them on slices of Corn Bread (page 255) that have been slathered in butter.

Vegetable oil for deep-frying
1 cup masa harina (available at Latin markets and many supermarkets)
1 tablespoon Emeril's Original Essence or Creole Seasoning (page 9)
1 teaspoon ground cumin
1 pint shucked oysters, drained
9 large eggs
1 teaspoon salt
3 tablespoons unsalted butter
¼ cup chopped green onions (green and white parts)
1 tablespoon minced red jalapeño or serrano chile
4 corn tortillas
2 cups Emeril's Pico de Gallo (recipe follows)
½ cup sour cream

1. **PREHEAT** the oven to 350°F.

2. **POUR** enough oil to come halfway up the sides of a large heavy pot or electric deep-fryer and heat over high heat to 360°F.

3. **COMBINE** the masa harina, Essence, and cumin in a shallow bowl. Dredge the oysters in the mixture, a few at a time, to coat evenly. Shake off any excess coating. In batches, without crowding, deep-fry the oysters, turning occasionally, until golden, about 2 minutes. Using a slotted spoon, transfer to paper towels to drain.

4. **LIGHTLY** beat the eggs and salt in a large bowl. Melt the butter in a large heavy skillet over medium-high heat. Add the green onions and chile pepper. Cook, stirring often, until softened, about 1 minute. Reduce the heat to medium. Add the eggs and, stirring constantly, scramble to the desired consistency.

5. **TO** serve, put one warm tortilla on each serving plate. Put an equal portion of the scrambled eggs and the oysters on each tortilla, then top each with ¼ cup of the pico de gallo and 2 tablespoons of the sour cream. Serve immediately, passing the remaining pico de gallo at the table.

Emeril's Pico de Gallo

MAKES ABOUT 3 CUPS

Pico de Gallo means rooster's beak, and the salsa is so called because its flavors are as sharp as a rooster's beak. You can make this ahead of time and store it in the refrigerator until serving time, but use it within 24 hours. This kicked-up salsa goes with the Chile-Scrambled Eggs and Fried Oysters, but it also would be good with the Hot Chorizo Tamales (page 198) and the Spicy Duck Empanadas (page 34)—or use it as a dip with a pile of tortilla chips.

1½ pounds plum tomatoes, cored, halved, seeded, and chopped
¾ cup finely chopped white onions
½ cup chopped fresh cilantro
1 tablespoon fresh lime juice
2 tablespoons minced seeded jalapeño or serrano chiles
1 teaspoon minced garlic
½ teaspoon salt
Pinch of cayenne

COMBINE all the ingredients in a bowl. Stir to mix, and let stand at room temperature for 1 hour for the flavors to blend.

CORNMEAL-CRUSTED REDFISH

MAKES 4 SERVINGS

We do this masa harina breading with lots of different fish at the restaurants. Masa harina is flour made from dried corn kernels that have been ground into a corn flour; it's finer than cornmeal. I used this particular procedure here to show the importance of breading fish fillets appropriately, because masa gives a great texture and corn flavor to any fish. You can substitute any white-fleshed, thin, flat fish fillets in place of the redfish. Try snapper, sole, or catfish. This is excellent with the Grown-Up Tartar Sauce (page 165) or Lemon–Black Pepper Tartar Sauce (page 157).

½ cup bleached all-purpose flour
1¼ teaspoons salt
2½ teaspoons Emeril's Original Essence or Creole Seasoning (page 9)
1 large egg
¾ cup masa harina (available at Latin markets and many supermarkets)
3 tablespoons olive oil, or as needed
Four 8-ounce redfish fillets

1. **BLEND** ¼ cup of the flour, ½ teaspoon of the salt, and 1 teaspoon of the Essence in a small mixing bowl. In another small bowl, combine the egg with 2 tablespoons water, ¼ teaspoon of the salt, and ½ teaspoon of the Essence. Whisk to blend. In a third bowl, combine the masa harina and the remaining ¼ cup flour, ½ teaspoon salt, and 1 teaspoon Essence. Stir to blend.

2. **LIGHTLY** dust both sides of the fillets with the flour mixture, then dip in the egg wash, and finally coat with the masa harina mixture. Shake off any excess.

3. **HEAT** the olive oil in a large heavy nonstick skillet over medium-high heat. Add two of the fillets and panfry until golden brown, 3 to 4 minutes on each side. Using a slotted spatula, transfer to paper towels to drain. Tent with aluminum foil to keep warm. Add more olive oil to the skillet as needed, and cook the remaining fillets. Serve immediately.

CHEDDAR CHEESE HUSH PUPPIES

MAKES 18 HUSH PUPPIES

Hush puppies got their name when folks tossed these delicious bite-size treats to howling puppies to make them hush. All I've got to say is "Lucky dogs!" I've taken these to the next level by adding Cheddar cheese and jalapeños. Try these with fried fish or fried chicken, or just serve them with beer for a summer afternoon snack.

1. **MIX** the cornmeal, flour, salt, baking powder, and baking soda in a large mixing bowl. Add the cheese, onions, jalapeños, and hot sauce and mix well. Add the eggs, buttermilk, and ½ cup water. Mix well.

2. **POUR** enough oil to come halfway up the sides of a large heavy pot or electric deep fryer and heat over high heat to 360°F. In batches, without crowding, drop tablespoons of the batter into the hot oil. Deep-fry on all sides until the hush puppies rise to the surface and are golden brown, 2 to 3 minutes. Using a slotted spoon, transfer to paper towels to drain.

3. **SPRINKLE** with the Essence if you wish, and serve hot.

1½ cups yellow cornmeal
½ cup bleached all-purpose flour
2 teaspoons salt
1 teaspoon baking powder
½ teaspoon baking soda
3 ounces grated sharp Cheddar cheese (about ¾ cup)
¼ cup minced yellow onions
1½ teaspoons minced jalapeños
1½ tablespoons Emeril's Red Pepper Sauce or other hot pepper sauce
2 large eggs
½ cup buttermilk
Vegetable oil for deep-frying
2 tablespoons Emeril's Original Essence or Creole Seasoning (page 9), (optional)

COUNTRY-FRIED STEAK
WITH WHITE GRAVY

MAKES 4 SERVINGS

This Southern staple can be found in just about any restaurant in every state south of the Mason-Dixon line. It's also called "chicken-fried steak," since the steak is pounded flat, coated in crumbs, then panfried like chicken. For a real blue-plate special, round this out with some Mashed Potatoes (page 14), Buttermilk Biscuits (page 259), and Southern Cooked Greens (page 209).

One 1¾-to 2-pound round steak, cut into 4 equal portions
3 tablespoons Emeril's Original Essence or Creole Seasoning (page 9)
½ pound bacon, chopped
1½ cups bleached all-purpose flour
1 large egg
2½ cups milk
1 cup fine dried bread crumbs
½ cup minced yellow onions
½ teaspoon salt
¼ teaspoon freshly ground black pepper

1. PLACE the steak on a plastic wrap–covered work surface and cover with another piece of plastic wrap. Pound the meat to a ¼-inch thickness with a meat mallet. Season both sides of the meat with 1½ teaspoons of the Essence.

2. FRY the bacon in a large skillet until just crisp, 6 to 8 minutes. Using a slotted spoon, transfer the bacon to paper towels to drain, leaving the fat in the pan. Set the pan aside.

3. COMBINE the flour with 1 tablespoon of the Essence in a large shallow bowl. Whisk the egg with ½ cup of the milk and 1½ teaspoons of the Essence in another bowl. Combine the bread crumbs and the remaining 1 tablespoon Essence in another shallow bowl or baking dish.

4. DREDGE the meat in the seasoned flour, then dip in the egg wash, letting the excess drip off. Dredge the meat in the seasoned bread crumbs, coating each side evenly. Shake off any excess bread crumbs. Reserve the seasoned flour.

5. REHEAT the bacon fat in the skillet over high heat until very hot but not smoking. In batches, without crowding (you may only be able to cook one portion at a time), carefully add the meat and fry until golden brown, 3 to 4 minutes on each side. Transfer to paper towels to drain.

6. ADD 3 tablespoons of the reserved seasoned flour to the pan. Cook over medium-high heat, stirring constantly, for about 2 minutes, to make a light roux. Add the onions and cook, stirring often, until softened, about 4 minutes. Whisk in the remaining 2 cups milk, the salt, and pepper and bring to a boil. Reduce the heat to medium-low and simmer until the sauce is thickened and there is no raw flour taste, about 5 minutes. Stir in the bacon.

7. SERVE the steaks with the hot gravy.

HAM HOCK AND
GOAT CHEESE WONTONS

MAKES 6 SERVINGS

We've given a Chinese spin to ham hock dumplings, an old Southern favorite, by putting them in wonton skins and deep-frying. These are great to serve as appetizers with the Creole Remoulade Sauce (page 103), or try serving them with the Asian Dipping Sauce (page 21) and Hot Mustard Sauce (page 23).

Two 1-pound smoked ham hocks
6 ounces goat cheese, crumbled
¼ cup minced green onions
   (green and white parts)
3 tablespoons extra-virgin
   olive oil
1 tablespoon chopped fresh
   flat-leaf parsley
1 teaspoon minced garlic
½ teaspoon salt
¼ teaspoon freshly ground black
   pepper
36 wonton skins
Cornstarch for dusting
Vegetable oil for deep-frying

1. **BRING** the ham hocks and 3 quarts water to a boil in a large saucepan over high heat. Reduce the heat to medium-low. Simmer, uncovered, until the meat is very tender, about 2 hours. Drain the ham hocks and let cool until easy to handle.

2. **REMOVE** the meat from the bones, discard the skin and bones, and coarsely chop the meat. Blend the meat and goat cheese in a large mixing bowl with a fork. Stir in the green onions, olive oil, parsley, garlic, salt, and pepper.

3. **LAY** 12 of the wonton skins on a work surface; have a cup of water at hand. Put a generous teaspoon of the meat mixture in the middle of each skin. Rub a bit of water along the edges of each skin and fold in half to make a triangle, pressing down the edges to seal. Transfer to a cornstarch-dusted baking sheet. Repeat with the remaining skins and meat mixture. (The filled wontons can be covered tightly with plastic wrap and refrigerated for up to 2 hours before frying.)

4. **POUR** enough oil to come halfway up the sides of a large heavy pot or electric deep fryer, and heat over high heat to 360°F. In batches, without crowding, deep-fry the wontons, stirring occasionally, until they float to the top and are golden brown, about 3 minutes. Using a slotted spoon, transfer to paper towels to drain.

5. **SERVE** immediately, with the dipping sauce of your choice.

CRAB CAKES WITH POACHED EGGS AND WILD MUSHROOM SAUCE

MAKES 6 SERVINGS

My mother loves this dish, so I prepared it for a Mother's Day show on *Essence of Emeril*. This elegant dish is an ideal main course for brunch, or serve just the crab cakes and sauce for an appetizer or as a main course for a luncheon. Make mini crab cakes for a passed starter, accompanied by a dish of mayonnaise kicked up with a bit of Essence and a squeeze of lemon juice. Try the mushroom sauce with grilled chicken breasts or broiled fish fillets.

1. **HEAT** 2 tablespoons of the olive oil in a large heavy skillet over medium-high heat. Add the onions, bell peppers, celery, salt, and cayenne and cook, stirring occasionally, until the vegetables are tender, about 5 minutes. Add the green onions and parsley and cook just until wilted, about 1 minute. Remove from the heat.

2. **PLACE** the crabmeat in a large bowl and add the cooked vegetables. Add the mayonnaise, cheese, and egg and stir gently with a large wooden spoon. Add the bread crumbs and stir gently, being careful not to break up the crabmeat too much. Form the mixture into twelve 2-inch-diameter cakes.

3. **COMBINE** the flour and Essence in a medium bowl. Lightly coat both sides of each cake with the flour mixture. Heat the remaining 2 tablespoons olive oil in a large heavy skillet over medium-high heat. In batches, without crowding, cook the cakes until golden brown, about 3 minutes per side, adding more oil as needed. Transfer to paper towels to drain.

4. **TO** serve, place two crab cakes on each plate, top each cake with 1 poached egg, and spoon about $1/3$ cup of the sauce over each serving.

¼ cup olive oil, or as needed
½ cup finely chopped yellow onions
¼ cup finely chopped green bell peppers
¼ cup finely chopped celery
1 teaspoon salt
½ teaspoon cayenne
2 tablespoons finely chopped green onions (green and white parts)
2 tablespoons finely chopped fresh flat-leaf parsley
1 pound lump crabmeat, picked over for shells and cartilage
¼ cup Mayonnaise (page 12) or store-bought mayonnaise
2 tablespoons freshly grated Parmigiano-Reggiano
1 large egg, lightly beaten
½ cup Italian-style bread crumbs
½ cup bleached all-purpose flour
1½ teaspoons Emeril's Original Essence or Creole Seasoning (page 9)
Poached Eggs (recipe follows)
Wild Mushroom Sauce (page 123)

Poached Eggs

MAKES 12 EGGS

12 large eggs
1 tablespoon distilled white
   vinegar

1. POUR cold water into a 10-inch sauté pan to a depth of about 2 inches. Bring to a simmer, then reduce the heat so that the surface of the water barely shimmers. Add the vinegar.

2. BREAK four of the eggs into individual saucers, then gently slide them out one at a time into the water and, with a large spoon, lift the white over the yolk. Repeat the lifting once or twice to completely enclose each yolk. Poach until the whites are set and the yolks feel soft when touched gently, 3 to 4 minutes.

3. REMOVE the eggs with a slotted spoon and either serve immediately, or place in a shallow pan or large bowl of cold water.

4. REPEAT with the remaining eggs, adding more water as needed to keep the depth at 2 inches, and bringing the water to a simmer before adding the eggs.

5. REHEAT the eggs by slipping them into simmering water for 30 seconds to 1 minute. Serve hot with the crab cakes.

Wild Mushroom Sauce

MAKES ABOUT 2 CUPS

1. **HEAT** the olive oil in a heavy medium saucepan over medium-high heat. Add the onions and cook, stirring often, until softened, about 4 minutes. Add the mushrooms, salt, and pepper and cook until the mushrooms start to give off their liquid, about 3 minutes. Add the green onions, parsley, and garlic and cook, stirring often, until fragrant, about 1 minute. Stir in the stock and heavy cream and bring to a boil over high heat. Reduce the heat to medium-low and simmer until thickened to a sauce consistency, about 30 minutes.

2. **SERVE,** or cover and keep warm until ready to use.

3 tablespoons olive oil
½ cup finely chopped yellow onions
3 cups sliced wild mushrooms, such as a shiitake, morel, chanterelle, wood ear, and/or oyster, stems trimmed and wiped clean
½ teaspoon salt
½ teaspoon freshly ground black pepper
2 tablespoons finely chopped green onions (green and white parts)
2 tablespoons chopped fresh flat-leaf parsley
1 tablespoon minced garlic
1½ cups Veal Stock (page 4) or canned low-sodium beef broth
1 cup heavy cream

CRAWFISH AND CORN CAKES

MAKES ABOUT 48 CAKES

These small cakes are very versatile. They are great as starters or as a side dish served with the Creole Remoulade Sauce (page 103) or Corn Remoulade (page 27). To kick them up a bit, cook another half-pound of peeled crawfish tails in some butter with a little garlic, green onions, Essence, and maybe a little cream, and serve the sauce spooned over the cakes. Or try sliced or chopped smoked salmon, sour cream, and caviar for something really special.

2 tablespoons olive oil plus about ¼ cup for frying
1¼ cups corn kernels (from 2 to 3 ears of fresh corn)
½ pound peeled crawfish tails (see Source Guide, page 282), chopped
2 tablespoons minced shallots
1 teaspoon minced garlic
1 teaspoon salt
¼ teaspoon cayenne
2 large eggs
1¼ cups milk
¾ cup yellow cornmeal
½ cup bleached all-purpose flour
½ cup masa harina (available at Latin markets and many supermarkets)
2 teaspoons baking powder
1 teaspoon Emeril's Original Essence or Creole Seasoning (page 9)
Sour cream for garnish (optional)
Sliced smoked salmon for garnish (optional)
Caviar for garnish (optional)

1. **HEAT** the 2 tablespoons oil in a medium heavy skillet over medium-high heat. Add the corn, crawfish, shallots, garlic, salt, and cayenne and cook, stirring often, to heat through and blend the flavors, about 5 minutes. Remove from the heat and let cool.

2. **BEAT** the eggs in a large mixing bowl. Add the milk, cornmeal, flour, masa harina, baking powder, and Essence and mix well. Stir in the crawfish mixture and mix well.

3. **HEAT** about 2 tablespoons of the remaining olive oil in a medium heavy skillet over medium-high heat. In batches, drop tablespoons of the batter into the skillet and cook, turning once, until golden brown on both sides, about 2 minutes. Transfer to paper towels to drain.

4. **SERVE** warm, topping each cake with a spoonful of sour cream and some sliced smoked salmon and caviar, if you wish.

ALLIGATOR SAUCE PIQUANTE

MAKES 6 SERVINGS

This is a traditional south Louisiana dish served during the fall, when it's alligator-hunting season. Though alligator is farm-raised these days—and generally the meat sold is from the loin—it can be hunted by special license on private property. Sauce piquante can be made with other meats or seafood, such as rabbit, chicken, or shrimp. Substitute a cut-up chicken for the alligator.

1. **HEAT** ¼ cup of the olive oil in large heavy nonstick pot or Dutch oven over medium-high heat. Stir in the onions, bell peppers, celery, salt, crushed red pepper flakes, cayenne, and bay leaves. Cook, stirring occasionally, until the vegetables are soft and lightly golden, about 5 minutes. Add 3 tablespoons of the flour and cook, stirring, to cook the flour without browning, 1 to 2 minutes. Add the tomatoes, chicken stock, Worcestershire, and pepper sauce. Bring to a boil, then reduce the heat to medium-low.

2. **PLACE** several pieces of alligator meat at a time on a work surface covered with plastic wrap. Cover the meat with plastic wrap and pound with a meat mallet until ¼ inch thick. Cut into 2-inch strips.

3. **COMBINE** the remaining ½ cup flour and the Essence in a medium bowl. Dredge the alligator pieces in the seasoned flour, shaking off any excess.

4. **HEAT** 2 tablespoons of the olive oil in a large nonstick skillet over medium-high heat. Add half of the meat and fry until golden brown, turning once, 3 to 4 minutes per side. Transfer to a platter. Heat the remaining 2 tablespoons oil in the skillet and repeat with the remaining alligator.

5. **ADD** the meat to the sauce. Increase the heat under the sauce to medium-high and bring to a gentle rolling boil. Reduce the heat to medium-low. Simmer uncovered, stirring occasionally, until the meat is tender, about 2 hours. Remove and discard the bay leaves.

6. **TO** serve, spoon the rice into soup bowls, top with the meat and sauce, and garnish with the green onions and parsley.

½ cup olive oil
1½ cups chopped yellow onions
¾ cup chopped green bell peppers
¾ cup chopped celery
1 teaspoon salt
1 teaspoon crushed red pepper flakes
½ teaspoon cayenne
4 bay leaves
½ cup plus 3 tablespoons bleached all-purpose flour
4 cups seeded and chopped plum tomatoes
3 cups Chicken Stock (page 2) or canned low-sodium chicken broth
1 teaspoon Worcestershire sauce
1 teaspoon Emeril's Red Pepper Sauce or other hot pepper sauce
1½ pounds alligator meat, cut into 2-inch strips (see Source Guide, page 282)
1½ teaspoons Emeril's Original Essence or Creole Seasoning (page 9)
½ cup chopped green onions (green and white parts)
¼ cup chopped fresh flat-leaf parsley
Perfect Rice (page 16), hot

OYSTER DRESSING SOUFFLÉS

MAKES 6 SERVINGS

At Emeril's New Orleans Fish House in Las Vegas, we often feature this dish as a special and, boy, does it fly out of the kitchen. Savory soufflés, like sweet ones, must be served immediately, as they will begin to deflate and fall as soon as they come out of the oven. Make the sauce while the soufflés are in the oven so both are ready at the same time. These soufflés are a festive first course for brunch or dinner, or a main course for a luncheon when followed or accompanied by a large salad and French bread. Or serve the dressing on its own as a Thanksgiving or Christmas side dish, as they do in southern Louisiana.

7 tablespoons unsalted butter
1½ cups finely chopped yellow onions
¾ cup finely chopped green bell peppers
¾ cup finely chopped celery
½ teaspoon salt
¼ teaspoon cayenne
2 bay leaves
1 teaspoon minced garlic
½ cup finely chopped green onions (green and white parts)
¼ cup finely chopped fresh flat-leaf parsley
½ cup Chicken Stock (page 2) or canned low-sodium chicken broth
6 cups 1-inch cubes day-old French bread
1 large egg, lightly beaten
1 pint shucked oysters with their liquor
1 cup freshly grated Parmigiano-Reggiano
3 tablespoons fine dried bread crumbs
6 large egg whites
Oyster-Tasso Sauce (recipe follows)

1. **PREHEAT** the oven to 350°F. Butter a 2-quart baking dish with 1 tablespoon of the butter, and set aside.

2. **MELT** 5 tablespoons of the butter in a large heavy saucepan over medium-high heat. Add the onions, bell peppers, celery, salt, cayenne, and bay leaves and cook until the vegetables are soft, about 7 minutes. Add the garlic, green onions, and parsley and cook, stirring constantly, until fragrant, about 1 minute. Add the chicken stock, remove from the heat, and stir in the bread cubes. Mix in the egg, then the oysters and their liquor, and the cheese.

3. **SPREAD** the mixture in the prepared pan. Bake until golden brown and bubbling on top, about 1 hour and 15 minutes.

4. **LET** cool, then refrigerate until well chilled, at least 6 hours and up to 8 hours.

5. **PREHEAT** the oven to 375°F. Butter six ½-cup ramekins with the remaining 1 tablespoon butter. Sprinkle the bread crumbs inside the ramekins and shake to coat evenly with the crumbs.

6. SCOOP the oyster dressing into a large mixing bowl with a spoon and break into ½- to 1-inch pieces. Remove and discard the bay leaves.

7. BEAT the egg whites in a large bowl with a hand mixer on high speed or a wire whisk until stiff peaks form. With a rubber spatula, gently fold the beaten whites into the dressing. Spoon into the prepared ramekins and place the ramekins on a baking sheet.

8. BAKE until the soufflés are golden brown and have risen above the edge of the ramekins, about 25 minutes. Serve immediately, with the sauce on the side. Have each guest make a hole in the center of his or her soufflé, and spoon in the sauce.

Oyster-Tasso Sauce

1 teaspoon olive oil

¼ pound Homemade Tasso
(page 17) or other spicy
sausage, cut into small dice
(about 1 cup)

¼ cup finely chopped yellow
onions

1 teaspoon minced garlic

1 cup heavy cream

2 tablespoons chopped green
onions (green and white
parts)

1 tablespoon Emeril's Original
Essence or Creole Seasoning
(page 9)

1 cup shucked oysters (about
12), with their liquor

Salt and freshly ground black
pepper

1. HEAT the olive oil in a heavy large skillet over medium-high heat. Add the tasso and cook, stirring constantly, until heated through, about 3 minutes. Mix in the onions and cook until just softened, about 2 minutes. Stir in the the garlic and cook until fragrant, about 30 seconds. Add the cream and bring to a boil over high heat. Add the green onions and Essence. Reduce the heat to medium. Cook until the sauce is thick enough to coat the back of a spoon, about 5 minutes.

2. ADD the oysters and cook just until the edges begin to curl, about 1½ minutes. Season to taste with salt and pepper. Serve immediately.

OYSTER AND SHRIMP PO'BOY

MAKES 2 LARGE SANDWICHES

Man, just writing this recipe makes me hungry for a po'boy! I wish I could describe the experience of biting into one of these sandwiches. There's that first bite, with a shatter of crumbs, then the crunch of the hot fried seafood and the sweet tang of the mayonnaise, spiced up with the hot sauce. Po'boys come in all kinds of combinations—from the mixed seafood here to fried trout, roast beef, ham and cheese, and French fries and gravy—you name it, somebody's made it. Each New Orleans shop makes po'boy sandwiches its own special way. Some butter the bread first, others use just mayonnaise. Some put on just a little gravy, while others put on so much it runs down your arms while you eat! Order your po'boy "dressed"— the New Orleans way of saying you want yours with mayo, lettuce, and tomatoes.

1. **CUT** the bread crosswise in half. Then, cut both pieces horizontally in half. Spread the mayonnaise on the cut sides of the bread. Arrange the tomatoes and lettuce on the bottom halves of the bread.

2. **POUR** enough oil into a large heavy pot or electric deep fryer to come halfway up the sides, and heat over high heat to 360°F.

3. **COMBINE** the cornmeal and Essence in a shallow bowl. Add the oysters and shrimp and toss to coat evenly. Shake off any excess cornmeal. In batches, without crowding, deep-fry the seafood, turning frequently, until golden brown, about 2 minutes. Using a slotted spoon, transfer to paper towels to drain.

4. **ARRANGE** the warm oysters and shrimp on top of the lettuce and tomatoes, season to taste with the hot sauce, and top with the remaining bread. Serve immediately.

1 large loaf French bread (20 to 24 inches long)
½ cup Mayonnaise (page 12) or store-bought mayonnaise
12 tomato slices
¾ cup shredded lettuce
Vegetable oil for deep-frying
1 cup yellow cornmeal
1 tablespoon Emeril's Original Essence or Creole Seasoning (page 9)
20 shucked oysters (about 1 pint), drained
8 large shrimp, peeled and deveined
Emeril's Red Pepper Sauce or other hot pepper sauce

ROASTED RED SNAPPER
IN CREOLE SAUCE

MAKES 6 SERVINGS

Red snapper is one of my favorite fish from the Gulf of Mexico. They vary in size, but here we're using a 4-pound snapper, which will yield 6 servings. However, you can do this with smaller fish, figuring that a 1-pound fish will feed one person. The sauce can also be used for all sorts of seafood—shrimp, crab, lobster—take your pick.

One 4-pound red snapper, cleaned and scaled
1 tablespoon salt
1 teaspoon Emeril's Original Essence or Creole Seasoning (page 9)
4 tablespoons (½ stick) unsalted butter
3 cups chopped yellow onions
1 cup chopped green bell peppers
1 cup chopped celery
¼ teaspoon cayenne
¼ teaspoon dried thyme
3 bay leaves
½ cup chopped green onions (green and white parts)
1 tablespoon chopped garlic
3 tablespoons bleached all-purpose flour
2 cups seeded and chopped tomatoes
2 cups Chicken Stock (page 2) or canned low-sodium chicken broth
1 teaspoon Worcestershire sauce
1 teaspoon Emeril's Red Pepper Sauce or other hot pepper sauce
1 tablespoon chopped fresh flat-leaf parsley

1. **RINSE** the fish under cold running water to remove any impurities and remaining scales. Put the fish in a large baking dish, and make shallow diagonal 3-inch-long slits on each side of the fish. Season each side with ½ teaspoon of the salt and ½ teaspoon of the Essence. Refrigerate while you make the sauce.

2. **PREHEAT** the oven to 300°F.

3. **MELT** the butter in a heavy medium stockpot over medium-high heat. Add the onions, bell peppers, celery, the remaining 2 teaspoons salt, the cayenne, thyme, and bay leaves. Cook, stirring often, until the onions are soft and golden, about 10 minutes. Stir in the green onions and garlic and cook until fragrant, about 1 minute. Stir in the flour and cook, stirring often, without browning the flour, about 2 minutes.

4. **ADD** the tomatoes, chicken stock, Worcestershire, and pepper sauce. Cook over medium heat for 10 minutes. Add the parsley, then remove the sauce from the heat and let cool for 15 minutes.

5. POUR the sauce over the snapper. Bake until the flesh is firm and cooked through, about 1 hour.

6. USING two large spoons, loosen the head from the flesh of the fish and remove. Run one spoon down the back of the fish to find the spine. Gently loosen the flesh from the spine and bones, slip a wide serving spatula under the flesh, lift the flesh away from the bones and lay the fillet of fish on a serving platter. Gently pull the fish skeleton away from the bottom fillet and discard. Lift the bottom fillet from the roasting pan and place on the serving platter. Remove and discard the bay leaves, and pour the sauce into a bowl.

7. SERVE the fish immediately, with the sauce spooned on top.

BARBECUED QUAIL WITH ANDOUILLE BREAD PUDDING

MAKES 6 SERVINGS

Quail has been featured on the menu at Emeril's since the day we opened more than ten years ago. Because of its popularity, we served this on a Father's Day show on *Emeril Live*. I've been seeing farm-raised quail in supermarkets, so look around, or ask the butcher if he can find some for you. Instead of baking the quail, feel free to cook them on your grill. Or use the andouille bread pudding to stuff the quail, then roast.

12 quail, split down the back and breastbones removed (about 3½ ounces each)
1 tablespoon Emeril's Original Essence or Creole Seasoning (page 9)
1 teaspoon salt
1 tablespoon vegetable oil, or as needed
1 cup Barbecue Sauce (page 229)
Andouille Bread Pudding (recipe follows)

1. **PREHEAT** the oven to 375°F.

2. **SEASON** the quail on both sides with the Essence and salt.

3. **HEAT** the oil in a large heavy skillet over medium-high heat. Add 4 quail, breast side down, and cook until browned, about 2 minutes. Arrange the quail breast side up in a baking pan just large enough to hold them all. Add more oil to the skillet as needed and sear the remaining quail in two batches.

4. **SPOON** the barbecue sauce over the quail and bake until the meat looks rosy when pierced at a thighbone, 12 to 15 minutes.

5. **SERVE** immediately with the bread pudding.

Andouille Bread Pudding

1. **PREHEAT** the oven to 375°F. Grease a 2-quart rectangular baking dish with the butter.

2. **HEAT** the oil in a large heavy skillet over medium heat. Add the sausage and cook, stirring for 3 minutes. Add the onions, celery, salt, and black pepper. Cook, stirring until the vegetables are soft, 2 to 3 minutes.

3. **ADD** the garlic and cook until fragrant, about 30 seconds. Remove from the heat and let cool.

4. **COMBINE** the eggs, cream, and milk in a large mixing bowl and whisk to blend well. Fold in the sausage mixture, cheese, and green onions. Add the bread cubes, pushing them into the sausage mixture.

5. **POUR** into the prepared baking dish. Bake until the top is golden brown, about 45 minutes. Remove from the oven and let rest for 5 minutes before serving.

1 tablespoon unsalted butter
2 tablespoons vegetable oil
1 pound andouille sausage, chopped
2 cups chopped yellow onions
½ cup chopped celery
½ teaspoon salt
¼ teaspoon freshly ground black pepper
2 tablespoons chopped garlic
5 large eggs
1 cup heavy cream
3 cups milk
8 ounces grated white Cheddar cheese
1 tablespoon finely chopped green onions (green part only)
8 cups 1-inch cubes white bread

RED BEANS AND RICE

MAKES 4 TO 6 SERVINGS

If there's one dish that is typically New Orleans, it's red beans and rice. It is still served on Mondays in restaurants of all kinds throughout the Crescent City, because traditionally Monday was wash day and a housewife could put on a pot of beans at the same time she was heating up the water for the family laundry.

I've made mine here in the time-honored way, with a ham hock and smoked sausage, and by giving the beans a good overnight soaking in water. These take time, but the result is worth it. Serve your beans and rice with a hot crusty loaf of French bread and plenty of butter, and a bottle of hot sauce on the side.

1 pound dried red beans
1 tablespoon vegetable oil
1 cup chopped yellow onions
½ cup chopped green bell peppers
2 tablespoons minced garlic
½ pound andouille or other spicy smoked sausage, cut into ¼-inch slices
1 teaspoon salt
1 teaspoon Emeril's Original Essence or Creole Seasoning (page 9)
½ teaspoon cayenne
½ teaspoon freshly ground black pepper
1 teaspoon dried thyme
2 bay leaves
One 1-pound ham hock
2 to 2½ quarts Chicken Stock (page 2) or canned low-sodium chicken broth
Perfect Rice (page 16), hot

1. **IN** a colander, rinse the beans under cold running water. Discard any broken beans or pebbles. Transfer the beans to a large bowl and add enough cold water to cover by 2 inches. Soak for at least 8 hours, or overnight. Or, bring the beans and enough water to cover by 2 inches to a boil in a large pot over high heat and cook for 2 minutes, then remove from the heat and cover tightly; let stand for 1 hour.

2. **HEAT** the oil in a large heavy stockpot over medium-high heat. Add the onions, bell peppers, and garlic and cook, stirring often, until softened, about 4 minutes. Add the sausage, salt, Essence, cayenne, black pepper, thyme, and bay leaves. Cook, stirring often, until the sausage is browned, about 4 minutes. Add the ham hock and cook for 2 minutes.

3. **DRAIN** the beans and add to the pot. Pour in enough stock to cover by about 1 inch. Bring to a boil over high heat. Reduce the heat to medium-low. Simmer uncovered, stirring occasionally, until the beans are tender, about 2 hours. Remove and discard the bay leaves.

4. **MASH** about one-fourth of the bean mixture against the side of the pot with a heavy spoon to thicken the juices. Remove the ham hock. Let cool slightly. Slice the meat from the bone, discarding the skin and bones. Return the meat to the pot and heat through.

5. **SPOON** the rice into bowls and top with the beans.

STEWED BLACK-EYED PEAS

Black-eyed peas are one of those old Southern favorites. I added tasso to perk them up. If you can't get tasso, substitute a little chopped pork butt or ham. Some folks cut the meat from the ham hocks when the cooking time is up and return it to the pot. If you want to take it up another notch, feel free to add minced jalapeños to the pot. Make it a real Southern supper with some Perfect Rice (page 16), Corn Bread (page 255), and stewed greens or a salad of sliced tomatoes.

1. WITH a sharp knife, score the fat on the ham hocks with ¼-inch-deep slashes.

2. HEAT the vegetable oil in a large heavy stockpot over medium-high heat. Add the tasso and cook, stirring often, until heated through, about 3 minutes. Add the onions and bell peppers and cook, stirring often, until softened, about 4 minutes. Add the ham hocks, garlic, salt, black pepper, cayenne, and bay leaves. Cook, stirring often, for 2 minutes.

3. ADD the black-eyed peas and chicken stock. Bring to boil over high heat. Reduce the heat to medium-low. Simmer uncovered, stirring occasionally, until the peas are tender, 45 minutes to 1 hour, skimming off any foam that forms on the surface.

4. REMOVE the bay leaves and discard. Cut the meat from the ham hocks, discarding the skin and bones. Return the meat to the pot. Stir in the parsley.

5. SERVE hot with rice and corn bread.

Two 6-ounce ham hocks, or one large
2 tablespoons vegetable oil
¼ pound Homemade Tasso (page 17) or other ham or sausage, chopped (about 1 cup)
1 cup chopped yellow onions
½ cup chopped green bell peppers
2 tablespoons minced garlic
1 teaspoon salt
½ teaspoon freshly ground black pepper
¼ teaspoon cayenne
2 bay leaves
1 pound dried black-eyed peas, rinsed and picked over
2 quarts Chicken Stock (page 2) or canned low-sodium chicken broth
2 tablespoons minced fresh flat-leaf parsley

FALL RIVER MEMORIES

the recipes

I will forever be indebted to my mother, Hilda, and my father, Mr. John, for showing me how to cook and how to enjoy eating! Man, did we eat well! I love recalling and re-creating the taste memories of my Portuguese–French Canadian heritage. The crispy Roasted Smothered Scrod with Onion Crisps is a tip of my hat to the crew at Al Mac's Diner, where I would eat the best scrod on Fridays or Saturdays. ■ For me, comfort means enjoying Hilda's Favas and Dad's Meat Loaf. My friend Inez at the St. John's Club inspired me to make old favorites like the Rice and Salt Cod Salad and the Portuguese Kale and Clam Soup. Ah, guys, thanks for the memories!

PORTUGUESE KALE AND CLAM SOUP

MAKES 8 TO 12 SERVINGS

When I was young, we spent a lot of time at the seashore, and there I'd be—ankle deep in the bay, digging for clams at low tide. They were fresh; I'd be drooling, thinking about this dish. There are two ways to present this soup—serve it with the clams still in their shells (put a large bowl on the table so everybody can discard the shells), or take a couple of minutes in the kitchen, remove the clams from their shells, and return them to the pot. Either way, have plenty of hot crusty French or Portuguese bread for dipping!

2 tablespoons olive oil
1 pound smoked chorizo sausage, removed from casings and finely chopped
2 cups chopped yellow onions
1 cup chopped celery
1 cup chopped carrots
1 teaspoon salt
½ teaspoon freshly ground black pepper
4 cups shredded kale
2 tablespoons chopped garlic
1 Bouquet Garni (page 7)
3 quarts Chicken Stock (page 2) or canned low-sodium chicken broth
¼ teaspoon crushed red pepper flakes
4 dozen littleneck clams, scrubbed well (discard any that are open)
¼ cup finely chopped fresh cilantro

1. **HEAT** the olive oil in a large heavy pot or Dutch oven over medium-high heat. Add the chorizo and cook, stirring often, until it has rendered its fat and is beginning to brown, 3 to 4 minutes. Add the onions, celery, and carrots and cook, stirring often, until softened, about 3 minutes. Add the salt and pepper and stir well.

2. **ADD** the kale, garlic, bouquet garni, chicken stock, and red pepper flakes. Bring to a boil over high heat, stirring occasionally. Reduce the heat to medium-low. Simmer, stirring occasionally, until the kale is tender, about 30 minutes.

3. **ADD** the clams and cook until they open, about 10 minutes. Discard any unopened clams.

4. **STIR** in the cilantro. Serve hot.

POTATO SOUP WITH SALT COD FRITTERS

MAKES 6 TO 8 SERVINGS

This soup was made on an *Essence* show on which we paid tribute to my mother, known to all as Hilda, and man, was it a hit! This combination of hearty potato soup and fritters is one of those comfort foods that takes me back to my childhood in Fall River. Salt cod fritters are the national snack of Portugal. Sold in every pastry shop, they are as common there as ice cream is here. Served hot, they make a perfect hors d'oeuvre with cocktails. If you can't get salt cod, make the soup anyway, and serve it with crusty French bread or hot garlic bread.

1. HEAT the olive oil in a large heavy pot or Dutch oven over medium-high heat. Add the salt, crushed red pepper flakes and bay leaves, and cook, stirring for 1 minute to extract the spice flavors into the oil. Add the sausage and cook, stirring often, until it begins to brown, about 2 minutes. Add the onions, bell peppers, and celery and cook, stirring occasionally, until they soften, about 4 minutes.

2. ADD the stock, potatoes, and garlic and bring to a boil over high heat. Season with salt to taste. Reduce the heat to medium-low and simmer until the soup has thickened, about 1 hour and 15 minutes.

3. STIR in the parsley and green onions. Serve immediately, topping each serving with two or three fritters.

2 tablespoons extra-virgin olive oil
1 teaspoon salt, or more to taste
½ teaspoon crushed red pepper flakes
3 bay leaves
½ pound chorizo sausage, cut crosswise into ½-inch slices
1½ cups finely chopped yellow onions
¼ cup finely chopped green bell peppers
¼ cup finely chopped celery
2 quarts Chicken Stock (page 2) or canned low-sodium chicken broth
2 Idaho potatoes (about 1½ pounds), peeled and cut into large dice (about 3 cups)
2 tablespoons minced garlic
¼ cup chopped green onions (green and white parts)
3 tablespoons chopped fresh flat-leaf parsley
Salt Cod Fritters (page 141)

Salt Cod

2 pounds salt cod, cut into
4-inch pieces

Growing up in Fall River, Massachusetts, I came to love salt cod. I learned as a young boy how to rehydrate it and cook it in many different ways. In this recipe, I've demystified the soaking process so that even if you're not Portuguese, you can enjoy salt cod at home!

1. **LAY** the cod in a single layer in a large glass or ceramic dish. Add enough water to cover the fish by 1 inch. Cover tightly with plastic wrap and refrigerate for 6 hours.

2. **DRAIN** the fish in a colander and rinse under cold running water. Place the fish on a work surface covered with paper towels. Press each piece of fish firmly with your hands. Pat the fish dry with paper towels and return to the dish. Cover with fresh water, soaking and draining a total of three more times. (Don't worry if you stretch the soaking times to 8 hours.)

3. **PUT** the rinsed salt cod in an airtight container until ready to use. It can be refrigerated for up to one week.

Salt Cod Fritters

MAKES 24 FRITTERS

1. **BRING** the potatoes and enough water to cover to a boil in a small saucepan. Reduce the heat to medium-low. Cook just until fork-tender, about 12 minutes. Drain and transfer to a large bowl. Let cool for about 10 minutes.

2. **MASH** the potatoes with a fork until fairly smooth. Add the salt cod, green onions, parsley, one egg, the salt, and cayenne, and mix until well blended.

3. **POUR** enough vegetable oil into a large deep heavy pot or electric deep fryer to come halfway up the sides and heat over high heat to 360°F.

4. **COMBINE** the flour and 1 teaspoon of the Essence in a small mixing bowl. In another bowl, whisk the remaining egg, the milk, and ¼ teaspoon Essence until combined. In a third bowl, combine the bread crumbs with the remaining 2 teaspoons Essence.

5. **USING** a heaping tablespoon of the Salt Cod mixture for each fritter, roll to coat evenly in the flour. Shake to remove any excess flour, dip in the egg wash, dredge in the seasoned bread crumbs, and place on a baking sheet.

6. **IN** batches, without crowding, deep-fry the fritters until golden, about 2½ minutes. Using a slotted spoon, transfer the fritters to a paper towel–lined baking sheet.

7. **SERVE** immediately in the Potato Soup or as a snack.

1 large Idaho potato (about ¾ pound), peeled and cubed (¾ cup)
6 ounces Salt Cod (preceding recipe), shredded (about 1 cup)
¼ cup finely chopped green onions (green and white parts)
2 tablespoons finely chopped fresh flat-leaf parsley
2 large eggs
¼ teaspoon salt
⅛ teaspoon cayenne
Vegetable oil for deep-frying
⅓ cup bleached all-purpose flour
3 tablespoons milk
1 tablespoon plus ¼ teaspoon Emeril's Original Essence or Creole Seasoning (page 9)
⅔ cup fine dried bread crumbs

LOBSTER PORTUGUESE-STYLE

MAKES 2 SERVINGS

For some, lobster is an extravagance, but where I grew up, they were always available and eaten regularly. We ate them frequently, prepared in all kinds of ways. This Fall River classic reminded me that a little pork sausage can add a world of flavor to just about any dish—even seafood. If you prefer not to split the live lobster in half yourself (it's really no big deal), have the guys at your local fish market do it for you. (Ask them to show you how to do it.) Oh, and make sure you serve this with piles of hot bread for sopping up the broth!

2 cups peeled and diced Idaho potatoes
2 tablespoons olive oil
6 ounces smoked spicy sausage, such as chorizo, removed from casings and chopped
1 cup finely chopped yellow onions
3 tablespoons finely chopped red bell peppers
2 bay leaves
2 tablespoons minced garlic
1 tablespoon minced shallots
2 tablespoons chopped fresh flat-leaf parsley
½ cup chopped pimiento-stuffed green olives
½ cup chopped pitted black olives
1½ cups seeded and chopped tomatoes
1 teaspoon salt, or more to taste
½ teaspoon crushed red pepper flakes, or more to taste
One 1½-pound live lobster, split lengthwise in half
½ cup dry white wine
¼ cup chopped green onions (green and white parts)

1. **BRING** the potatoes and enough water to cover to a boil in a small saucepan over high heat. Cook until the potatoes are just tender, about 6 minutes. Drain.

2. **HEAT** the olive oil in a large skillet over medium-high heat. Add the sausage and cook, stirring occasionally, until just beginning to brown, about 5 minutes. Stir in the onions, red bell peppers, and bay leaves and cook until beginning to soften, about 3 minutes. Add the garlic, shallots, and parsley and cook, stirring until fragrant, about 1 minute. Add the olives, potatoes, tomatoes, salt, and crushed red pepper flakes, stir well to combine, and cook for 1 minute.

3. **ADD** the split lobster, shell side down. Add 1 cup water and the wine, cover, and simmer until the lobster shells are deep red and the meat is cooked through, about 10 minutes.

4. **WITH** tongs, transfer each lobster half to a shallow soup bowl. Season the broth if necessary, remove the bay leaves, and spoon the broth over the lobster. Garnish with the chopped green onions and serve immediately.

HILDA'S FAVAS

Boy, does this dish take me back to my childhood, when my mother, Hilda, used to make this for holiday dinners and special occasions, particularly during those cold New England winter months. As with any bean, favas only get better the next day, and the next day after that. So, do as Hilda does, and cook these three days ahead of when you're planning to actually serve them.

1. **BRING** 3 quarts water to a boil in a large heavy saucepan over high heat. Reduce the heat to medium-low and add the favas and 2 teaspoons of the salt. Cover and simmer until the beans are tender, about 1½ hours. Drain in a colander and rinse under cold running water until cool enough to handle.

2. **TO** peel the beans, gently pull open the dark end of the skin of each bean with the tip of a small sharp knife, or with your fingernail, and peel back the skin. Put the peeled beans in a bowl.

3. **HEAT** the olive oil in a heavy large saucepan over medium-high heat. Add the bay leaves, crushed red pepper flakes, and the remaining 1 teaspoon salt and heat for 1 minute, stirring occasionally. Add the onions and bell peppers and cook, stirring occasionally, until softened, about 5 minutes. Stir in the parsley and garlic and cook, stirring, until fragrant, about 1 minute.

4. **STIR** in the tomato paste and 7½ cups water. Bring to a boil over high heat, then reduce the heat to medium-low, and simmer until slightly thickened, about 30 minutes.

5. **ADD** the fava beans and continue simmering until the beans are tender, about 1 hour. Serve immediately, or cool, cover, and refrigerate for up to three days.

2 pounds dried fava beans
1 tablespoon salt
3 tablespoons extra-virgin olive oil
4 bay leaves, torn into quarters
1½ teaspoons crushed red pepper flakes
2 cups finely chopped yellow onions
1 cup finely chopped green bell peppers
½ cup chopped fresh flat-leaf parsley
1 tablespoon minced garlic
Two 6-ounce cans tomato paste

ROASTED SMOTHERED SCROD WITH ONION CRISPS

MAKES 4 SERVINGS

Scrod (young cod weighing less than 2½ pounds) is a firm white-fleshed fish found on menus and in homes throughout New England. Like chicken, scrod can be served with many sauces and toppings. Here I cook the fish with a topping, then top both with crispy onion rings. Now, here's a warning—these onion crisps are completely addictive, and you might not want to share. Think about doubling the recipe so you can be sure everybody gets enough!

Four 6-ounce scrod fillets
1 tablespoon Emeril's Original Essence or Creole Seasoning (page 9)
2 tablespoons olive oil
1¼ pounds eggplant, peeled and cut into ½-inch dice (about 6 cups)
1 cup chopped yellow onions
8 plum tomatoes (about 1 pound), cored and cut into quarters
¼ cup chopped fresh basil
2 teaspoons minced garlic
1 teaspoon salt, or more to taste
¼ teaspoon cayenne
¼ teaspoon crushed red pepper flakes
1 cup Chicken Stock (page 2) or canned low-sodium chicken broth
Onion Crisps (recipe follows)

1. **PREHEAT** the oven to 400°F.

2. **SEASON** both sides of the fish fillets with the Essence. Set aside.

3. **HEAT** the oil in a large nonstick ovenproof skillet over medium-high heat. Add the eggplant and onions and cook, stirring, until the eggplant is softened, about 6 minutes. Add the tomatoes, basil, garlic, salt, cayenne, and crushed red pepper flakes, and cook, stirring, for 2 minutes. Add the stock, bring to a simmer, and simmer for 2 minutes. Season with more salt to taste if necessary.

4. **ADD** the fish to the skillet and spoon the vegetables over the fish to cover it. Transfer to the oven and roast until the fish is cooked through and the vegetables are tender, about 20 minutes.

5. **USING** a spatula, transfer the fish fillets to four shallow soup or pasta bowls. Top with the vegetable sauce, garnish with the onion crisps, and serve immediately.

Onion Crisps

MAKES 4 SERVINGS

1. **POUR** enough oil to come halfway up the sides into a large heavy pot or electric deep-fryer and heat over high heat to 360°F.

2. **COMBINE** the flour and 1 tablespoon of the Essence in a shallow bowl. Whisk the egg and 2 tablespoons water in another shallow bowl. Dip the onions in the egg mixture, then toss in the seasoned flour, shaking to remove any excess flour. In batches, without crowding, deep-fry the onions until crisp and golden, 2 to 3 minutes. Using a slotted spoon, transfer to a paper towel–lined baking sheet.

3. **JUST** before serving, season with the remaining 1 teaspoon Essence and the salt. Serve hot.

Vegetable oil for deep-frying
¾ cup bleached all-purpose flour
1 tablespoon plus 1 teaspoon
    Emeril's Original Essence or
    Creole Seasoning (page 9)
1 large egg
2 cups thinly sliced yellow
    onions, separated into rings
½ teaspoon salt

RICE AND SALT COD SALAD

MAKES 12 SERVINGS

A Portuguese tradition, rice and salt cod salad is served at family-style gatherings from big bowls on the table so everyone can help themselves. My friend Inez at the St. John's Club in Fall River still has this dish on her menu, and every time we visit her, I get to enjoy this great favorite from my childhood. This is my twist on the salad, kicked up with a lot more garnishes than you'd usually find in Fall River.

- 1 pound salt cod, soaked as directed on page 140
- 1/4 cup plus 2 tablespoons extra-virgin olive oil
- 1 cup finely chopped yellow onions
- 1/4 cup finely chopped green bell peppers
- 1/4 cup finely chopped celery
- 1/2 teaspoon salt
- 1/4 teaspoon cayenne
- 1 teaspoon minced garlic
- 1 cup seeded and chopped tomatoes
- 1 cup dry white wine
- 2 tablespoons chopped fresh flat-leaf parsley
- 2 tablespoons finely chopped green onions (green and white parts)
- 1 cup frozen green peas, thawed
- 1/2 head iceberg lettuce, washed and separated into leaves
- 7 cups Perfect Rice (page 16), cooled
- 12 pimiento-stuffed green olives, sliced in half
- 1 tablespoon chopped fresh cilantro
- 3 tablespoons fresh lemon juice
- 4 Perfect Hard-Boiled Eggs (page 16), sliced

1. **BREAK** the soaked salt cod into small flakes in a mixing bowl. Set aside.

2. **HEAT** 2 tablespoons of the olive oil in a heavy medium saucepan over medium-high heat. Add the onions, bell peppers, celery, salt, and cayenne, and cook, stirring, until the vegetables are softened, about 4 minutes. Stir in the garlic, then the tomatoes and wine. Bring to a boil. Reduce the heat to medium-low and simmer for 4 minutes.

3. **ADD** the parsley, green onions, and salt cod, stir, and simmer for 10 minutes. Remove from the heat and add the peas and 2 tablespoons of the olive oil. Let cool.

4. **LINE** a large serving platter with the lettuce leaves. Arrange the rice over the lettuce, gently spreading it and making a groove down the center. Pour the cooled sauce into the groove and top with the olives and cilantro. Drizzle with the lemon juice and the remaining 2 tablespoons olive oil. Arrange the sliced eggs around the edge of the platter and serve.

PORTUGUESE CHORIZO PIZZA

When I was a youngster in Fall River, my first job was at a neighborhood pizzeria, where one of the most popular pizzas was made with chorizo. Once you try it, you'll see why it's become one of my favorites! Although I can eat an entire pizza myself, there's probably enough here to serve four people with a big green salad on the side. Or serve these as appetizers while you're preparing other dishes.

Pizza Dough (page 10)
1 cup Tomato Sauce (page 8)
½ pound smoked chorizo sausage, thinly sliced
8 ounces mozzarella, grated

1. PREHEAT the oven to 500°F. Lightly grease two baking sheets.

2. ONE at a time, pull and gently stretch each pizza dough portion into a 6-inch round. Put each piece of dough on a greased baking sheet. Pat each out to a 10- to 12-inch round, about ⅛ inch thick. Spread ½ cup of the tomato sauce on each round, leaving a 1-inch border. Arrange the chorizo on top of the sauce and top with a thin layer of the cheese.

3. BAKE until the dough is golden brown and the cheese is bubbly, about 20 minutes, switching the pans from top to bottom after 10 minutes.

4. SERVE immediately.

HILDA'S STEWED CHICKEN

MAKES 4 SERVINGS

When I was a young boy, my cooking inspirations came from my mother, Hilda. Serve my Mom's chicken with crusty bread and some red wine; you'll love it as much as I do.

One 3½- to 4-pound chicken, cut into 8 pieces
1 tablespoon plus 1 teaspoon Emeril's Original Essence or Creole Seasoning (page 9)
½ cup bleached all-purpose flour
¼ cup olive oil
1 pound smoked chorizo sausage, cut crosswise into 2-inch pieces
1 pound Idaho potatoes, peeled and diced (about 2 cups)
1 cup finely chopped yellow onions
½ cup thinly sliced red bell peppers
½ cup thinly sliced yellow bell peppers
2 cups chopped tomatoes
1 head garlic, separated into cloves and peeled
1 cup kalamata or other black brine-cured olives, pitted and sliced in half
1 teaspoon salt
½ teaspoon freshly ground black pepper
⅛ teaspoon crushed red pepper flakes
1 cup dry white wine
½ cup finely chopped fresh flat-leaf parsley
½ cup green onions (green and white parts)
Perfect Rice (page 16)
½ cup freshly grated Parmigiano-Reggiano

1. **SEASON** the chicken with 1 tablespoon of the Essence. In a shallow bowl, season the flour with the remaining 1 teaspoon Essence. Add the chicken and toss to coat evenly, shaking to remove any excess flour.

2. **HEAT** the oil in a large heavy skillet over medium-high heat. Add the chicken and cook until lightly browned, about 2½ minutes on each side.

3. **TRANSFER** the chicken to a plate and add the chorizo to the pan. Cook, stirring often, until the chorizo is beginning to brown, about 2 minutes. Add the potatoes, onions, and bell peppers. Cook, stirring often, until the onions soften, about 2 minutes. Add the tomatoes, garlic cloves, olives, salt, black pepper, and crushed red pepper flakes and stir well. Add the white wine and parsley, and return the chicken to the pan. Bring to a boil, then reduce the heat to medium-low. Simmer, covered, until the chicken falls from the bone, about 45 minutes.

4. **STIR** in the green onions. Serve with the hot rice, allowing two pieces of chicken per person, and sprinkle the cheese on top.

DAD'S MEAT LOAF

MAKES 4 SERVINGS

Growing up, I was always guided by Mr. John, my father. On Sundays, when he often took over the cooking, he made this one simple dish and it has remained one of my favorites. As Jay Leno said on a recent *Tonight* show when I made this, "We'll hide the sausage for a kicked-up meat loaf."

1. PREHEAT the oven to 350°F. Grease a large roasting pan with the butter.

2. COMBINE the beef, pork, onions, bell peppers, garlic, eggs, cream, bread crumbs, salt, pepper, and Essence in a large mixing bowl and stir with a wooden spoon to mix. Pat half of the meat mixture into a rectangle about 9 × 4 inches on the prepared pan. Layer the sausage on top of the loaf. Mold the remaining meat mixture around and over the sausage to cover it completely. Pour the chili sauce on top.

3. BAKE, basting occasionally with the pan juices, for 1½ hours. With a large spatula, carefully transfer the meat loaf to a serving platter.

4. HEAT the roasting pan over high heat on the stovetop. Add the veal stock, stir up the browned bits in the pan, and bring to a boil. Whisk the flour and 2 tablespoons of water in a small bowl until smooth. Then whisk into the stock. Bring to a boil and cook, whisking often, until the gravy thickens slightly, about 2 minutes. Season to taste.

5. SERVE the meat loaf with the hot mashed potatoes and gravy.

---

2 teaspoons unsalted butter
1 pound ground beef
½ pound ground pork
1 cup finely chopped yellow onions
½ cup finely chopped green bell peppers
1 tablespoon minced garlic
2 large eggs
½ cup heavy cream
½ to 1 cup fine dried bread crumbs (depending on how firm you want the meat loaf)
1 teaspoon salt
½ teaspoon freshly ground black pepper
1 tablespoon Emeril's Original Essence or Creole Seasoning (page 9)
½ pound smoked chorizo sausage, chopped into ½-inch pieces
1 cup bottled chili sauce
2 cups Veal Stock (page 4) or canned low-sodium beef broth
2 tablespoons bleached all-purpose flour
Mashed Potatoes (page 14)

MEAT PIES WITH SPICY PORTUGUESE SAUCE

MAKES ABOUT 36 APPETIZER PIES

My mother's people came from Portugal, and I had always wanted to visit the country I'd heard so much about. I did visit, and what a trip! I ate many familiar dishes, but I also discovered new versions of others. I was so impressed by Portuguese food that I did a couple of *Essence of Emeril* shows on the topic. Man, these meat pies are so good! And the sauce will blow your mind!

1½ pounds ground veal
¾ cup fine dried bread crumbs
2 tablespoons chopped fresh cilantro
2 tablespoons chopped fresh flat-leaf parsley
2 tablespoons buttermilk
2 large eggs
1 teaspoon minced garlic
2 teaspoons salt
½ teaspoon crushed red pepper flakes
1 tablespoon Emeril's Original Essence or Creole Seasoning (page 9)
½ cup bleached all-purpose flour
Vegetable oil for frying
Spicy Portuguese Sauce (recipe follows)

1. **PLACE** the veal, ¼ cup of the bread crumbs, the cilantro, parsley, buttermilk, 1 egg, the garlic, salt, and crushed red pepper flakes in a large bowl and mix quickly but thoroughly. Form the mixture into meatballs the size of a large walnut, about 2 tablespoons each.

2. **BEAT** the remaining egg with 2 tablespoons water and 1 teaspoon of the Essence in a shallow bowl. Combine the flour and 1 teaspoon of the Essence in a shallow bowl. Combine the remaining bread crumbs with the remaining 1 teaspoon Essence in another shallow bowl.

3. **DIP** each meat pie first into the seasoned flour, then into the egg wash, letting the excess drip off, and finally into the bread crumbs, coating evenly. Flatten each ball slightly to form a patty and place on a baking sheet lined with waxed paper. Cover tightly with plastic wrap and refrigerate until ready to cook. The balls may be made ahead of time and kept in the refrigerator up to 5 hours.

4. **ADD** enough oil to come ½ inch up the sides of a large heavy skillet and heat over high heat until very hot. In batches, fry the meat patties in the oil until deep golden brown, 3 to 4 minutes on each side. Using a slotted spatula, transfer to paper towels to drain. Serve hot with the sauce.

Spicy Portuguese Sauce

MAKES ABOUT 2½ CUPS

This sauce is awesome with the meat pies, but I also like it as a pasta or pizza topping.

1. **HEAT** the olive oil in a saucepan over medium-high heat. Add the onions and garlic and cook, stirring, until soft, about 4 minutes. Add the anchovy fillets, olives, and crushed red pepper flakes and cook, stirring often, until the anchovies dissolve, about 2 minutes.

2. **ADD** the tomatoes, tomato paste, and ¼ cup water. Stir well. Simmer, uncovered, until the sauce has thickened, about 20 minutes.

3. **ADD** the parsley and cilantro, and season with salt and pepper. Serve hot.

2 tablespoons olive oil
¾ cup finely chopped yellow onions
1 tablespoon minced garlic
2 anchovy fillets, minced
¼ cup chopped pitted cured black olives, such as kalamata
¾ teaspoon crushed red pepper flakes
One 16-ounce can crushed tomatoes
1 tablespoon tomato paste
2 tablespoons chopped fresh flat-leaf parsley
2 tablespoons chopped fresh cilantro
Salt and freshly ground black pepper

MADEIRA-BRAISED SHORT RIBS

MAKES 8 SERVINGS

Madeira is a wine named for the Portuguese island where it's produced. Madeira can be dry or sweet in taste, light or dark in color. I call for sweet Rainwater Madeira here, but if you can't find it in your area, substitute another Portuguese fortified wine, like a ruby port. I use boneless beef short ribs for this dish; just ask your butcher to remove the ribs for you.

4½ pounds boneless beef short ribs, cut into 1½-inch pieces
2 tablespoons Emeril's Original Essence or Creole Seasoning (page 9)
1 teaspoon salt
½ teaspoon freshly ground black pepper
½ cup bleached all-purpose flour
¼ cup plus 1 tablespoon extra-virgin olive oil, or as needed
4 large carrots, coarsely chopped
4 celery ribs, coarsely chopped
1 large yellow onion, coarsely chopped
3 bay leaves
8 garlic cloves, minced
1 large jalapeño, quartered through the stem
3 tablespoons tomato paste
1½ cups Rainwater Madeira
6 cups Veal Stock (page 4) or canned low-sodium beef broth
3 tablespoons finely chopped fresh flat-leaf parsley

1. **SEASON** the meat with the Essence, salt, and pepper. Dredge it in the flour, shaking to remove any excess.

2. **HEAT** 3 tablespoons of the olive oil in a large enameled casserole or Dutch oven. In batches, brown the meat on all sides, about 10 minutes per batch, adding more oil to the pot as needed. Transfer the meat to a large platter. Discard the oil.

3. **ADD** the remaining 3 tablespoons oil to the pot and heat over medium-high heat. Add the carrots, celery, onions, and bay leaves and cook, stirring often, until the onions are softened, about 5 minutes. Add the garlic and jalapeño and stir until fragrant, about 1 minute. Add the tomato paste and cook, stirring, until heated through, about 1 minute.

4. **ADD** the Madeira, stirring to scrape up any browned bits from the bottom of the pot. Add the stock and bring to a boil. Return the meat to the pot. Lower the heat to medium-low and simmer, partially covered, stirring occasionally, until the meat is tender, about 2½ hours. (During cooking, make sure there is always at least 1 inch of liquid in the pot; add more stock or water as necessary.)

5. **REMOVE** the pot from the heat. Skim any fat from the surface of the cooking liquid, and remove and discard the bay leaves. Sprinkle the ribs with the parsley and serve immediately.

PORTUGUESE FIVE-EGG EASTER BREAD

MAKES 5 LOAVES

I'm really sentimental about this bread because it's one all the Fall River families of Portuguese descent make each Easter. This recipe has been handed down for generations, and, as a matter of fact, Hilda dictated this one to me on the phone when we were getting ready to film a new *Essence of Emeril* show featuring Mediterranean Easter traditions. Now, I know the rising and kneading process sounds a bit crazy, but trust me, this works. Hilda's favorite flours to use when making this bread are either St. Elizabeth or Rose brand, but if you don't live in New England and can't find those, any all-purpose flour will work. The five eggs are the decoration on the top of the breads; you add one to each loaf during the final rising, and then bake them in. Originally, this was one large loaf with five eggs decorating the top. To simplify things, this recipe makes five smaller loaves with one egg each. (If you want to freeze the dough, add the eggs when you bake it.)

1. **IN** a saucepan combine the milk, salt, and lard and bring to a boil. Set aside.

2. **IN** a small bowl combine the yeast, 1 cup of the flour, and ½ cup warm water and set aside.

3. **IN** a large bowl, with a whisk, combine the eggs, sugar, and lemon zest and mix thoroughly. Add the milk mixture, yeast mixture, and remaining flour and thoroughly combine. Set aside to rise, kneading 6 times every half hour. The bread will take 6 hours to rise.

4. **PREPARE** 5 round loaf pans with butter or lard. Divide the batter among the pans (pans should be half full). Press the dough evenly in the pan and let it rise again until it reaches the top of the pan.

5. **PREHEAT** the oven to 350 °F. Brush with beaten egg and bake for about 1 hour, until golden brown.

NOTE: If you choose to add the five eggs for Easter, place an egg on top of each loaf during the final rising.

4 cups milk
1 teaspoon salt
½ pound lard
Three ¼-ounce envelopes active dry yeast
5 pounds flour (St. Elizabeth or Rose brand preferred)
12 large eggs
4 cups sugar
Zest of 1 lemon, grated
1 large egg beaten with 1 tablespoon water, for glaze
5 eggs (optional)

THE FLOPPIN'  FISH MARKET

the recipes

TEMPURA STONE CRAB
CLAWS WITH LEMON–BLACK
PEPPER TARTAR SAUCE

SEARED SCALLOPS ON
TRUFFLE–WHITE BEAN PURÉE
WITH WILD MUSHROOM SAUCE

RED SNAPPER WITH TAPENADE

VODKA-AND-CITRUS-
CURED SALMON

PANFRIED CATFISH WITH WARM
ANDOUILLE POTATO SALAD AND
GROWN-UP TARTAR SAUCE

PROSCIUTTO-WRAPPED HALIBUT
WITH TOMATO-CAPER
BUTTER SAUCE

ROAST FLOUNDER
STUFFED WITH EGGPLANT–CORN
BREAD DRESSING

PAN-SEARED SALMON WITH
BLACK BEAN RELISH

REDFISH BAKED IN FOIL WITH
CASHEW-GARLIC BUTTER

When fish is so fresh that it's still floppin' when you're about to cook it, I call it floppin' fish. ■ I grew up eating plenty of fresh-caught fish from the Atlantic Ocean. Since I've moved to New Orleans and traveled all over the world, I've eaten and cooked all kinds of seafood from oceans, lakes, rivers, bayous, and streams. Seafood, be it fish, shrimp, plump oysters, crawfish, or sweet lump crabmeat, is endlessly versatile, and each dish here is a winner.

TEMPURA STONE CRAB CLAWS WITH LEMON–BLACK PEPPER TARTAR SAUCE

Light, delicate tempura batter is best when allowed to stand in the refrigerator for 30 minutes to an hour before using it. Stone crab claws can be found in some fish markets around the country, or you can have them sent overnight to you. Leave some of the shell attached as a handle for easy eating.

1 large egg
1 cup cold club soda
⅔ cup bleached all-purpose flour
½ cup cornstarch
1 tablespoon Emeril's Original Essence or Creole Seasoning (page 9)
1 teaspoon salt
24 Florida stone crab claws (see Source Guide, page 282), shells cracked
Vegetable oil, for deep-frying
Lemon–Black Pepper Tartar Sauce (recipe follows)

1. BEAT the egg in a large mixing bowl. Add the club soda, flour, cornstarch, Essence, and salt and whisk until smooth. Cover and refrigerate for 30 minutes to 1 hour.

2. POUR enough oil into a large heavy pot or electric deep fryer to come halfway up the sides and heat to 360°F.

3. IN batches, dip the crab claws into the batter and deep-fry until golden brown, 2 to 3 minutes. Using a slotted spoon, transfer the claws to paper towels to drain.

4. SERVE immediately with the tartar sauce.

Lemon–Black Pepper Tartar Sauce

You'll find that this sauce is a terrific accompaniment to just about any boiled or fried seafood.

1. COMBINE the egg, lemon juice, lime juice, mustard, and onions in a food processor or a blender. Process until smooth, about 15 seconds. With the machine running, slowly add the oil in a steady stream. The mixture will thicken. Add the salt and pepper and pulse for 10 seconds.

2. POUR the sauce into a decorative bowl, cover, and chill for one hour before serving.

1 large egg
2 tablespoons fresh lemon juice
1 tablespoon fresh lime juice
2 teaspoons Dijon mustard
¼ cup minced yellow onions
1 cup olive oil
1 teaspoon salt
1 teaspoon freshly ground black pepper

SEARED SCALLOPS ON TRUFFLE–WHITE BEAN PURÉE WITH WILD MUSHROOM SAUCE

MAKES 4 APPETIZER OR 2 MAIN-COURSE SERVINGS

Normally, I make my wine selection once I have a meal planned. In this case, I had a wonderful full-bodied California Chardonnay and needed a main course to serve with it. This scallop dish filled the bill and the white bean purée gave the whole thing a very sophisticated taste. I recommend making the bean purée ahead of time. You can try this with seared shrimp for an equally good result.

WHITE BEAN PURÉE
1 tablespoon unsalted butter
¼ cup finely chopped yellow onions
½ teaspoon salt
¼ teaspoon freshly ground black pepper
1 tablespoon minced shallots
1 teaspoon minced garlic
½ cup heavy cream
1 cup Basic Beans (white) (page 13)
¼ cup white truffle oil

WILD MUSHROOM SAUCE
2 tablespoons olive oil
¼ cup minced yellow onions
½ teaspoon salt
¼ teaspoon freshly ground black pepper
2 tablespoons minced shallots

1. TO make the purée: Melt the butter in a medium saucepan over medium-high heat. Add the onions, salt, and pepper, and cook, stirring, for 3 minutes. Add the shallots and cook, stirring, for 2 minutes. Add the garlic and cook, stirring, until fragrant, about 1 minute. Add the cream and the beans. Bring to a boil, then reduce the heat to medium-low and simmer for 5 minutes. Remove from the heat.

2. POUR the mixture into the bowl of a food processor or blender. Add additional salt and pepper if necessary, and process on high speed for 30 seconds. With the motor running, add the truffle oil and process until smooth, about 1 minute. Set aside and keep warm.

3. TO make the mushroom sauce: Heat the olive oil in a heavy medium saucepan over medium-high heat. Add the onions, salt, and pepper, and cook, stirring, for 2 minutes. Add the shallots and mushrooms, and cook, stirring, for 2 minutes. Add the garlic and cook until fragrant, about 1 minute. Add the stock and bring to a boil over high heat. Reduce the heat to medium-low and cook until the sauce has thickened, about 4 minutes.

4. REMOVE from the heat, cover, and keep warm.

5. TO prepare the scallops: Heat the olive oil in a large heavy skillet on medium-high heat. Season the scallops with the salt and white pepper. Add them to the skillet and sear until lightly golden brown, about 2 minutes on each side.

6. TO serve, spoon about 1/3 cup of white bean purée on each of four plates, place three scallops on the purée, and top with about 1/2 cup of the mushroom sauce.

1/2 pound assorted wild mushrooms, such as porcini, chanterelle, oyster, or wood ear, wiped clean, stems removed, and thinly sliced

2 teaspoons minced garlic

1 1/2 cups Brown Chicken Stock (page 3), or commercial demi-glace

SCALLOPS

2 tablespoons olive oil

12 divers scallops, or other large sea scallops, rinsed and patted dry

1 teaspoon salt

1/2 teaspoon freshly ground white pepper

RED SNAPPER WITH TAPENADE

MAKES 6 TO 8 SERVINGS

Whatever the time of year, this dish, with its flavors of briny olives, fresh tomatoes, and onions, will bring the magic of Provence to your table. Serve it over rice, like saffron rice or pilaf, or with rice-shaped orzo pasta. The Provençal Tapenade makes a great appetizer served on toasted French or Italian bread croutons, topped with a little bit of goat cheese.

One 4-pound red snapper, cleaned and scaled
3 tablespoons extra-virgin olive oil
1 tablespoon plus 1 teaspoon kosher salt
1½ teaspoons freshly ground black pepper
1 tablespoon herbes de Provence or 1 teaspoon each dried basil, thyme, and rosemary
4 large plum tomatoes, cored and sliced lengthwise, ¼ inch thick
1 tablespoon minced fresh basil
Tapenade (recipe follows)
1½ cups sliced yellow onions

1. PREHEAT the oven to 400°F.

2. RINSE the snapper under cold running water and pat dry with paper towels. Place in a large glass or ceramic baking dish. Make five 3-inch slits in each side. Season each side of the fish with 1 tablespoon of the olive oil, 1½ teaspoons of the salt, ½ teaspoon of the pepper, and 1½ teaspoons of the herbes de Provence. Bake the fish for 30 minutes.

3. MEANWHILE, toss the tomatoes with the remaining 1 tablespoon olive oil, 1 teaspoon salt, and ½ teaspoon pepper and the fresh basil in a large bowl. Cover and set aside at room temperature.

4. REMOVE the fish from the oven and thickly coat the top side of the fish, from just behind the head to just before the tail, with the tapenade. Layer the tomatoes on top of the tapenade, then top with the onions. Return the fish to the oven and bake until the juices run clear and the onions are beginning to crisp and slightly blacken around the edges, about 30 minutes.

5. REMOVE from the oven.

6. WITH a large spatula, gently lift the tomato and onion topping and underlying tapenade from the fish, and arrange around the edges of a serving platter. With two spoons, loosen the head from the body of the fish, lift it away, and discard. Run one of the spoons down the back of the fish and gently separate the flesh into the two fillets. Lift the top fillet onto the serving platter. Carefully lift the spine and other bones out of the fish and discard. Place the remaining fish fillet on the platter and serve.

Tapenade

MAKES 1½ CUPS

COMBINE all the ingredients except the basil in the bowl of a food processor. Purée, then transfer to a bowl. Fold in the basil and set aside until needed, up to two hours, or refrigerate for up to three days in an airtight container.

2 cups pitted Niçoise or other brine-cured black olives
¼ cup extra-virgin olive oil
2 tablespoons fresh lemon juice
1 tablespoon minced shallots
1 tablespoon minced garlic
1 tablespoon capers, drained
1 tablespoon chopped fresh flat-leaf parsley
4 anchovy fillets
⅛ teaspoon freshly ground black pepper
1 tablespoon chopped fresh basil

VODKA-AND-CITRUS-CURED SALMON

MAKES 8 SERVINGS

Curing salmon is easy. I've paired this with the Caramelized Ruby Red Grapefruit Salad (page 62), but the cured salmon also is super when served traditionally on toast points with a dollop of sour cream and snipped chives. A little salmon roe or sturgeon caviar on top is an elegant touch. You can double this for a crowd.

One 2-pound salmon fillet,
   with skin
½ cup kosher salt
3 tablespoons sugar
¼ cup chopped fresh dill
¼ cup lemon-flavored vodka
   (such as Absolut Citron)
2 tablespoons grated lemon zest
   (from about 6 lemons)
2 tablespoons grated orange zest
   (from about 3 oranges)
2 tablespoons grated lime zest
   (from about 8 limes)

1. **REMOVE** any tiny pinbones from the salmon with a pair of needle-nose pliers or tweezers. Rinse the salmon under cold running water and pat dry. Place it, skin side down on several large sheets of plastic wrap.

2. **COMBINE** the salt, sugar, dill, vodka, and lemon, orange, and lime zests in a small mixing bowl. Spread evenly over the flesh side of the fish, pressing it into the flesh. Wrap the salmon tightly in the plastic wrap and place skin side down in a baking dish. Place a flat glass or ceramic dish on top of the salmon and weight the dish with several heavy cans or a brick. Refrigerate for at least 24 hours and up to 48 hours.

3. **REMOVE** the salmon from the refrigerator and unwrap. Rinse under cold running water to completely remove the curing mixture. Pat dry.

4. **WITH** a sharp knife, slice the salmon diagonally into paper-thin slices, holding the knife almost parallel to the work surface. Serve as desired.

PANFRIED CATFISH WITH WARM ANDOUILLE POTATO SALAD AND GROWN-UP TARTAR SAUCE

MAKES 4 SERVINGS

Fried catfish is a Southern staple. When I did an *Essence* show on Southern favorites, we included this incredible dish. If you want to blow yourself into outer space, serve Stewed Black-Eyed Peas (page 135) and cracklin' corn bread with this! Now, that is what I call a rib-sticking meal!

1. **COMBINE** the flour and 1 teaspoon of the Essence in a shallow bowl. Season the fish with the salt.

2. **HEAT** the vegetable oil in a large heavy skillet. Dredge two of the fillets in the flour, coating evenly, and shake to remove excess flour. Fry the fillets until golden brown, about 4 minutes on each side. Remove with a slotted spatula and drain on paper towels. Repeat with the remaining fish. Season the fillets with the remaining ½ teaspoon Essence.

3. **MOUND** equal amounts of the potato salad in the centers of four serving plates. Lay one catfish fillet on each, top with a dollop of tartar sauce, and serve.

¼ cup bleached all-purpose flour
1½ teaspoons Emeril's Original Essence or Creole Seasoning (page 9)
Four 6- to 7-ounce catfish fillets
1 teaspoon salt
½ cup vegetable oil
Andouille Potato Salad (recipe follows)
Grown-Up Tartar Sauce (page 165)

Andouille Potato Salad

1½ pounds new potatoes, scrubbed

1½ teaspoons salt

1 tablespoon vegetable oil

½ cup andouille or other spicy smoked sausage, removed from casings and chopped

2 cups thinly sliced yellow onions

2 tablespoons minced shallots

1 tablespoon minced garlic

1 cup heavy cream

2 tablespoons Creole or other spicy whole-grain mustard

¼ teaspoon freshly ground black pepper

1. CUT the potatoes into quarters and put into a medium saucepan. Add enough water to cover and 1 teaspoon of the salt. Bring to a boil over medium-high heat and cook, uncovered, until just fork-tender, about 15 minutes. Drain.

2. HEAT the oil in a large heavy skillet over medium-high heat. Add the andouille and cook, stirring often, until beginning to brown, about 2 minutes. Add the onions and cook, stirring often, until softened, about 3 minutes. Add the shallots and cook until beginning to soften, about 1 minute. Add the garlic and stir until fragrant, about 30 seconds. Add the cream and cook until reduced by half, 2 to 3 minutes. Stir in the mustard and mix well.

3. ADD the potatoes, the remaining ½ teaspoon salt, and the pepper and cook, stirring, for 2 minutes.

4. REMOVE from the heat and serve, or cover to keep warm until ready to serve.

Grown-Up Tartar Sauce

MAKES ABOUT 1 1/4 CUPS

1. **MELT** the butter in a small skillet over medium-high heat. Add the corn, salt, and cayenne and cook, stirring occasionally, until the corn is a deep golden brown, 5 minutes. (The corn will make popping sounds as it cooks.) Transfer to a large mixing bowl and let cool completely.

2. **ADD** the remaining ingredients to the corn and mix well. (The sauce can be covered and refrigerated for up to five days.)

1 1/2 teaspoons unsalted butter
1/2 cup fresh or thawed frozen corn kernels
Pinch of salt
Pinch of cayenne
1 cup Mayonnaise (page 12) or store-bought mayonnaise
1/4 cup seeded and chopped tomatoes
2 tablespoons chopped green onions (green parts)
1 tablespoon minced jalapeño
1 tablespoon chopped fresh flat-leaf parsley
1 teaspoon minced garlic
1/2 teaspoon Emeril's Original Essence or Creole Seasoning (page 9)

PROSCIUTTO-WRAPPED HALIBUT
WITH TOMATO-CAPER BUTTER SAUCE

MAKES 4 SERVINGS

Prosciutto is the Italian word for ham. When we did a "Hamming It Up" show, we wrapped halibut in prosciutto, sautéed it, and topped it with a rich tomato-caper butter sauce. You can substitute grouper, snapper, or cod in place of the halibut. Try wrapping fish, shrimp, or even steak with ham or bacon to give it a smoky flavor. Be creative—wrap scallops, pork chops, or veal! That's what it's all about, right?

Four 6-ounce halibut fillets (or other firm-fleshed white fish, such as snapper or grouper)
1½ teaspoons salt
½ teaspoon freshly ground white pepper
8 thin slices prosciutto
3 tablespoons olive oil
1 tablespoon minced shallots
1 teaspoon minced garlic
1 cup seeded and chopped tomatoes
¼ cup capers, drained
½ cup dry white wine
¼ cup heavy cream
8 tablespoons (1 stick) unsalted butter, cut into ¼-inch cubes and chilled
2 tablespoons chopped fresh flat-leaf parsley
¼ teaspoon freshly ground black pepper

1. **SEASON** both sides of the fillets with 1 teaspoon of the salt and the white pepper. Lay 2 slices of the prosciutto side by side on a piece of plastic wrap. Put 1 fillet skin side down on top of the prosciutto and wrap the fish in it, folding the prosciutto tightly around the sides to completely enclose the fish. Repeat the procedure with the remaining prosciutto and fish.

2. **HEAT** 2 tablespoons of the oil in a large heavy skillet over medium-high heat until it begins to smoke. Place the fillets skin side down in the pan and cook until the prosciutto is golden brown and the fillets are opaque throughout, about 3 minutes on each side. Transfer the fish to a platter and tent with aluminum foil to keep warm.

3. **ADD** the remaining 1 tablespoon oil to the skillet. Add the shallots and garlic and cook, stirring, until fragrant, about 30 seconds. Add the tomatoes and capers and cook, stirring often, until the tomatoes are heated through, about 3 minutes. Add the white wine and increase the heat to high. Boil until the liquid is reduced by two-thirds, about 2 minutes. Add the cream and reduce by half, about 2 minutes.

4. **REMOVE** the pan from the heat. One cube at a time, whisk in the butter until it makes a smooth sauce. Add the parsley, the ½ teaspoon remaining salt, and the black pepper. Transfer to a sauceboat or bowl.

5. **SERVE** the fish with the sauce passed on the side.

ROAST FLOUNDER STUFFED WITH EGGPLANT—CORN BREAD DRESSING

Talk about North meets South! When I was a young boy, I often went fishing with my father, Mr. John, near our hometown, Fall River, Massachusetts. When I moved to New Orleans to work at Commander's Palace, I tasted my first sensational eggplant and corn bread dressing! I only wish I'd known at an earlier age to stuff flounder with that dressing! This simple dressing also can be used as a topping or stuffing for other fish, such as red snapper and catfish, or try it with pork chops.

1. HEAT the oil in a large skillet over medium heat. Add the eggplant and season with ½ teaspoon of the salt and ¼ teaspoon of the cayenne. Cook, stirring often, until the eggplant softens, 3 to 4 minutes. Add the onions and celery and cook, stirring often, until they soften and the eggplant is just tender, about 5 minutes. Transfer to a large bowl and cool completely.

2. STIR the garlic, and then the corn bread, into the eggplant. Stir in 1 cup of the chicken stock and let stand for 20 minutes.

3. PREHEAT the oven to 400°F.

4. SEASON the fillets with the remaining 1 teaspoon salt and ¼ teaspoon cayenne. Place the fillets skinned side up (the skinned side will have a few shiny streaks) on a lightly oiled baking sheet lined with parchment paper.

5. IF the dressing seems too dry, moisten it with more stock. Put about 1 cup of the dressing on one half of each fillet, fold the fillet over to cover the dressing, pressing gently but firmly, and secure with a wooden toothpick. Bake until the fish is opaque when pierced with a knife and the dressing is warmed through, 10 to 15 minutes.

6. GARNISH each serving with a sprinkling of parsley and and serve.

¼ cup olive oil
1 large eggplant (about 1¼ pounds), peeled and cut into ½-inch dice
1½ teaspoons salt
½ teaspoon cayenne
1 cup chopped yellow onions
½ cup chopped celery
1 teaspoon minced garlic
4 cups crumbled Corn Bread (page 255)
1 to 1½ cups Chicken Stock (page 2) or canned low-sodium chicken broth
Four 6-ounce flounder fillets, skin removed
1 tablespoon chopped fresh flat-leaf parsley

PAN-SEARED SALMON WITH BLACK BEAN RELISH

MAKES 6 SERVINGS

You know, flavors like this say "food of love" to me. Food of love doesn't have to be fancy, just the very best flavors coming through, and when you have a quick, simple preparation like this, it's all the easier to share with others. If the weather's good, go ahead and fire up the grill for this one—otherwise, just a quick pan sear on both sides will do you right. Try the Drunken Hominy (page 240) alongside this for a total Southwestern meal, or the Smashed Potato Salad (page 239). Now you're talkin'!

4 cups Basic Beans (black),
    drained and rinsed
    (page 13)
2 cups cooked corn kernels
½ cup finely chopped red bell
    peppers
½ cup minced green onions
    (green and white parts)
1½ teaspoons minced garlic
4 teaspoons minced jalapeño
⅓ cup chopped cilantro
2 tablespoons fresh lime juice
½ cup extra-virgin olive oil
1¾ teaspoons salt
¼ teaspoon cayenne
Six 6-ounce salmon fillets
1 tablespoon Emeril's Original
    Essence or Creole Seasoning
    (page 9)
3 tablespoons canola oil

1. IN a large bowl combine the beans, corn, bell peppers, green onions, garlic, jalapeño, cilantro, lime juice, and olive oil. Stir well to combine, and season with ¾ teaspoon of the salt and the cayenne. Let the flavors blend for 30 minutes before serving.

2. SEASON the salmon fillets with the Essence and remaining teaspoon salt.

3. HEAT the canola oil in one large or two small skillets over high heat. Add the salmon and sear for 2 to 3 minutes on each side for medium-rare. Serve immediately with the black bean relish.

REDFISH BAKED IN FOIL WITH CASHEW-GARLIC BUTTER

MAKES 6 SERVINGS

The French term *en papillote* refers to baking in parchment paper, and New Orleanians love their pompano cooked in this manner. But, hey, you can cook chicken cutlets, shrimp, vegetables, and other things the same way. We did an entire *Essence* show on this cooking method; it's a simple way of intensifying flavors and drawing out natural juices. The packets also make a dramatic presentation for dinner parties. If you don't have parchment paper, use aluminum foil to enclose the ingredients. The secret is a tight seal to keep in all the juices and flavors.

CASHEW-GARLIC BUTTER
1 cup salted roasted cashews
½ pound (2 sticks) unsalted
    butter, at room temperature
1½ teaspoons fresh lemon juice
1 tablespoon minced garlic
1 teaspoon salt
1 teaspoon Emeril's Red Pepper
    Sauce or other hot pepper
    sauce

POTATO SALAD
6 medium Idaho potatoes,
    peeled and cut into 1-inch
    dice
2 tablespoons Dijon mustard
¼ cup red wine vinegar
¾ cup finely chopped yellow
    onions
⅓ cup finely chopped celery
4 Perfect Hard-Boiled Eggs
    (page 16), chopped

1. **TO** make the cashew butter, pulse the cashews in a food processor until coarsely chopped. Add the butter, lemon juice, garlic, salt, and hot pepper sauce, and pulse until the cashews are finely chopped and the other ingredients are well blended. Transfer the butter to a small bowl, cover, and set it aside.

2. **TO** make the potato salad, boil the potatoes in a large pot of lightly salted water until fork-tender, about 12 minutes. Drain.

3. **MEANWHILE,** in a large bowl, whisk together the mustard and red wine vinegar. Add the hot potatoes. Toss to mix. Add the onions, celery, eggs, heavy cream, and parsley. Season with the salt, white pepper, and black pepper. Cover to keep warm.

4. **PREHEAT** the oven to 350°F.

5. **PLACE** a collapsible steamer in a large pot. Add water to reach just below the bottom of the steamer and bring to a boil over high heat. Add the spinach and cover tightly. Cook until the spinach is tender and wilted, about 5 minutes. Transfer the spinach to a colander and let cool completely.

6. TRANSFER the spinach, a handful at a time, to a bowl, squeezing the liquid from the spinach. Season with ½ teaspoon of the salt and ¼ teaspoon of the pepper.

7. DIVIDE the spinach among six 15-inch squares of aluminum foil or parchment paper. Season the fillets with the remaining ½ teaspoon salt and ¼ teaspoon pepper. Using a flat metal spatula, smear both sides of each fillet liberally with the cashew butter. Lay a fillet on top of each portion of spinach, fold up to enclose the fillets, and tightly crimp the edges to seal the pouches.

8. BAKE for 20 minutes.

9. TO serve, transfer the papillotes to warmed dinner plates. Open at the table, using scissors. Serve the potato salad on the side.

1 cup heavy cream, boiled until reduced to ½ cup
¼ cup chopped fresh flat-leaf parsley
1 teaspoon salt
¼ teaspoon freshly ground white pepper
¼ teaspoon freshly ground black pepper
1½ pounds fresh spinach
1 teaspoon salt
½ teaspoon freshly ground black pepper
Six 8-ounce redfish fillets or other white-fleshed fish fillets, such as snapper

FROM THE BARNYARD

On the road, people always ask me, "Hey, Emeril, do you have any new chicken recipes?" ▪ Well, I do. But I also have recipes for quail, turkey, Cornish hens, and duck. Availability of guinea fowl or free-range chickens has increased dramatically; you can find them in many markets now. ▪ Try the Pecan-Crusted Chicken for something different. Chicken Clemenceau, an old New Orleans favorite, adds the right touch of elegance to a dinner party. ▪ If you want something a little more adventurous, try the Funky Bird, Pan-Seared Squab with Dried Cherry Reduction, or perhaps the Garlic-Schmeared Rosemary Roasted Chicken.

GARLIC-SCHMEARED ROSEMARY ROASTED CHICKEN

MAKES 4 SERVINGS

When we first opened the doors of Emeril's in New Orleans, this chicken dish was on the menu. We couldn't roast the chickens fast enough for our customers. You know how much I love garlic; well, this has plenty of it. Mashed Potatoes (page 14), and plenty of them, are perfect with this.

One 3½-pound chicken
2 tablespoons olive oil
1½ teaspoons salt
¼ teaspoon freshly ground black pepper
2 tablespoons finely chopped rosemary, stems reserved
⅓ cup Roasted Garlic Purée (page 11)

1. **PREHEAT** the oven to 425°F.

2. **RINSE** the chicken well under cool running water. Pat dry with paper towels. Rub the chicken all over with the olive oil. Season the cavity and the outside of the chicken with the salt and pepper. Sprinkle the rosemary all over the chicken, and place the reserved stems inside the cavity. Place in a small roasting pan.

3. **ROAST** until an instant-read thermometer inserted in the thickest part of the thigh reads 170°F, 1 to 1¼ hours.

4. **REMOVE** the chicken from the oven and "schmear" (that means rub and smear in my language) the garlic pureé all over the chicken. Return to the oven and roast until the thermometer reads 180°F when inserted in the thigh, about 15 minutes longer. Let stand for a few minutes before carving.

PECAN-CRUSTED CHICKEN

MAKES 4 SERVINGS

With its crunchy nut coating, this oven-baked chicken comes close to fried. Boy, the pecan flavor is delicious! This is a great dish to make when you have a hankering for fried chicken, but don't have the time to spend in front of the stove. Make it ahead and take it along with you on a picnic or to a tailgate party, like we did on a food-to-go show.

1. **COMBINE** the buttermilk, 1 tablespoon of the Essence, and 1 teaspoon of the salt in a large (1-gallon) plastic storage bag. Add the chicken pieces, seal, and gently squeeze to coat the chicken evenly. Refrigerate for at least 1 hour, or up to 4 hours.

2. **PREHEAT** the oven to 400°F. Grease a heavy baking sheet with the olive oil and set aside.

3. **PULSE** the pecans in a food processor or blender until finely chopped into a meal.

4. **COMBINE** the ground pecans, the flour, the remaining 2 tablespoons Essence and 1 teaspoon salt, and the pepper in another large plastic bag.

5. **REMOVE** the chicken from the buttermilk mixture. Add the chicken one piece at a time to the pecan-flour mixture, and shake to coat evenly. Put the chicken skin side down on the prepared baking sheet.

6. **BAKE** the chicken for 30 minutes, then turn it. Return to the oven and bake until the juices run clear when pierced with a fork, about 30 minutes. Serve hot, or let cool to room temperature.

1 cup buttermilk
3 tablespoons Emeril's Original Essence or Creole Seasoning (page 9)
2 teaspoons salt
One 3½-pound chicken, cut into 8 pieces (or 8 chicken parts of your choosing)
2 tablespoons olive oil
¾ cup pecan pieces
¾ cup bleached all-purpose flour
½ teaspoon freshly ground black pepper

CHICKEN CLEMENCEAU

When we reopened Delmonico Restaurant and Bar in New Orleans, we researched this old, classic New Orleans–Creole dish that has been a longtime favorite for generations at the city's older restaurants. Named for George Benjamin Eugene Clemenceau, a French statesman born in 1841 who became the premier of France in 1906, this dish was created in New Orleans to honor him. Chicken Clemenceau is an impressive collection of ingredients topped with béarnaise sauce. To simplify the preparation for the home cook, instead of using a whole chicken as we do in the restaurant, we've substituted four chicken breast halves, but by no means is the dish any less impressive or delicious.

2 tablespoons vegetable oil

4 boneless, skinless chicken breast halves, each 6 to 8 ounces

1 tablespoon unsalted butter

½ cup minced yellow onions

2 teaspoons chopped garlic

½ pound boiled ham, finely sliced

½ pound assorted wild mushrooms, such as shiitake, chanterelle, porcini, and oyster, wiped clean, stemmed, and thinly sliced

½ pound fresh small green peas (or frozen and defrosted)

½ pound Brabant Potatoes (recipe follows)

1 recipe Béarnaise Sauce (page 178)

1. **HEAT** the oil in a large, heavy skillet over high heat. Add the chicken breasts and cook for 3 to 3½ minutes on each side. Transfer to a platter and keep warm.

2. **WIPE** the skillet with paper towels and return to the stove. Heat the butter in the skillet over medium heat. Add the onions and cook, stirring, for 3 minutes. Add the garlic and cook, stirring, for 30 seconds. Add the ham and cook, stirring occasionally, for 3 minutes. Add the mushrooms and continue cooking for 5 minutes. Add the peas and cook for 2 minutes. Add the Brabant Potatoes and the chicken breasts, and cook for 1 minute.

3. **TO** serve, put about ¾ cup of the ham-vegetable mixture on each dinner plate, and top with a chicken breast. Spoon about ¼ cup of the Béarnaise Sauce over the chicken.

Brabant Potatoes

MAKES 2 SERVINGS

Brabant potatoes are fried potato cubes that have been quickly cooked in water before frying, which gives them a light, crunchy texture. They are a great accompaniment to roast meats and chicken, and are an important component of Chicken Clemenceau (page 176), but you can also serve them for brunch with scrambled eggs and sausage.

2 pounds Idaho potatoes, peeled
4 cups vegetable oil, for frying
½ teaspoon salt

1. **CUT** each potato into an even rectangular shape: cut off the bottom, top, and sides, then cut into ½-inch cubes. Put the potatoes in a medium, heavy saucepan and add enough water to cover. Bring to a boil and cook until the potatoes are slightly tender, about 10 minutes.

2. **REMOVE** from the heat and drain. Pat dry with paper towels.

3. **HEAT** the oil in a large, deep, heavy pot or an electric deep fryer to 360°F. Add the potatoes and fry, turning to brown evenly, for 3 to 4 minutes.

4. **REMOVE** and drain on paper towels. Season with salt, and serve hot.

Béarnaise Sauce

MAKES 1 CUP

This classic French butter sauce, with its rich tarragon flavor, is extremely versatile. Try it on a simple grilled steak or roasted beef tenderloin, poached salmon, or poached eggs.

2 tablespoons dried tarragon
1 tablespoon minced shallots
½ teaspoon salt
Pinch of freshly ground black pepper
½ cup white vinegar
2 egg yolks
⅛ teaspoon cayenne
1 stick (¼ pound) unsalted butter, melted
1 teaspoon fresh lemon juice
1 tablespoon minced fresh tarragon
1 tablespoon minced fresh chervil

1. **COMBINE** the tarragon, shallots, ¼ teaspoon of the salt, pepper, and vinegar in a small saucepan. Simmer the ingredients over medium-high heat until almost all the vinegar evaporates and 1 tablespoon is left, about 15 minutes. Remove the pan from the heat and allow the syrup to cool slightly.

2. **IN** the top of double boiler, or in a stainless steel bowl set over a pot of simmering water, whisk the egg yolks and cayenne into the syrup over a very low heat. As soon as the egg yolks have thickened, slowly add the melted butter a bit at a time, whisking continuously. Add the lemon juice and adjust the seasoning to taste, then whisk in the fresh herbs. Serve immediately over the Chicken Clemenceau, or keep warm, covered, over a pot of simmering water, for a short time.

TANGERINE-GLAZED ROASTED CHICKEN

MAKES 4 SERVINGS

I have great childhood memories of cooking with tangerines during the holiday season. Fresh tangerines are available throughout the winter months and this bright, sweet flavor adds a wonderful note to many dishes. By not peeling the fruit, you give this chicken intense tangerine flavor while roasting.

1. PREHEAT the oven to 400°F.

2. RUB the outside of the chicken with the butter. Season the outside and the cavity with the salt, pepper, and Essence. Stuff the cavity with the onion, tangerines, and rosemary. Place on a rack in a roasting pan.

3. ROAST for 15 minutes. Reduce the oven temperature to 350°F. Continue roasting until the chicken is golden brown and a meat thermometer inserted in the thickest part of the thigh reads 180°F, 1 hour to 1 hour and 15 minutes.

4. TRANSFER the chicken to a platter and let stand for 10 minutes.

5. MEANWHILE place the roasting pan on top of two burners over medium-high heat. Add the wine and stir for 1 minute to deglaze the pan and dislodge any browned bits from the bottom. Stir in the tangerine juice and bring to a boil. Cook, stirring often, until the liquid is reduced by half, about 3 minutes. Add the honey and any juices accumulated around the chicken and bring to a boil. Pour into a bowl or sauceboat.

6. TO serve, carve the chicken (discard the onions and tangerines) and serve with the sauce.

One 3- to 3½-pound chicken
2 tablespoons unsalted butter, at room temperature
¾ teaspoon salt
½ teaspoon freshly ground black pepper
1 teaspoon Emeril's Original Essence or Creole Seasoning (page 9)
1 large yellow onion, peeled and quartered
3 tangerines, quartered
4 sprigs fresh rosemary
½ cup dry white wine or dry vermouth
1 cup fresh tangerine juice
1 tablespoon honey

EMERIL'S CHICKEN POTPIES

As far as I'm concerned, potpies are just as American as apple pie. Growing up in Fall River, we had them often. Loaded with chicken and vegetables, these individual pies are satisfying and make a great presentation.

3 large carrots
3 celery ribs
2 medium yellow onions
One 3½-pound chicken
2 bay leaves
½ teaspoon whole black
   peppercorns

PIECRUST
2¼ cups bleached all-purpose
   flour
1 teaspoon salt
10 tablespoons (1¼ sticks) cold
   unsalted butter, cut into thin
   slices
4 to 6 tablespoons ice water

1 cup fresh or thawed frozen peas
4 tablespoons (½ stick) unsalted
   butter
½ pound shiitake mushrooms,
   stemmed, wiped clean, and
   finely sliced
2 teaspoons chopped garlic
2 teaspoons Emeril's Original
   Essence or Creole Seasoning
   (page 9)
¼ cup bleached all-purpose flour

1. COARSELY chop 1 carrot and 1 celery rib. Peel and quarter 1 onion. Put them in a large stockpot and add the chicken, 1 bay leaf, the peppercorns, and enough water to cover by 1 inch. Bring to a boil over high heat. Reduce the heat to medium-low. Simmer until the chicken is tender, about 45 minutes, skimming off any foam that forms on the surface.

2. REMOVE the chicken from the pot and transfer to a platter. Strain the stock into a large saucepan and bring to a boil over high heat. Boil until the stock is reduced to 3 cups. Let cool.

3. WHEN the chicken is cool enough to handle, remove the skin, cut the meat from the bones, and cut it into 1-inch pieces. Set the meat aside and discard the skin and bones.

4. TO make the piecrust, combine the flour and salt in a mixing bowl. Add the butter and cut it in with a pastry blender (or rub the mixture between your fingers) until the mixture resembles coarse crumbs. Using a fork, stir in the water, 1 tablespoon at a time, just until the mixture is moist enough to hold together when gathered up. Shape into a smooth ball, being careful not to overwork the dough, then press into a disk. Wrap in plastic wrap and refrigerate for 30 minutes.

5. MEANWHILE, chop the remaining carrots, celery, and onion. Bring a medium saucepan of water to a boil. Blanch the carrots and the peas in the boiling water until just tender, 2 to 3 minutes. Drain and set aside.

6. PREHEAT the oven to 400°F.

7. MELT the butter in a large heavy pot over medium-high heat. Add the onions and celery, and cook, stirring often, until softened, about 3 minutes. Add the mushrooms, garlic, and Essence. Cook until the mushrooms are soft and give off their liquid, about 5 minutes. Sprinkle the flour over the vegetables and stir. Cook until the mixture thickens, about 2 minutes. Stir in the wine, cream, and the reserved stock. Add the chicken, carrots, peas, and parsley. Season with the salt and pepper, and stir well.

8. TRANSFER the chicken mixture to a casserole dish or a large ovenproof skillet, or divide it among eight individual 2-cup baking dishes.

9. ROLL out the dough on a floured surface until 1/8 inch thick. Cut it into a round or other appropriate shape a little larger than the dish or dishes. Cover the chicken mixture with the dough, and press the dough against the sides of the dish(es) to seal. Brush the top of the pastry with the egg glaze and cut several slits in it.

10. BAKE until the crust is golden brown and the filling is hot and bubbly, about 15 minutes. Serve hot.

1/2 cup dry white wine
1/3 cup heavy cream
2 tablespoons chopped fresh
 flat-leaf parsley
1 teaspoon salt
1/4 teaspoon freshly ground black
 pepper
1 large egg beaten with
 1 tablespoon water, for glaze

APRICOT-GLAZED CORNISH GAME HENS WITH SAUSAGE—RICE PILAF STUFFING

MAKES 4 SERVINGS

Cornish hens (also known as Rock Cornish hens) are ideal for dinner parties, since the smaller ones, weighing 1 to 1½ pounds, can be served one to a person. The sausage-rice stuffing is Moroccan-inspired with orange zest, raisins, almonds, and cinnamon.

1 tablespoon olive oil
¼ pound sweet Italian sausage, removed from casings
½ cup finely chopped onions
¼ cup finely chopped carrots
¼ cup finely chopped celery
2 teaspoons chopped garlic
½ teaspoon minced orange zest
1 cup long-grain white rice
⅓ cup golden raisins
2 tablespoons toasted almond slivers
1 tablespoon chopped fresh flat-leaf parsley
1½ teaspoon chopped fresh thyme
½ teaspoon ground cinnamon
2 cups Chicken Stock (page 2) or canned low-sodium chicken broth
2 cups apricot jam
½ teaspoon minced orange zest
1 tablespoon sugar
1 cup fresh orange juice
4 Cornish game hens (1¼ to 1½ pounds each)
1½ teaspoons salt
½ teaspoon freshly ground black pepper

1. **PREHEAT** the oven to 375°F.

2. **HEAT** the oil in an ovenproof saucepan over medium-high heat. Add the sausage and cook, breaking it up with a spoon, until browned, about 5 minutes. Add the onions, carrots, and celery and cook, stirring, until softened, about 3 minutes. Add the garlic and orange zest and stir until fragrant, about 30 seconds. Add the rice and stir until it turns opaque, about 3 minutes. Stir in the raisins, almonds, parsley, thyme, and cinnamon.

3. **ADD** the chicken stock and bring to a boil. Stir, cover the saucepan and transfer to the oven. Bake until the rice is tender and the liquid is absorbed, about 30 minutes. Remove the rice from the oven and spread it evenly on a large plate or baking pan to cool. Increase the oven temperature to 400°F.

4. **WHISK** the apricot jam, orange zest, sugar, and orange juice in a small saucepan over high heat. Cook until reduced by half, 8 to 10 minutes. Set aside to cool slightly.

5. **SEASON** the hens, inside and out, with the salt and pepper. Loosely stuff each hen with the cooled rice pilaf. Place the remaining pilaf in a small baking dish and cover with aluminum foil. Set aside.

6. **PLACE** the hens breast side up in a roasting pan. Brush some of the glaze on the hens. Roast, brushing every 15 minutes with more of the glaze, until the juices run clear and an instant-read thermometer inserted into the thickest part of the thigh registers 180°F, about 1 hour. Place the dish of rice pilaf in the oven to reheat during the last 10 minutes.

7. **SERVE** the hens with the extra rice pilaf on the side.

FUNKY BIRD (A.K.A. SOUTHWESTERN TURKEY BREAST)

MAKES 4 TO 6 SERVINGS

This year for my Thanksgiving *Good Morning America* segment, I presented a taste test of sorts—deep-fried turkey versus this brine-soaked bird. I referred to it as Funky Bird because it was so different from other turkey preparations. I gotta tell you this, all of us at the studio—Charlie Gibson, Diane Sawyer, and the crew—were truly amazed by the flavors of this dish. The turkey absorbs moisture and seasoning during the overnight brining process, which ensures a moist, flavorful bird that doesn't require basting. You're not going to believe how tender and juicy this turkey is! Serve this with the Poblano-Chocolate Mole for a really amazing flavor combination.

1. **TO** make the brining liquid, combine all the ingredients with 1 gallon water in a large nonreactive container and stir to dissolve the sugar and salt.

2. **PUT** the turkey in a large colander and rinse under cold running water. Add the turkey breast to the brine, cover, and refrigerate, turning the breast occasionally, for at least 12 hours, and up to 24 hours. (If you don't have a large nonreactive container, put the turkey breast in a large heavy-duty plastic garbage bag. Make the marinade in a large bowl and pour the marinade into the bag. Put the bag inside a large container or roasting pan in case it should leak or drip.)

3. **PREHEAT** the oven to 375°F.

4. **REMOVE** the turkey from the brine (discard the brine) and put it breast side up in a large heavy roasting pan. Pat dry with paper towels. Rub the turkey with the vegetable oil, and sprinkle on both sides with the Essence.

5. **ROAST** until deep golden brown and an instant-read thermometer inserted in the thickest part of the breast reads 180°F, about 1 hour and 45 minutes. Transfer to a platter and let stand for 15 minutes before carving.

6. **CARVE** the turkey and serve with the mole if desired.

BRINE
1 cup fresh lemon juice
3/4 cup fresh orange juice
1 cup kosher salt
1 cup packed light brown sugar
1 cup chopped yellow onions
2 oranges, cut in half
2 jalapeños, minced (with their seeds)
1/4 cup chopped fresh cilantro
2 tablespoons chopped garlic
1 tablespoon chili powder
1 tablespoon ground cumin
1 teaspoon dried oregano, preferably Mexican

One 6- 6½-pound whole turkey breast
1 tablespoon vegetable oil
1 tablespoon Emeril's Original Essence or Creole Seasoning (page 9)
Poblano-Chocolate Mole (recipe follows), optional

Poblano-Chocolate Mole

MAKES 1½ QUARTS; 8 TO 10 SERVINGS

Mole is a thick Mexican sauce made with a variety of ingredients, from nuts and seeds to onions and chile peppers, and always a small amount of chocolate that adds a richness to the sauce. ■ The rich, smoky, and nutty flavors in this mole make it absolutely killer with the Funky Bird or the Aw Nuts Pork Chops (page 211). This makes a lot of sauce, and you won't finish the mole in one sitting with either of these dishes. It can be refrigerated for up to one week in an airtight container. It's also great served with roasted pork loin or grilled chicken. Or, to tell the truth, I like to just dip bread or chips in it and slurp it up!

1 pound poblano chiles (available at Latin grocers and specialty produce markets)
1 large yellow onion, peeled and halved (root ends left on)
1 tablespoon vegetable oil
½ cup shelled pistachio nuts
½ cup pumpkin seeds
½ cup pine nuts
2 teaspoons chili powder
1 teaspoon minced garlic
1 teaspoon ground cumin
1 teaspoon ground coriander
1 teaspoon salt
½ teaspoon freshly ground black pepper
4 cups Chicken Stock (page 2) or canned low-sodium chicken broth
½ cup coarsely chopped fresh cilantro
2 ounces semisweet chocolate, finely chopped
½ cup heavy cream

1. TO roast the peppers, place them directly on the burners of a gas stove over medium heat and turn them frequently with tongs until all sides are charred black, 7 to 10 minutes. (Alternatively, the peppers can be roasted under a broiler, or over a hot gas or charcoal grill.) Transfer the peppers to a plastic or paper bag, seal the bag, and let cool for about 15 minutes.

2. ROAST the two onion halves over medium heat, using the same procedure, until the cut surfaces are lightly charred and the onion is slightly softened, about 10 minutes. Remove from the heat and let cool.

3. PEEL the peppers, remove the seeds and stems, and coarsely chop the flesh. Remove the root ends from the onions and coarsely chop them. (The chopped peppers and onions will yield about 2 cups.)

4. HEAT the vegetable oil in a medium saucepan over medium-high heat. Add the pistachio nuts, pumpkin seeds, and pine nuts and cook, stirring occasionally, until the nuts are browned, about 5 minutes. (The nuts will make popping sounds as they cook.) Cover the skillet if the nuts start to jump out of the skillet.

5. ADD the chopped peppers and onions, the chili powder, garlic, cumin, coriander, salt, and pepper and stir for 1 minute. Add the chicken stock and cilantro and bring to a boil over high heat. Reduce the heat to medium-low and simmer for 45 minutes.

6. ADD the chocolate and stir until melted. Add the cream, stir well, and simmer for an additional 15 minutes.

7. PURÉE the mole with an immersion blender, or in batches in a blender. Serve warm.

OYSTER-AND-SPINACH-STUFFED TURKEY BREAST WITH GARLIC-WINE SAUCE

A lot of people turn their noses up at turkey, probably because the turkeys to which they are accustomed are easily overcooked. Well, here's a recipe that uses just the breast, boned, stuffed, and rolled up, and I promise you, it will be moist. To simplify preparation, ask your butcher to bone and butterfly the turkey breast for you.

One 2½- to 3-pound half turkey breast, boned and skinned
1 tablespoon plus 1 teaspoon Emeril's Original Essence or Creole Seasoning (page 9)
8 large spinach leaves, stemmed and washed
¼ cup olive oil
¼ pound andouille or other spicy sausage, removed from casings and chopped
½ cup chopped yellow onions
¼ cup chopped celery
¼ cup chopped green bell peppers
1 teaspoon salt
½ teaspoon freshly ground black pepper
¼ cup chopped fresh flat-leaf parsley
2 tablespoons minced garlic
1 teaspoon Worcestershire sauce
1 pint shucked oysters, with their liquor
3 cups crumbled Corn Bread (page 255)
½ cup Chicken Stock (page 2) or canned low-sodium chicken broth
¼ cup chopped green onions (green parts only)
Garlic-Wine Sauce (recipe follows)

1. **PUT** the turkey smooth side down on a work surface lined with plastic wrap. With a thin sharp knife, cut a slit lengthwise through the center of the meat, being careful not to cut all the way through. Gently open the two flaps of meat as though opening a book, and lay another piece of plastic wrap on top. With a flat meat mallet, pound the meat to an even ½-inch thickness to form a rough rectangle. Remove the plastic wrap and season the turkey on both sides with 1 tablespoon of the Essence.

2. **BLANCH** the spinach leaves in a saucepan of boiling water just until wilted, about 15 seconds. Drain and rinse under cold running water. Drain well on paper towels and pat dry. Turn the breast so that a long side faces you. Lay the spinach leaves in a line across the upper third of the turkey, leaving a 1-inch border.

3. **PREHEAT** the oven to 400°F.

4. **HEAT** 2 tablespoons of the oil in a large heavy skillet over high heat. Add the andouille, onions, celery, and bell peppers, the remaining 1 teaspoon Essence, ½ teaspoon of the salt, and ¼ teaspoon of the pepper and cook, stirring often, until the vegetables soften, about 4 minutes. Add the parsley, garlic, and Worcestershire and stir until fragrant, about 30 seconds. Add the oysters and their liquor and cook just until the oysters' edges curl, about 1 minute. Add the corn bread, stock, and green onions and stir to combine. Remove from the heat and let cool for about 5 minutes.

5. SPREAD the stuffing on top of the spinach leaves, leaving a 1-inch border on all three sides. Fold the breast lengthwise over the stuffing, tucking in the edges. Then roll up the breast jelly-roll fashion to completely enclose the stuffing. Tie every 2 inches with kitchen twine. Rub the remaining 2 tablespoons oil over the turkey and season with the remaining ½ teaspoon salt and ¼ teaspoon pepper. Place on a baking sheet.

6. ROAST until an instant-read thermometer inserted in the thickest part of the breast reads 180°F, about 1 hour.

7. TRANSFER to a cutting board and let rest for 10 minutes. Remove and discard the string. Carve into ½-inch-thick slices and serve immediately with the sauce.

Garlic-Wine Sauce

MAKES 2 CUPS

Now this sauce is deceptively simple to make, but, man, is it delicious. This is also a great match for roasted chicken.

BRING the stock, wine, shallots, garlic, salt, and pepper to a boil in a medium heavy nonreactive saucepan, over medium-high heat. Boil until the liquid is reduced by half, about 15 minutes. Remove from the heat. Whisk in the butter, one piece at a time, until the sauce is smooth. Serve immediately.

3 cups Veal Stock (page 4), Brown Chicken Stock (page 2), or canned low-sodium beef broth
1 cup dry red wine
¼ cup plus 2 tablespoons minced shallots
¼ cup plus 2 tablespoons minced garlic
½ teaspoon salt
⅛ teaspoon freshly ground black pepper
4 tablespoons (½ stick) unsalted butter, cut into 4 pieces

TURKEY CHILI

This dish is best if made a day ahead, and refrigerated overnight to let the flavors marry, then slowly reheated before serving. Put out some bowls of grated Cheddar cheese and minced green onions or chopped yellow onions, so everyone can have it their way. I'd definitely make some Corn Bread (page 255) that's been kicked up with a tablespoon or two of minced jalapeños and a little Cheddar cheese melted on top. If you prefer only white or only black beans, be my guest.

1. **HEAT** the oil in a large heavy stockpot over medium-high heat. Add the turkey, chili powder, cumin, salt, and cayenne and cook, stirring to break up the meat, until the turkey loses its pink color, about 5 minutes. Add the onions, bell peppers, and celery and cook until they soften, about 4 minutes. Add the tomatoes, cilantro, jalapeños, and garlic and cook to blend the flavors, about 3 minutes.

2. **STIR** in the white beans, black beans, and chicken stock. Bring to a boil over high heat. Reduce the heat to medium-low. Simmer, uncovered, stirring occasionally, until the mixture has thickened, about 45 minutes. Serve immediately.

2 tablespoons olive oil
1 to 1¼ pounds lean ground turkey
2 tablespoons chili powder
½ teaspoon ground cumin
2 teaspoons salt
¼ teaspoon cayenne
1 cup chopped yellow onions
½ cup chopped green bell peppers
½ cup chopped celery
½ cup seeded and chopped tomatoes
2 tablespoons minced fresh cilantro
2 teaspoons seeded and minced jalapeños
2 teaspoons chopped garlic
2 cups each black and white Basic Beans (page 13)
4 cups Chicken Stock (page 2) or canned low-sodium chicken broth

DUCK AND SAUSAGE ÉTOUFFÉE

In southern Louisiana, *étouffée* is a cooking method that means "to smother," or to cook something in its own juices. It's frequently made with seafood, such as crawfish or shrimp, but we've kicked ours up a notch with duck and sausage, perfect for a winter supper. I start my étouffée with a roux, which won't sit well with many Louisianans. They'll say once you add a roux, you have a stew, not an étouffée. Hey, this is how I like it. We've put a pastry dome on top for an elegant presentation, but you can serve this with scoops of steamed rice.

One 4- to 5-pound duck, skinned and cut into quarters (reserve the skin)
½ teaspoon salt
⅛ teaspoon cayenne
¼ teaspoon freshly ground white pepper
¾ cup bleached all-purpose flour
1 cup finely chopped yellow onions
½ cup finely chopped celery
½ cup finely chopped bell peppers
2 teaspoons chopped garlic
One 12-ounce bottle amber or dark lager beer
4 cups Chicken Stock (page 2) or canned low-sodium chicken broth
¼ cup minced fresh flat-leaf parsley
2 bay leaves
¾ pound andouille or other spicy smoked sausage, cut crosswise into ¾-inch rounds
1 sheet puff pastry (half of a 17.3-ounce box), thawed
1 large egg beaten with 1 tablespoon water, for glaze

1. **CUT** the duck skin into strips. Season the duck quarters lightly with salt, cayenne, and white pepper.

2. **HEAT** a large heavy pot or Dutch oven over medium-high heat. Add the strips of duck skin and the duck quarters and cook, turning the duck once, until the fat is rendered and the duck is brown on both sides, 5 to 7 minutes for each side. Remove the skin with a slotted spoon and discard. Transfer the duck pieces to paper towels to drain.

3. **WHISK** the flour into the fat in the pot. Reduce the heat to medium and cook, stirring with a wooden spoon, to make a brown roux, for about 15 minutes. Add the onions, celery, and bell peppers and cook stirring often, until softened, about 4 minutes. Add the garlic and cook until fragrant, about 1 minute. Stir in the beer, scraping the pot to remove any browned bits from the bottom.

4. **ADD** the stock, parsley, bay leaves, and duck quarters and bring to a boil. Reduce the heat to medium-low and simmer until the duck is tender, about 1½ hours, skimming off any foam that forms on the surface.

5. **MEANWHILE,** cook the andouille, stirring occasionally, in a skillet over medium-high heat until browned, about 10 minutes. Set aside.

6. PREHEAT the oven to 400°F.

7. USING tongs or a slotted spoon, carefully remove the duck pieces from the pot and let cool, then remove the meat from the bones, discarding the bones.

8. RETURN the meat to the pot, along with the andouille. Continue cooking until the étouffée is slightly reduced and thickened. Transfer the étouffée to a large casserole or ovenproof skillet. Cool for 10 minutes.

9. ROLL out the puff pastry on a lightly floured work surface to a round ⅛-inch thickness, slightly larger than the casserole dish. Carefully lay the puff pastry sheet on top of the dish, turning the edges under and crimping them. Brush the top with the egg glaze.

10. BAKE until the pastry is puffed and golden brown, about 15 minutes. Serve hot.

PAN-SEARED SQUAB WITH DRIED CHERRY REDUCTION

MAKES 2 SERVINGS

Looking for a recipe for two for a romantic dinner at home? Here you go. And talk about easy, as well as appealing! Squabs, if not fresh, are usually available in the frozen poultry section. Serve this on a bed of creamy grits, polenta, or Perfect Rice (page 16), and pair with a nice bottle of Pinot Noir.

1½ cups Brown Chicken Stock (page 3) or store-bought demi-glace
⅔ cup dried cherries
2 squabs (1 pound each)
2 teaspoons Emeril's Original Essence or Creole Seasoning (page 9)
3 tablespoons olive oil
¼ cup thinly sliced shallots
1 teaspoon minced garlic
½ teaspoon salt
¼ teaspoon freshly ground black pepper
2 tablespoons unsalted butter
2 tablespoons finely chopped fresh flat-leaf parsley, for garnish

1. **BRING** the stock to a gentle boil in a small saucepan over medium-high heat. Remove from the heat, add the cherries, and allow to soften for at least 5 minutes.

2. **SEASON** the outside and cavity of each squab with 1 teaspoon Essence.

3. **HEAT** the oil in a medium heavy skillet over medium-high heat. Add the squab and cook, turning to brown evenly on all sides, about 20 minutes total for medium-rare squab. Transfer the squab to a platter and cover with aluminum foil to keep warm.

4. **ADD** the shallots to the skillet and cook, stirring often, until softened, about 1 minute. Add the garlic and stir until fragrant, about 30 seconds. Add the chicken stock, cherries, salt, and pepper and bring to a boil. Reduce the heat to medium-low and simmer for 2 minutes. Whisk in the butter until melted. Return the squab and any accumulated juices to the pan and cook over medium-low heat to warm through, about 1 minute.

5. **GARNISH** the squab with the chopped parsley and serve immediately with the sauce.

FRIED QUAIL WITH CREAMY HAM GRAVY

MAKES 6 SERVINGS

In the South, quail are often served for brunch, but they're good for dinner, too. We prepared this for an *Emeril Live* brunch show. And, remember, be sure to serve the quail with mashed potatoes.

1. SEASON the quail with 1 tablespoon of the Essence. Combine the eggs and 1/4 cup of the milk in a shallow bowl and whisk to blend. Combine 2 cups of the flour with the remaining 2 tablespoons Essence in another shallow bowl.

2. POUR enough oil to come halfway up the sides of a large deep heavy skillet, and heat over high heat to 360°F.

3. DREDGE the quail in the seasoned flour, then dip in the egg wash. Dredge the quail again in the flour, coating completely, and shake off any excess. In batches, without crowding, fry the quail until golden brown, turning once, 3 to 4 minutes. Using a slotted spoon, transfer the quail to paper towels to drain.

4. DISCARD all except about 2 tablespoons of the oil in the skillet. Add the ham and cook over medium heat for about 1 minute. Add the remaining 2 tablespoons flour and whisk until the mixture thickens, about 2 minutes. Whisk in the remaining 1 cup milk and bring to a boil. Reduce the heat to medium and simmer until the gravy is thick, about 3 minutes. Season with the salt and pepper.

5. MOUND equal portions of the hot mashed potatoes in the centers of six serving plates. Put two quail each on the potatoes, and top with the gravy.

Twelve 4-ounce quail
3 tablespoons Emeril's Original Essence or Creole Seasoning (page 9)
2 large eggs
1 1/4 cups milk
2 cups plus 2 tablespoons bleached all-purpose flour
Vegetable oil for deep-frying
1/4 cup finely chopped ham or Homemade Tasso (page 17)
1 teaspoon salt
1/2 teaspoon freshly ground black pepper
Mashed Potatoes (page 14)

PORK

FAT

the recipes

You know how much I love pork. And I know I've joked with y'all about how pork fat makes your skin moist and smooth, but you don't have to eat it at every meal. For years now, Dan Crutchfield has been raising pigs for me, and every Wednesday, the day he delivers them to Emeril's in New Orleans, the entire staff can't wait for his arrival. Wednesdays are now called pig day. ■ Chef Neal's Baby Back Ribs will satisfy any pork-loving crowd (double or triple the recipe). The Spiced Baked Ham with Sweet Potatoes could become your traditional Christmas family meal. The Roasted Pork Loin is simple enough for Sunday supper, and The King's Creole Fried Pork Chops are, well, fit for a king!

HAM CROQUETTES

MAKES 48 CROQUETTES

When we did an *Emeril Live* show on Cuban food, these little croquettes were a hit. They make a good starter. Seasoning ham is great stuff. It's available in supermarkets in the meat section, and comes in sealed packets of about 1 pound. Basically it's cooked ham that's cut into chunks, making it perfect for adding to red beans, jambalaya, and other slow-cooked dishes that need some kicking up. I've used it here because I really like the texture of the meat. If you can't find seasoning ham, substitute chopped ham. Make the croquettes ahead and reheat them in the oven.

1 pound Idaho potatoes, peeled
1¾ teaspoons salt
1 tablespoon vegetable oil, plus
    more for deep-frying
1 cup chopped yellow onions
1 tablespoon chopped fresh
    flat-leaf parsley
1 teaspoon minced garlic
1 teaspoon minced jalapeño
¾ teaspoon freshly ground black
    pepper
1 pound seasoning ham, cut into
    ¼-inch dice
1½ cups bleached all-purpose
    flour
4 large eggs
2 tablespoons plus ½ teaspoon
    Emeril's Original Essence or
    Creole Seasoning (page 9),
    plus extra for sprinkling if
    desired
1 cup fine dried bread crumbs
Vegetable oil for deep-frying

1. COMBINE the potatoes, enough cold water to cover by 1 inch, and 1 teaspoon of the salt in a medium saucepan, and bring to a boil over high heat. Reduce the heat to medium-low. Cook, uncovered, until the potatoes are fork-tender, about 15 minutes. Drain and transfer to a large bowl.

2. HEAT 1 tablespoon oil in a large heavy skillet over medium heat. Add the onions, parsley, garlic, jalapeño, the remaining ¾ teaspoon salt, and the pepper. Cook, stirring often, until the onions soften, about 2 minutes. Add the ham and cook until heated through, about 2 minutes.

3. ADD the ham mixture to the potatoes. Mash until blended but slightly lumpy. Set aside to cool for 15 minutes.

4. ADD ½ cup of the flour and 1 egg to the potatoes and stir well with a wooden spoon to blend. Divide the mixture into 3 equal portions. Lightly dust a work surface with flour. Shape each portion into a 14-inch-long cylinder, about 1½ inches in diameter, by rolling under your palms, coating it with flour to prevent sticking as you shape it. Cut each cylinder into 16 equal pieces. Place ½ cup of the flour in a small dish. Roll each piece in the flour into a ball about 1½ inches in diameter. Put the balls on a baking sheet.

5. PUT the remaining ½ cup flour in a shallow dish and season with 1½ teaspoons of the Essence. Beat the remaining 3 eggs with 2 teaspoons of the Essence and 3 tablespoons water in a shallow bowl. Toss the bread crumbs with the remaining 1 tablespoon Essence in a shallow dish. Dredge each croquette in the seasoned flour, then in the egg wash, then in the seasoned bread crumbs, and return to the baking sheet.

6. POUR enough oil to come halfway up the sides of a large heavy pot or electric deep fryer and heat to 360°F. In batches, without crowding, fry the croquettes, turning to cook evenly, until golden brown, 3 to 4 minutes.

7. SPRINKLE with some Essence, if desired, and serve hot.

HOT CHORIZO TAMALES WITH BLACK BEAN AND ROASTED PEPPER SALSA

MAKES 32 TO 36 TAMALES

Traditionally tamales are made with masa harina (coarse corn flour) forming a crust around a meat, or meat and vegetable filling, so that when you bite into them, there's a layer of dough, then a filling inside. What I did here was mix together the masa harina and the filling to simplify things, and also to get a unique flavor and texture. It'll also save you a bunch of time. You're not going to need the entire 8-ounce package of corn husks, but you will need to soak them all in order to find the best ones. When you're making these tamales, use only the large husks, so that the filling will be completely enclosed; set the smaller or torn ones aside to line the steamer.

One 8-ounce package corn husks (about 40 husks)

FILLING

2 tablespoons vegetable shortening
1 pound smoked chorizo sausage, finely chopped
1 cup chopped yellow onions
1 cup fresh or thawed frozen corn kernels
½ cup chopped green bell peppers
¼ cup chopped green onions (green and white parts)
2 tablespoons chopped fresh flat-leaf parsley
1 tablespoon chopped garlic
1 tablespoon minced jalapeños
2 teaspoons chili powder
1 teaspoon ground cumin
1 teaspoon salt
½ teaspoon cayenne

1. **SEPARATE** the corn husks and remove any corn silks. Bring a large pot of water to a boil, then remove from the heat. Place the husks in the water, and weight them down with a large heavy baking dish to submerge them. Soak until the husks are pliable, 30 minutes to 1 hour.

2. **MEANWHILE,** to make the filling, melt the shortening in a large heavy skillet over medium heat. Add the chorizo and cook, stirring often, until browned, about 4 minutes. Add the onions, corn, bell peppers, green onions, parsley, garlic, jalapeños, chili powder, cumin, salt, and cayenne. Cook, stirring, for 4 minutes longer. Remove from the heat and let cool for 20 to 30 minutes.

3. **TO** make the dough, put the ⅔ cup shortening in the bowl of a heavy-duty electric mixer fitted with the whisk attachment and cream on high speed until light and fluffy, about 3 minutes. Mix the masa harina and salt in a bowl. With the mixer on medium speed, alternately add the masa harina mixture and the chicken stock to the whipped shortening, mixing thoroughly after each addition. Gradually add the ⅓ cup melted shortening and whip until light.

4. PLACE 1 large soaked corn husk on a work surface. Spoon about ¼ cup of the filling into the middle of the husk. Fold the sides of the husk over the filling, then bring the bottom and the top over, overlapping them as much as possible to tightly enclose the filling. (You should now have a small package measuring about 3 × 2 inches.) Wrap a piece of kitchen twine horizontally, and then vertically, around the tamale, like wrapping a gift box, and knot the twine at the top. Put the tamale on a large platter. Repeat with the remaining husks and filling, stacking the tamales as you go.

5. PLACE a steamer rack in a large pot about 2 inches above gently boiling water. Lay the tamales on the rack, being careful not to pack them too tightly. Cover the tamales with a layer of the torn and smaller corn husks, and cover tightly with a lid. Steam the tamales for 2 hours, replenishing the boiling water as needed so the pot does not go dry.

6. WITH tongs, remove the tamales from the steamer and let cool for 10 minutes before serving.

7. SERVE hot with the salsa.

DOUGH

⅔ cup vegetable shortening, plus ⅓ cup melted shortening

4 cups masa harina (available at Latino markets and many supermarkets)

1 teaspoon salt

3 cups Chicken Stock (page 2) or canned low-sodium chicken broth

Black Bean and Roasted Pepper Salsa (recipe follows)

Black Bean and Roasted Pepper Salsa

4 large red bell peppers
1 cup Basic Beans (black)
   (page 13)
½ cup minced red onions
7 tablespoons fresh lime juice
¼ cup extra-virgin olive oil
2 tablespoons chopped fresh
   cilantro
2 tablespoons minced green
   onions (green and white
   parts)
1 tablespoon plus 1 teaspoon
   minced jalapeños
1 teaspoon minced garlic
1 teaspoon salt
1 teaspoon minced and seeded
   habanero chile
1 teaspoon red wine vinegar

1. TO roast the peppers, place them on an open gas flame and turn them frequently with tongs until all sides are charred black, 7 to 10 minutes. (Alternatively, the peppers can be roasted under a broiler or on top of a gas or charcoal grill.) Place the blackened peppers in a plastic or paper bag, seal the bag, and let stand until cool enough to handle, about 15 minutes.

2. PEEL the peppers and remove the seeds and the stems. Chop the pepper flesh and place in a medium mixing bowl. (The chopped peppers will yield approximately 2 cups.) Add the remaining ingredients and stir to mix well. The salsa may be kept in the refrigerator for 2 to 3 days. Serve at room temperature.

CHEF NEAL'S BABY BACK RIBS WITH ORANGE-CHIPOTLE GLAZE

MAKES 4 TO 6 SERVINGS

I made these on a *Good Morning America* summertime show, and you just can't believe the responses we got from viewers. Everyone loves these! Now, I know it sounds weird to roast the ribs wrapped in both plastic wrap *and* aluminum foil, but trust me, this is the secret to really tender, juicy meat that you just won't believe. Plus, smoking the ribs first in a smoker, or grill outfitted to smoke, before roasting really gives them a great flavor. And talk about kicked up—wait till you try the Orange-Chipotle Glaze with these—there's definitely some heat going on in there!

2 to 3 cups wood chips
   (any kind)
2 tablespoons kosher salt
1 tablespoon Chinese five-spice
   powder
1 tablespoon coarsely ground
   black pepper
6 slabs baby back ribs
   (10 to 12 ribs per slab)
Orange-Chipotle Glaze
   (recipe follows)

1. **SOAK** the wood chips in water to cover for at least 30 minutes. Drain well.

2. **PREHEAT** a home smoker with the chips to 200°F. (If you have a Weber grill, it may be used for smoking. See the Weber website for information.)

3. **COMBINE** the salt, five-spice powder, and pepper in a small bowl. Rub 2 teaspoons of the spice mixture into each slab of ribs, seasoning both sides. Smoke for 20 minutes. Remove the ribs from the smoker and let cool enough to handle.

4. **PREHEAT** the oven to 350°F.

5. **WRAP** the ribs tightly in plastic wrap, then in foil. Place on baking sheets, and bake for 1½ hours. Remove from the oven and cool slightly, still wrapped, about 20 minutes.

6. **BEFORE** serving, liberally coat both sides of the ribs with the glaze. Serve 1 to 1½ slabs, or more, per person, and pass the remaining glaze at the table.

Orange-Chipotle Glaze

MAKES 4 CUPS

There's one secret to making this glaze, and that's using a big pot, since this has a tendency to boil over quickly. Watch the pot carefully as you're reducing the glaze, and simply remove it from the heat for ten seconds or so if necessary to prevent it from boiling over; then return it to the heat and continue cooking until it has thickened. This sauce is really amazing, and it has quite a bit of a kick. It also would be good served on grilled pork chops or chicken. And while you'll think this recipe makes a lot, watch out; it'll go fast.

1 cup fresh orange juice
8 cups sugar
2 cups apple cider vinegar
1 cup soy sauce
One 7-ounce can chipotle peppers
    in adobo sauce, puréed in the
    blender (or finely chopped,
    with their liquid)

1. BRING the orange juice to a boil in a large heavy nonreactive stockpot or a Dutch oven over high heat, and boil until reduced to about ¼ cup and thick.

2. REDUCE the heat to medium-high. Add the sugar, vinegar, soy sauce, and puréed chiles. Boil, stirring often, until the sugar has dissolved and the sauce has reduced to 4 cups and coats the back of a spoon, 20 to 30 minutes.

3. THIS keeps for three to four days in the refrigerator.

ANDOUILLE-STUFFED DOUBLE-CUT PORK CHOPS WITH WHISKEY-BRAISED APPLESAUCE

MAKES 4 SERVINGS

We did a show on "Dad's Day Off" (not Father's Day), and we thought these pork chops would be just the thing to make him king for the day! Now don't get scared off by the size of these chops. When you stuff the pork chops, remember that the side dish is inside, so you've really got two dishes in one. But these definitely are manly man portions.

3 tablespoons vegetable oil
½ pound andouille or other spicy smoked sausage, removed from casings and finely chopped
½ cup chopped yellow onions
¼ cup chopped green bell peppers
¼ cup chopped celery
1 teaspoon salt
½ teaspoon freshly ground black pepper
1 teaspoon minced garlic
2 cups crumbled Corn Bread (page 255)
1 cup Chicken Stock (page 2) or canned low-sodium chicken broth
2 tablespoons finely chopped fresh flat-leaf parsley
4 double-cut, bone-in loin pork chops (about 14 ounces each)
1 tablespoon Emeril's Original Essence or Creole Seasoning (page 9)
16 slices bacon
2 cups Veal Stock (page 4) or canned low-sodium beef broth
Whiskey-Braised Applesauce (recipe follows)

1. **HEAT** 1 tablespoon of the oil in a large heavy skillet over medium-high heat. Add the andouille and cook, stirring, until it browns, about 3 minutes. Add the onions, bell peppers, and celery and cook, stirring often, until tender, about 4 minutes. Add ½ teaspoon of the salt and the black pepper, then add the garlic and stir until fragrant, about 1 minute. Add the corn bread and chicken stock and cook, stirring, until the corn bread is soft, about 1 minute. Remove from the heat and mix in the parsley. Let cool for about 10 minutes.

2. **PREHEAT** the oven to 400°F.

3. **WITH** a thin sharp knife, cut a slit into the side of each pork chop, about 2½ inches across and 1 inch deep. Season the chops with the remaining ½ teaspoon salt and the Essence, then stuff each chop with about ½ cup of the corn bread stuffing. (The chops will be very full.) Wrap 4 slices of bacon around each chop, making sure that each end of bacon overlaps the next, so that the chop is completely wrapped.

4. **HEAT** the remaining 2 tablespoons oil in a very large heavy ovenproof skillet over medium-high heat. Carefully lay the chops in the pan. Cook until the bacon is crispy, about 4 minutes on each side.

5. TRANSFER the skillet to the oven and roast for 20 minutes. Transfer the chops to a platter and tent with aluminum foil to keep warm. Pour out the fat in the skillet and discard.

6. POUR the veal stock into the skillet and bring to a boil over medium-high heat, stirring constantly with a wooden spoon. Cook until slightly thickened, about 10 minutes.

7. SERVE the pork chops with the pan gravy spooned over the top and the applesauce on the side.

Whiskey-Braised Applesauce

MAKES ABOUT 2 CUPS

Believe me, this applesauce is a long way from that stuff your mom made. This is the grown-up kind, and, boy, does it ever go well with the pork chops. This also is excellent served with turkey, and the recipe can be easily doubled to feed a crowd.

8 tablespoons (1 stick) unsalted butter, cut into 8 pieces, plus 1 tablespoon
1½ tablespoons finely chopped fresh ginger (from about a 2-inch piece)
6 Granny Smith apples (about 3 pounds), peeled, cored, and coarsely chopped
1 cup bourbon
1 cup packed dark brown sugar
1 teaspoon ground cinnamon
½ teaspoon salt

1. MELT 1 tablespoon of the butter in a medium, heavy saucepan over medium-high heat. Add the ginger and cook, stirring, for 1 minute. Add the apples, bourbon, brown sugar, cinnamon, and salt. Simmer, uncovered, over medium-low heat until the apples are very tender, about 45 minutes.

2. PUREÉ the mixture in a blender or food processor. Return the purée to the saucepan and place over medium heat. Whisk in the remaining butter, 1 tablespoon at a time. Serve immediately, or cover and keep warm until ready to serve.

SPICED BAKED HAM
WITH SWEET POTATOES

MAKES 8 SERVINGS

This is the way to go when you have a crowd of people over for Super Bowl, New Year's Day, or Easter Brunch. When you bake a ham like this, you can count on 10 to 15 minutes baking time per pound, but make sure your instant-read thermometer reaches an internal temperature of 170°F to guarantee that the ham is baked through.

One 6- to 7-pound cooked, bone-
  in, butt portion ham
1 loosely packed cup dark brown
  sugar
¾ cup fresh orange juice
¾ cup Creole mustard or other
  spicy, whole-grained mustard
½ cup dark molasses
3 tablespoons prepared
  horseradish
½ teaspoon ground allspice
½ teaspoon cayenne

FOR THE POTATOES
7 small sweet potatoes
  (about 3 pounds), peeled
1 tablespoon vegetable oil
½ teaspoon salt
½ teaspoon ground cinnamon
¼ teaspoon ground allspice
2 teaspoons dark brown sugar

1. **RINSE** the ham under cold running water. Pat dry and place on a work surface. With a sharp knife, score parallel lines, 1 inch apart and ¼ inch deep, across the rounded skin side of the ham. Turn the ham 180° and score in a similar fashion to create a grid pattern across the ham. Put the ham in a 2-gallon plastic garbage bag.

2. **COMBINE** the remaining ingredients in a large mixing bowl, whisking to mix. Pour the mixture into the bag with the ham and seal. Gently squeeze the bag to evenly distribute the marinade around the ham. Refrigerate for 24 hours.

3. **PREHEAT** the oven to 350°F.

4. **FOR** the potatoes: Cut the potatoes in quarters lengthwise and put in a large mixing bowl. Toss with the vegetable oil, salt, cinnamon, allspice, and sugar. Arrange the potatoes in a layer on the bottom of a large roasting pan. Remove the ham from the bag and reserve the marinade. Set the ham, scored side up, on top of the potatoes. Bake for 45 minutes. Pour the marinade into a medium saucepan and bring to a gentle boil over medium-high heat. Reduce the heat to low and simmer, uncovered, until it has thickened and will coat the back of a spoon, about 20 minutes.

5. **REMOVE** the ham from the oven and evenly baste all sides with the marinade. Return to the oven and bake for 15 minutes. Remove the ham from the oven and baste again. Turn the sweet potatoes. Return the ham to the oven and bake, basting every 15 minutes, for 1½ hours.

6. **REMOVE** from the oven and allow to stand for 15 minutes before carving. Serve with the sweet potatoes.

ROASTED PORK LOIN

MAKES 4 SERVINGS

When you want to put a meal together without a whole lot of fuss, make this roast and serve it with the Cabbage and Potato Bake (page 238).

1. **PREHEAT** the oven to 400°F.

2. **RUB** the olive oil over the pork loin, and season with the salt and pepper. Heat a large ovenproof skillet over medium-high heat. Add the loin and sear, turning it to brown evenly on all sides, about 4 minutes per side.

3. **TRANSFER** the roast to the oven. Roast until a meat thermometer inserted in the center of the meat reads 160°F, 40 to 50 minutes. Transfer the loin to a platter and let rest for 15 minutes. Set the skillet aside.

4. **MEANWHILE,** bring veal stock to a boil, in a medium heavy saucepan over high heat and boil until it reduces by half, about 5 minutes. Set aside.

5. **IN** the same skillet you used for the pork, fry the bacon over medium-high heat until just crispy, about 4 minutes. Using a slotted spoon, transfer the bacon to paper towels to drain.

6. **ADD** the onions to the fat remaining in the skillet. Cook over medium-high heat, stirring often, for 2 minutes. Add the shallots and garlic and stir until fragrant, about 1 minute. Add the red wine and bring to a boil, stirring to release any brown bits from the bottom of the pan. Add the reduced veal stock and cook, stirring often, until the liquid is reduced by one-third.

7. **REMOVE** from the heat and whisk in the butter. Stir in the reserved bacon. Cover to keep warm.

8. **CARVE** the pork loin into ½-inch slices and serve with the sauce.

---

2 tablespoons olive oil
One 2- to 2½-pound boneless
  pork loin roast, rolled and tied
½ teaspoon salt
2 tablespoons cracked black
  pepper
2 cups Veal Stock (page 4) or
  canned low-sodium beef broth
1 pound bacon, cut into ½-inch-
  wide pieces
2 cups thinly sliced yellow onions
2 tablespoons minced shallots
1 tablespoon minced garlic
½ cup dry red wine
2 tablespoons unsalted butter

THE KING'S CREOLE
FRIED PORK CHOPS WITH
MASHED SWEET POTATOES AND
SOUTHERN COOKED GREENS

MAKES 4 SERVINGS

I have a feeling that Elvis, The King, would have liked this meal! We all know Elvis's reputation for eating great Southern favorites. I understand he loved fried peanut butter and banana sandwiches, and pork chops are said to have been his absolute favorite!

1½ pounds sweet potatoes,
  peeled and quartered
¾ teaspoon salt
4 tablespoons (½ stick) unsalted
  butter
¼ cup heavy cream
1 teaspoon pure vanilla extract
⅛ teaspoon freshly ground black
  pepper
3 Granny Smith apples, peeled,
  cored, and cut into ¼-inch
  slices
1 tablespoon fresh lemon juice
2 tablespoons Steen's 100% Pure
  Cane Syrup (see Source Guide,
  page 282)
1 tablespoon bourbon
4 pork loin chops, about 1 inch
  thick; double-cut, bone-in
2 tablespoons plus 2 teaspoons
  Emeril's Original Essence
2 cups bleached all-purpose flour
⅓ cup vegetable oil
Southern Cooked Greens
  (recipe follows)

1. **PUT** the potatoes in a large saucepan and add enough water to cover. Add ½ teaspoon of the salt and bring to a boil. Reduce the heat to medium and cook until fork-tender, about 20 minutes. Drain and transfer to a bowl. Mash the potatoes with a fork, then add 3 tablespoons of the butter, the cream, vanilla, the remaining ¼ teaspoon salt, and the pepper. Mix well, cover to keep warm, and set aside.

2. **HEAT** the remaining 1 tablespoon butter in a large skillet over medium heat. Add the apples and cook, stirring gently, until soft, about 5 minutes. Add the lemon juice, cane syrup, and bourbon. Cook, stirring, until golden, about 3 minutes.

3. **SEASON** the pork chops with 2 teaspoons of the Essence. Combine the flour and 2 tablespoons of Essence in a shallow bowl.

4. **HEAT** the vegetable oil in a large skillet over medium high heat. Dredge the chops in the seasoned flour, shaking off any excess. Fry the chops in the oil for 5 to 6 minutes on each side.

5. **TO** serve, spoon equal amounts of the sweet potatoes in the center of serving plates. Place a pork chop on top of the potatoes, then top with the apples. Arrange equal amounts of the greens around the chops. If you wish, spoon some of the "pot likker" over the greens.

Southern Cooked Greens

FRY the bacon in a large pot until crispy. Add the onions and cook, stirring, until they are soft and lightly golden, 6 to 7 minutes. Add the salt, black pepper, and cayenne. Add the shallots and garlic and cook for 2 minutes. Stir in the beer, vinegar, and molasses. Add the greens, a third at a time, pressing them down in the pot as they wilt. Cook, uncovered, stirring occasionally, for about 1 hour and 15 minutes.

½ pound bacon
3 cups thinly sliced yellow onions
½ teaspoon salt
¼ teaspoon freshly ground black pepper
⅛ teaspoon cayenne
2 tablespoons minced shallots
1 tablespoon minced garlic
One 12-ounce bottle of Dixie Beer
¼ cup rice wine vinegar
1 tablespoon molasses
6 pounds greens, such as mustard greens, collard greens, turnip greens, kale, and spinach, cleaned and stemmed

HAM HOCKS WITH BLACK BEANS

MAKES 4 SERVINGS

The hock is the lower portion of a hog's hind leg. It may not sound all that appetizing, but once they're smoked, they have great flavor. You're gonna love the flavor of the hocks with the black beans . . . I promise.

Four ½-pound ham hocks
3 tablespoons olive oil
1 cup minced yellow onions
¼ cup minced celery
¼ cup minced green bell peppers
½ teaspoon crushed red pepper flakes
¼ teaspoon dried oregano, preferably Mexican
¼ teaspoon dried thyme
2 bay leaves
1 tablespoon minced garlic
2 quarts Chicken Stock (page 2) or canned low-sodium chicken broth
1 pound dried black beans, rinsed, picked over, soaked overnight in water to cover, and drained
1 teaspoon salt
½ cup minced green onions (green and white parts)
¼ cup minced fresh flat-leaf parsley

1. **SCORE** the skin of each ham hock with a sharp knife.

2. **HEAT** the oil in a large deep pot or Dutch oven over medium-high heat. Add the ham hocks, onions, celery, bell peppers, crushed red pepper flakes, oregano, thyme, and bay leaves and cook, stirring, until the vegetables are softened, about 5 minutes. Stir in the garlic, and cook until fragrant, about 1 minute. Add the stock and bring to a boil over high heat. Reduce the heat to medium-low, cover, and simmer, stirring occasionally, for 1½ hours.

3. **ADD** the beans and stir. Continue simmering over medium-low heat until the beans are just tender and ham hocks are very tender, 45 minutes to 1 hour. Season with the salt and continue cooking for 15 to 30 minutes, until the beans are tender and the ham hocks are beginning to fall apart. Remove from the heat.

4. **SPOON** the ham hocks and beans into bowls (or cut the meat from the bones and stir the meat back into the pot of beans before ladling into bowls) and sprinkle with the green onions and parsley.

AW NUTS PORK CHOPS

MAKES 4 SERVINGS

These pork chops, each weighing in at over a pound, make a real manly meal. Giving the chops a quick sear in the pan before roasting seals in the juices . . . just make sure you don't overcook them. The nut crust on these chops is greatly complemented by the Poblano-Chocolate Mole (page 184).

1. **COMBINE** ¼ cup of the bread crumbs, the pistachio nuts, pine nuts, and pumpkin seeds in the bowl of a food processor or blender. Process on high speed until the mixture is the consistency of fine bread crumbs, about 1 minute. Transfer to a mixing bowl and add ¼ cup plus 2 tablespoons bread crumbs, and 2 tablespoons Essence.

2. **PAT** the pork chops dry with paper towels. Season both sides with 1 teaspoon Essence.

3. **PREHEAT** the oven to 375°F.

4. **HEAT** 1 tablespoon of the oil in each of two heavy, large skillets over medium-high heat. Add the pork chops and cook for 2 minutes on each side. Transfer the chops to a baking sheet lined with aluminum foil. Cool for 5 minutes.

5. **RUB** each chop with 1½ tablespoons of the mustard, and coat each with ¼ cup of the bread crumb mixture, pressing to make the crumbs stick to the meat.

6. **PUT** the chops on a baking sheet and roast for 30 minutes. Remove from the oven and serve hot with the mole.

½ cup plus 2 tablespoons dried fine bread crumbs
¼ cup shelled pistachio nuts
2 tablespoons pine nuts
2 tablespoons shelled pumpkin seeds
2 tablespoons plus 4 teaspoons Emeril's Original Essence
Four double-cut pork chops, about 2 inches thick, 6 to 18 ounces each
2 tablespoons olive oil
6 tablespoons Creole mustard, or other spicy, whole-grain mustard
Poblano-Chocolate Mole (page 184)

MACHO

the recipes

Yep, I do like a good steak. But I like all kinds of meat—rabbit, lamb, venison, veal chops, and other cuts of beef. The Rustic Rabbit Stew with Drop Biscuit Topping is a hearty winter dish that I often serve to friends as a casual supper. For a small, fancy-schmancy dinner party, try the simple but awesome Prime Rib of Beef. The Chili-Rubbed Pesto-Stuffed Leg of Lamb is ideal for a crowd. If you like comfort foods, try the Pot Roast. You should hear my wife, Alden, rave about it!

RUSTIC RABBIT STEW WITH DROP BISCUIT TOPPING

MAKES 4 SERVINGS

When I first came to New Orleans, I became involved with a Mississippi farm cooperative that supplied many of my fresh menu ingredients, including game, organically grown hogs, quail, and rabbits. Farmer Dan Crutchfield has become a great friend and continues to supply me with the best rabbits I can find. Rabbit holds up well to slow cooking and is a delicious ingredient in stews, gumbos, pâtés, and terrines. This is a tasty country version of rabbit stew that we did for a show on potpies. Rather than making the traditional piecrust, just drop the biscuit topping over the stew.

One 2½-pound rabbit, cut into serving pieces
1 tablespoon Emeril's Original Essence or Creole Seasoning (page 9)
¼ cup plus 1 tablespoon olive oil
1 cup dry red wine
¼ pound andouille or other spicy smoked sausage, removed from casings and finely chopped (about ½ cup)
¼ cup bleached all-purpose flour
2½ cups thinly sliced yellow onions
1 cup chopped carrots
1 cup chopped celery
3 cups sliced mixed wild mushrooms, such as chanterelles, morels, and stemmed shiitakes
½ teaspoon salt
¼ teaspoon freshly ground black pepper
2 tablespoons minced shallots
1 teaspoon minced garlic
2 cups Chicken Stock (page 2) or canned low-sodium chicken broth

1. **SEASON** the rabbit with the Essence. Heat 2 tablespoons of the oil in a large heavy ovenproof pot or Dutch oven over medium-high heat. Add the rabbit and cook, turning occasionally, until evenly browned, about 10 minutes. Transfer the rabbit to a platter.

2. **ADD** the red wine to the pot, stirring to deglaze and remove the browned bits on the bottom. Pour the pan juices into a bowl and set aside. Wipe out the pot with a paper towel and remove any burned bits sticking to the bottom.

3. **HEAT** the remaining 3 tablespoons oil in the pot over medium-high heat. Add the andouille and cook, stirring occasionally, until browned, about 5 minutes. Add the flour and cook, stirring constantly, to make a medium-dark, peanut butter–colored roux, 10 to 15 minutes.

4. **ADD** the onions and cook, stirring often, until softened, about 3 minutes. Add the carrots and celery and cook, stirring often, until they soften, about 3 minutes. Add the mushrooms, salt, and pepper. Cook, stirring often, until the mushroom liquid evaporates, about 8 minutes. Add the shallots and garlic and stir until the shallots soften, about 2 minutes. Stir the reserved pan juices into the pot and bring to a boil. Cook over high heat until the liquid reduces by half, about 5 minutes.

5. RETURN the rabbit to the pot and add the chicken stock, oregano, and bay leaves. Bring to a boil. Reduce the heat to medium low and simmer, uncovered, until the rabbit is tender, about 45 minutes. Remove and discard the bay leaves.

6. MEANWHILE, preheat the oven to 350°F.

7. DROP the dumpling dough by heaping tablespoons, about 1 inch apart, on top of the stew. Bake until the biscuits are golden, about 20 minutes.

8. TO serve, spoon the stew and biscuits onto serving plates. Garnish with the green onions.

1 tablespoon chopped fresh
    oregano
2 bay leaves
¼ cup chopped green onions
    (green and white parts)
Drop Biscuit Topping
    (recipe follows)

Drop Biscuit Topping

SIFT the flour, baking powder, baking soda, and salt into a mixing bowl. Add the shortening and work it with your fingers, or with a fork or pastry blender, until the mixture resembles coarse meal. Add the milk and black pepper and stir with a fork just until a soft dough forms. Use immediately.

1 cup bleached all-purpose flour
1 teaspoon baking powder
⅛ teaspoon baking soda
¼ teaspoon salt
2 tablespoons plus 1 teaspoon
    vegetable shortening
¼ cup plus 1 tablespoon milk
½ teaspoon freshly ground black
    pepper

TO CUT UP A RABBIT

Cut and remove the two forelegs where they attach to the body.

Cut between the second and third ribs (counting from the rear) on one side and cut all the way down to the backbone, then repeat on the other side.

Cut off the whole rib cage and neck section where you've cut down to the backbone between the ribs.

Cut the rib cage into chunks.

Detach the thighs. Cut away the tailbone, leaving the saddle. Spread out the flaps of the saddle and cut away from the remaining two ribs. Snap off the ribs.

KICKED-UP VENISON AND SAUSAGE CASSOULET

MAKES 6 SERVINGS

Cassoulet, a slow-cooked meat-and-bean dish from southwestern France, is ideal for those bone-chilling winter months. It's traditionally made with pork sausage, lamb, duck confit, and beans, but I give it a Louisiana twist with andouille and venison. Use loin or shoulder cuts.

BEANS
1 pound dried white beans, soaked for at least 8 hours, or overnight (see page 13), and drained
2 quarts Chicken Stock (page 2) or canned low-sodium chicken broth
Two 1-pound ham hocks
½ cup chopped yellow onions
1 tablespoon minced garlic
1 tablespoon fresh thyme
2 bay leaves

1½ pounds boneless lean venison (such as loin or shoulder), cut into ½-inch cubes
2 teaspoons Emeril's Original Essence or Creole Seasoning (page 9)
½ cup bleached all-purpose flour
¼ cup vegetable oil, or as needed
1 cup chopped yellow onions
½ cup chopped celery
½ cup chopped green bell peppers

1. **TO** make the beans, combine the first 7 ingredients in a large, heavy stockpot and bring to a boil. Reduce the heat to medium-low and simmer, uncovered, until the beans are tender, 45 minutes to 1 hour. Skim from time to time to remove any foam that forms on the surface.

2. **DRAIN** the beans, reserving the cooking liquid; discard the bay leaves.

3. **WHEN** the ham hocks are cool enough to handle, cut the meat off the bones, discarding the skin and bones. Chop the meat and set aside.

4. **PREHEAT** the oven to 375°F.

5. **SEASON** the venison with 1 teaspoon of the Essence. Combine the flour and the remaining 1 teaspoon Essence in a shallow bowl. Dredge the venison in the flour, shaking off the excess. Reserve the remaining flour.

6. **HEAT** the oil in a large heavy ovenproof pot or Dutch oven over medium-high heat. In batches, add the venison and cook, turning occasionally, until evenly browned, about 4 minutes. Using a slotted spoon, transfer the meat to paper towels to drain, leaving the oil in the pot.

7. ADD more oil to the pot if needed to make ¼ cup. Add the onions, celery, bell peppers, salt, and cayenne, and cook, stirring often, until the vegetables soften, about 5 minutes. Add the andouille and garlic and cook, stirring often, until the andouille is hot, about 3 minutes.

8. ADD ¼ cup of the reserved seasoned flour and cook, stirring constantly, to make a medium-dark, peanut butter–colored roux, 10 to 15 minutes. Add the Worcestershire. Slowly add the reserved bean cooking liquid and the chicken stock, stirring to a blend. Bring to a simmer and cook over medium heat for 10 minutes. Stir in the reserved ham hock meat, venison, and beans.

9. MEANWHILE, preheat the oven to 375°F.

10. TO make the crust, pulse all the ingredients in a food processor for 30 seconds, or until blended.

11. TOP the cassoulet with the bread crumb mixture and bake until the crust is golden brown and crispy, 30 to 45 minutes.

12. TO serve, spoon onto dinner plates and serve hot.

½ teaspoon salt
¼ teaspoon cayenne
1 pound andouille or other spicy
    smoked sausage, cut into
    1-inch pieces
1 teaspoon minced garlic
1 tablespoon Worcestershire
    sauce
2 cups Chicken Stock (page 2) or
    canned low-sodium chicken
    broth

BREAD CRUMB CRUST
2 cups fine dried bread crumbs
8 tablespoons (1 stick) unsalted
    butter, melted
¼ cup freshly grated Parmigiano-
    Reggiano
2 large egg yolks
1 tablespoon chopped fresh
    thyme
1 teaspoon salt
1 teaspoon freshly ground black
    pepper

VENISON MEDALLIONS WITH BACON AND WHITE BEAN RAGOUT AND CREOLE MUSTARD SAUCE

MAKES 4 SERVINGS

Because of the meat's leanness and great flavor, venison's popularity is on the rise. On a game show we did (a show where we cooked game; there were no contestants), we found that venison is so lean, it easily dries out. Wrapped with bacon, however, it will be moist and succulent.

2 pounds venison loin, trimmed and cut into 4 medallions (6 to 7 ounces each after trimming)
½ teaspoon Emeril's Original Essence or Creole Seasoning (page 9)
½ teaspoon salt
¼ teaspoon freshly ground black pepper
1 cup olive oil
¼ cup dry sherry or dry red wine
2 tablespoons chopped fresh thyme
2 tablespoons minced garlic plus 1 teaspoon
2 cups Veal Stock (page 4) or store-bought demi-glace (see Source Guide, page 282)
1 cup dry white wine
½ cup Creole or other spicy whole-grain mustard

1. **SEASON** the venison medallions on both sides with the Essence, ¼ teaspoon of the salt, and ⅛ teaspoon of the pepper. Put into a large self-sealing plastic bag. Whisk the olive oil, sherry, thyme, and 2 tablespoons garlic in a bowl. Pour over the venison. Seal the bag and place in a large bowl. Refrigerate for 2 to 4 hours.

2. **COMBINE** 1 cup of the veal stock, the white wine, mustard, and shallots in a medium saucepan and bring to a boil over high heat. Reduce the heat to medium and simmer until the mixture has reduced by half, about 5 minutes. Set aside.

3. **FRY** the bacon in a large skillet over high heat, stirring frequently, until just crisp, about 5 minutes. Add the onions and cook, stirring often, until softened, about 2 minutes. Add the spinach and the remaining 1 teaspoon garlic and cook, stirring often, until the spinach has wilted, about 2 minutes. Stir in the beans and season with the remaining ¼ teaspoon salt and ⅛ teaspoon pepper. Cook for 2 minutes to heat the beans through. Cover to keep warm.

4. **REMOVE** the venison from the marinade and pat completely dry; discard the marinade.

5. **HEAT** the vegetable oil in a large heavy skillet over medium-high heat. Add the venison and cook for 5 minutes on the first side, then turn and cook for 3 minutes on the other side for medium-rare. Transfer to a platter and let stand for 5 minutes.

6. **MEANWHILE,** add the remaining 1 cup veal stock to the skillet and deglaze the pan over high heat, scraping up any browned bits on the bottom. Boil to reduce the stock by half, about 3 minutes. Stir in the reserved white wine mixture and bring to a boil. Remove from the heat.

7. **TO** serve, spoon equal amounts of the ragout onto the centers of four plates. Cut each venison medallion into ½-inch-thick slices, and fan around the ragout. Spoon the sauce over the meat and serve.

¼ cup minced shallots
8 slices bacon, chopped
½ cup finely chopped yellow
    onions
2 cups thinly sliced spinach
    leaves
2 cups Basic Beans (white)
    (page 13)
2 tablespoons vegetable oil

GRILLED MARINATED FLANK STEAKS

MAKES 4 SERVINGS

There's nothing like grilling some meat on the barbecue pit to make a weekend complete. Go ahead and serve this with the Smashed Potato Salad (page 239). Oh, and remember, when slicing flank steak or London broil, you always want to cut across the grain. I made this for a kicked-up tailgating show on *Emeril Live*, and it definitely was one of the hits of the party out in the parking lot!

One 2-pound flank steak
1 cup dry sherry or dry red wine
½ cup soy sauce
¼ cup packed brown sugar
2 tablespoons Emeril's Original Essence or Creole Seasoning (page 9)
2 tablespoons minced garlic
2 tablespoons tomato paste
1 teaspoon freshly ground black pepper

1. **PUT** the flank steak in a large self-sealing plastic bag. Whisk the sherry, soy sauce, brown sugar, Essence, garlic, tomato paste, and pepper in a medium bowl. Pour into the bag and seal. Refrigerate for at least 4 hours, and up to 24 hours.

2. **PREHEAT** a gas or charcoal grill.

3. **REMOVE** the steak from the marinade and pat it dry. Grill the steak for about 6 minutes on each side for rare. While it cooks, pour the marinade into a small heavy saucepan and bring to a boil over high heat. Lower the heat to medium-low and simmer until reduced and thickened, about 10 minutes.

4. **TRANSFER** the steak to a cutting board and let stand for 5 minutes before slicing.

5. **CUT** the steak across the grain into thin diagonal slices, and serve with the sauce on the side.

MY FAVORITE VEAL CHOPS

MAKES 4 SERVINGS

When veal chops like this are served in Italy, you have the option of having the chopped arugula on top or on the side, but always with a squeeze of fresh lemon. Now, there are a couple of special directions in this recipe that will help you achieve perfect results. First, you need to pound the chops really thin, to just ¼-inch thickness, then cook them in clarified butter. This way, the chops are going to have a great flavor that just can't be reached any other way. It's definitely worth the extra effort to clarify your own butter.

Four 12-ounce bone-in veal chops
2 tablespoons plus 2 teaspoons Emeril's Original Essence or Creole Seasoning (page 9)
1 cup bleached all-purpose flour
1 cup fine dried bread crumbs
2 large eggs
1 cup milk
½ cup clarified butter (see Note)
1 bunch arugula, stemmed, washed, patted dry, and chopped (about 1½ cups)
4 ripe plum tomatoes (about 1¼ pounds), cored and chopped
2 tablespoons extra-virgin olive oil
2 teaspoons fresh lemon juice
½ teaspoon kosher salt
¼ teaspoon freshly ground black pepper
1 lemon, cut into 4 wedges

1. **ONE** at a time, using a thin sharp knife, cut a slit into the side of the meaty part of each chop, about 3 inches long and 1 inch deep, being careful not to cut all the way through to the bone. Gently open out the chop so the meat surface is about twice as wide as before. Place the chop between two large pieces of plastic wrap on a work surface. Using a flat meat mallet, pound the meat until ¼ inch thick.

2. **SEASON** both sides of each chop with ½ teaspoon of the Essence. Combine the flour with 1 tablespoon of the Essence in a shallow bowl. Put the bread crumbs in another shallow bowl and season with the remaining 1 tablespoon Essence. Combine the eggs and milk in another shallow bowl and whisk to blend.

3. **DREDGE** the chops in the seasoned flour and shake off excess. Dip in the egg wash, and then coat both sides with the bread crumbs. Set on a baking sheet.

4. **HEAT** the clarified butter in a large heavy nonstick skillet over medium-high heat. Two at a time, add the chops and cook until golden brown, about 3 minutes per side. Cut into a chop at the bone to check for doneness—they should be barely pink. Using a slotted spatula, transfer the chops to a baking sheet and keep warm in the oven while you cook the other chops.

5. **MEANWHILE,** toss the arugula, tomatoes, olive oil, lemon juice, salt, and pepper in a large bowl.

6. PLACE a chop on each plate. Mound a portion of the arugula salad on top of each chop, and serve with a lemon wedge on the side.

NOTE: What makes clarified butter so great is its higher smoke point. This means you can cook meats and fish at a higher temperature than with regular butter, making it ideal for panfrying. By clarifying the butter during a slow cooking process, you're able to strain out the milk solids that burn quickly, as well as the water and salt.

To make your own clarified butter at home, just cut unsalted butter into 1-inch pieces and melt it slowly over low heat in a heavy saucepan. Remove the pan from the heat and let the melted butter stand for 5 minutes. Skim the foam from the top, and slowly pour the clarified butter into a container, discarding the milky solids in the bottom of the pan. You'll lose about one-quarter of your original butter amount during the process. Clarified butter will keep tightly covered in the refrigerator for about one month.

STUFFED RACK OF LAMB

MAKES 4 SERVINGS

Become buddies with your butcher; he can be your best friend. I paid tribute to butchers on a show with this dish! I stuffed the inside of the tenderloin, with the meat still on the bone, as well as coating the outside of the racks as they usually are before being roasted. By inserting a knife into the meat and pushing through the stuffing, you save yourself the effort of butterflying and pounding the meat, then stuffing and tying it. This dried fruit stuffing has a definite winter taste, and the nuts and port wine give it a richness that's almost chutney-like.

Four 1-pound half-racks of lamb (about 16 chops)
2 tablespoons Emeril's Original Essence or Creole Seasoning (page 9)
1 tablespoon unsalted butter
1/4 cup finely chopped yellow onions
2 tablespoons finely chopped celery
1 tablespoon minced shallots
3/4 teaspoon salt
1/8 teaspoon freshly ground black pepper
1/2 teaspoon minced garlic
1/4 cup finely chopped dried apricots
1/4 cup golden raisins
1/4 cup finely chopped pitted prunes
1 cup ruby port wine
1/4 cup ground walnuts
1 tablespoon chopped fresh mint
1 cup fine dried bread crumbs
2 tablespoons extra-virgin olive oil
1/2 cup Creole or other spicy whole-grain mustard

1. **SEASON** the meaty side of each rack with 3/4 teaspoon of the Essence.

2. **MELT** the butter in a medium skillet over medium-high heat. Add the onions, celery, shallots, 1/4 teaspoon of the salt, and the pepper and cook, stirring often, until the vegetables begin to soften, about 1 minute. Add the garlic and stir until fragrant, about 30 seconds. Add the apricots, raisins, and prunes and cook until softened, 2 to 3 minutes. Add the port wine and cook until almost all the liquid has evaporated, about 5 minutes. Stir in the walnuts and mint.

3. **REMOVE** from the heat and let cool for 10 minutes. (If desired, the stuffing can be made 1 day ahead and refrigerated, tightly covered.)

4. **PREHEAT** the oven to 400°F.

5. **ONE** rack at a time, with a thin sharp knife, cut into the center of the lamb loin from one end, going into the meat as deep as you can. Turn the lamb and cut into the center from the other end, to make one long hole through the meat. Insert a long-handled wooden spoon into the hole and push the handle through to the other side. Gently work the spoon handle to enlarge the hole to 1/2 to 3/4 inch in diameter.

6. **WITH** your fingers, work about one-fourth of the fruit stuffing into the center of the meat so that the hole is filled with stuffing. Repeat with the remaining racks and stuffing.

7. **HEAT** a heavy nonstick skillet over medium-high heat. In batches, add the racks to the skillet and sear, turning occasionally, until browned on all sides, about 7 minutes.

8. **MEANWHILE** combine the bread crumbs, olive oil, the remaining 1 tablespoon essence, and the remaining ½ teaspoon salt in a shallow bowl.

9. **SPREAD** 2 tablespoons of the mustard on each rack, then dredge in the seasoned bread crumbs, coating evenly. Place the lamb on the meaty side in a roasting pan. Cover the bones with aluminum foil to prevent them from burning. Roast for 20 to 25 minutes, until an instant-read thermometer inserted in the thickest part of the racks reads 125°F, for medium-rare.

10. **LET** stand for 5 minutes before slicing into chops.

CHILI-RUBBED PESTO-STUFFED LEG OF LAMB

MAKES 6 TO 8 SERVINGS

Don't underestimate the idea of stuffing a leg of lamb! You will make a lot of friends with this dish. It might seem like the pesto recipe would make way too much for stuffing the boned leg of lamb, but trust me, it's really the perfect amount. Same thing with the chili powder rub—use it all, for an amazing crust and pan gravy. This would be a really terrific contribution to a buffet table, thinly sliced and served with different side dishes, such as the Roasted Vegetable Salad (page 61), the Grape Tomato, Arugula, and Red Onion Salad (page 69), or the Bulghur Wheat–Stuffed Tomatoes (page 235).

½ cup olive oil
¼ cup plus 1 tablespoon Emeril's Original Essence or Creole Seasoning (page 9)
¼ cup chili powder
¼ cup ground cumin
1 tablespoon salt
2 tablespoons freshly ground black pepper
One 4 to 5-pound boned leg of lamb, boned and butterflied
Cilantro, Pine Nut, and Walnut Pesto (recipe follows)

1. **PREHEAT** the oven to 400°F.

2. **COMBINE** the olive oil, ¼ cup of the Essence, the chili powder, cumin, salt, and pepper in a small bowl.

3. **PUT** the lamb on a work surface lined with plastic wrap. With a thin sharp knife, cut a slit lengthwise through the thickest part of the meat, being careful not to cut all the way through to the other side. Gently pry open the flap of meat. Lay another piece of plastic wrap on top of the meat. With a flat meat mallet, pound the meat to an even ¾-inch thickness. Remove the plastic wrap and season with the remaining 1 tablespoon Essence.

4. **SPREAD** the pesto over the inside of the meat, leaving a ½-inch border along the edges. Starting at a short side, roll up the meat tightly, jelly-roll style, to enclose the stuffing. Tie at 1-inch intervals with kitchen twine. Spread the chili rub all over the outside of the lamb.

5. **PLACE** the meat on a rack in a roasting pan. Roast until an instant-read thermometer inserted in the thickest part of the roast reads 125°F, about 1¼ hours, for medium-rare.

6. **TRANSFER** the lamb to a platter and let stand for 15 minutes before carving.

Cilantro, Pine Nut, and Walnut Pesto

MAKES ABOUT 1¼ CUPS

Pesto is really adaptable. You can vary the usual basil, pine nuts, garlic, olive oil, salt and black pepper, and Parmesan recipe to suit your needs. For instance, I've given this pesto a Southwestern twist by substituting cilantro for the basil and red pepper for the black. You could also change it around by substituting pumpkin seeds for the walnuts and adding chili powder and cumin. Your choice—it's just a matter of what you're in the mood for. Pesto can definitely be made ahead of time. Cover it tightly; it will keep for up to a week in the refrigerator. You'll find, though, that the longer you keep this, the darker it'll get—but the taste won't be affected.

2 cups packed fresh cilantro leaves, rinsed and patted dry
½ cup freshly grated Parmigiano-Reggiano
¼ cup toasted pine nuts (see Note)
¼ cup toasted walnuts (see Note)
1 tablespoon minced garlic
¼ teaspoon salt, or more to taste
¼ teaspoon cayenne, or more to taste
⅓ cup extra-virgin olive oil

1. **COMBINE** the cilantro, cheese, pine nuts, walnuts, garlic, salt, and cayenne in a food processor and process for 20 seconds. Or process in a blender on high speed.

2. **WITH** the machine running, slowly add the olive oil in a steady stream to form a thick, smooth paste. Season with more salt and red pepper if needed.

NOTE: Toasting nuts really brings out their flavor. To toast pine nuts, place them in an empty skillet. Cook over medium heat, stirring often, until light brown, then pour onto a plate to cool. To toast walnuts, pecans, or almonds, spread them on a baking sheet and bake in a preheated 350°F oven, stirring occasionally, until fragrant.

BARBECUED BEEF BRISKET

MAKES 10 SERVINGS

If you cook this right, man, this is melt-in your-mouth good! During the summer, I usually cook my brisket on the pit, but during the winter I do it in the oven, like this. I did this on one of the shows, and I had to fight off the television crew, because the aroma while it bakes is out of sight! Serve with warm onion rolls and some hearty side dishes, like the Smashed Potato Salad (page 239) and baked beans.

One 5- to 6-pound beef brisket, trimmed
3 tablespoons Emeril's Original Essence or Creole Seasoning (page 9)
3½ teaspoons salt
1 tablespoon olive oil
4 cups Barbecue Sauce (recipe follows)
2 cups Veal Stock (page 4) or canned low-sodium beef broth

1. **PREHEAT** the oven to 325°F.

2. **SEASON** the brisket on both sides with the Essence and 1½ teaspoons of the salt.

3. **HEAT** the oil in a large heavy skillet or large roasting pan over high heat. Add the meat and sear, turning once, until evenly browned, about 3 minutes per side. Transfer to a large roasting pan.

4. **COMBINE** the barbecue sauce, stock, and the remaining 2 teaspoons salt in a large mixing bowl and mix well. Pour the mixture over the brisket and cover tightly with aluminum foil. Bake for 2½ hours.

5. **TURN** the meat over, cover again, and continue baking for another 2½ hours, or until very tender.

6. **LET** stand for 15 minutes before carving. Slice the meat across the grain and serve with the pan juices spooned over each serving.

Barbecue Sauce

MAKES 5 CUPS

Everyone seems to have an opinion about what constitutes a good barbecue sauce. I like mine with some heat. You can make yours hotter by adding more jalapeños and pepper sauce. So simple! On one of our tailgate party shows, I smeared this on marinated flank steaks and everyone went wild! But hey, you can slather it on just about any kind of meat. You'll notice that it isn't a "cooked" sauce, but I assure you that it works for me!

COMBINE all the ingredients in a large mixing bowl. Stir to mix well. Use immediately, or store in an airtight container in the refrigerator for up to three days.

4 cups ketchup
1 cup finely chopped yellow onions
½ cup Steen's 100% Pure Cane Syrup (see Source Guide, page 282)
½ cup dry red wine
2 tablespoons fresh lemon juice
2 tablespoons Creole or other spicy whole-grain mustard
2 tablespoons dark brown sugar
1 tablespoon minced garlic
1 tablespoon minced jalapeños
1 tablespoon Worcestershire sauce
1 teaspoon Emeril's Red Pepper Sauce or other hot pepper sauce
1 teaspoon salt
½ teaspoon cayenne

EMERIL'S POT ROAST

MAKES 6 TO 8 SERVINGS

Pot roast has received a bad rap. Too often people use the wrong cut of meat, or don't sear the meat before ever-so-slowly cooking it in the oven for hours. The aroma of this roasting in the oven will attract even die-hard pot roast haters. The roast cooks on a bed of carrots, celery, onions, and new potatoes. Feel free to add whatever vegetables are in season and whatever suits your taste—parsnips, baby turnips, sweet potatoes, and fennel are just a few ideas. If you can hold your guests off, this is even better the next day.

One 4- to 5-pound sirloin tip roast, netted or tied at 1-inch intervals

12 garlic cloves, peeled and cut lengthwise in half

1½ tablespoons Emeril's Original Essence or Creole Seasoning (page 9)

1¼ teaspoons salt

1¼ teaspoons freshly ground black pepper

2 tablespoons vegetable oil

8 large carrots

4 medium celery ribs, cut crosswise in half

4 medium yellow onions, quartered

16 small red potatoes (each about 1½ inches in diameter), scrubbed

2 bay leaves

1 cup dry red wine

3 tablespoons tomato paste

1. **PREHEAT** the oven to 400°F.

2. **WITH** a small sharp knife, make twenty-four 1½-inch-deep slits about 2 inches apart in the roast. Insert the garlic pieces into the slits. Mix 1 tablespoon of the Essence, 1 teaspoon of the salt, and 1 teaspoon of the pepper and rub all over the roast.

3. **HEAT** the oil in a heavy large skillet over medium-high heat. Add the roast and brown on all sides, about 8 minutes total. Set aside.

4. **LAY** the carrots and celery, alternating them, in the bottom of a roasting pan. Scatter the onions and potatoes over the carrots and celery. Season the vegetables with the remaining Essence and salt and pepper. Put the bay leaves on top of the vegetables. Put the roast on top of the vegetables.

5. **WHISK** 1 cup water, the red wine, and tomato paste in a small mixing bowl. Pour the mixture over the roast. Cover the pan tightly with aluminum foil and bake for 1½ hours.

6. **REMOVE** the pot roast from the oven and baste with the pan juices. Reduce the heat to 350°F. Cover, return to the oven, and continue cooking until the meat is very tender, about 2 hours, basting the roast every 30 minutes. Remove from the oven and baste with the pan juices. Remove and discard the bay leaves. Let stand for 15 minutes.

7. **CARVE** the roast and serve with the vegetables and the pan juices.

PRIME RIB OF BEEF

MAKES 4 SERVINGS

As far as I'm concerned, the prime rib roast is most flavorful—but it's also the most expensive cut. I say get the best if you're going to plunk down some money, and you'll get what you pay for. This preparation is quite simple, and the taste will blast you off into outer space.

1. PREHEAT the oven to 400°F.

2. PUT the roast in a small roasting pan, bone side down. With a small sharp knife, make sixteen ½-inch-deep slits in the meaty side of the roast. Insert 1 garlic clove into each slit, pressing it into the meat. Pinch with your thumb and index finger to close the openings.

3. COMBINE the chopped thyme, salt, Essence, and pepper in a small bowl. Slowly stir in the oil to make a paste. Rub the paste on both sides of the roast, and place the thyme sprigs under the roast.

4. ROAST for 1 hour. Remove the pan from the oven and turn the roast for even browning. Reduce the oven temperature to 350°F and continue roasting until an instant-read thermometer inserted in the thickest part of the roast reads 125° to 130°F for medium-rare, about 45 minutes, or 140°F for medium, about 1 hour.

5. LET stand for 15 minutes before carving.

One 4½- to 5-pound standing rib roast
16 garlic cloves, peeled
1 tablespoon chopped fresh thyme, plus 12 sprigs
2 teaspoons salt
1 teaspoon Emeril's Original Essence or Creole Seasoning (page 9)
1 teaspoon freshly ground black pepper
2 tablespoons vegetable oil

the recipes

VEGETABLES

Eat your vegetables. And I'm not talking about a pile of plain steamed broccoli or carrots. Try the Celery Root Fries with Creole Remoulade Sauce. Tomatoes stuffed with bulghur are a great go-with for any lamb dish. Eggplant, Tomato, and Feta Cheese Napoleons make a perfect side dish with grilled fish or shrimp. Looking for something simpler? The Smashed Potato Salad and the Twice-Baked Potatoes are just the ticket.

BROCCOLI AND CAULIFLOWER AU GRATIN

MAKES 6 TO 8 SERVINGS

Sometimes people become lost and confused when preparing a special-occasion or holiday meal. They spend all their time concentrating on the main course, and side dishes are somehow ignored. Not only is this dish impressive and rich but you can assemble it ahead of time. Refrigerate, let it come to room temperature, spoon on the bread crumb topping, and bake.

1 tablespoon salt
3 pounds cauliflower, cut into large florets
1 to 1½ pounds broccoli, cut into large florets
8 tablespoons (1 stick) plus 2 teaspoons unsalted butter
½ cup bleached all-purpose flour
¼ teaspoon cayenne
6 cups milk
8 ounces Cheddar cheese, shredded (about 2 cups)
1 cup fine dried bread crumbs
2 teaspoons Emeril's Original Essence or Creole Seasoning (page 9)
¼ cup extra-virgin olive oil

1. **PREHEAT** the oven to 375°F.

2. **FILL** a large pot three-quarters full with water and add 1 teaspoon of the salt. Bring to a boil over high heat. Add the cauliflower and cook until just tender, 8 to 10 minutes. Using a slotted spoon, transfer the cauliflower to a colander. Rinse under cold running water until cool. Drain well.

3. **ADD** the broccoli to the boiling water. Cook until just tender, about 5 minutes. Drain the broccoli in a colander. Rinse under cold running water to cool. Drain well.

4. **BUTTER** a 15 × 10-inch baking dish (or 2 smaller dishes) with 2 teaspoons of the butter. Arrange the cauliflower evenly in the dish, then arrange the broccoli on top.

5. **MELT** the remaining 8 tablespoons butter in a heavy medium saucepan over medium heat. Whisk in the flour and cook, whisking, until the roux is a blond color, about 3 minutes. Add the remaining 2 teaspoons salt and the cayenne. Gradually whisk in the milk and whisk constantly until the mixture boils and thickens, about 4 minutes. Whisk in the cheese until it melts.

6. **POUR** the cheese sauce over the cauliflower and broccoli, and gently rap the dish on the countertop to remove any air bubbles.

7. **COMBINE** the bread crumbs, Essence, and olive oil in a small bowl, mixing well. Spoon the mixture evenly over the top of the vegetables.

8. **BAKE** until golden brown, about 30 minutes. Serve hot.

BULGHUR WHEAT—STUFFED TOMATOES

MAKES 4 SERVINGS

Here's a salad that we featured on an *Essence* show that can easily be a main course. It would also make a nice side dish to serve with grilled lamb chops or a leg of lamb. Bulghur wheat, which comes in coarse, medium, and fine grinds, is actually wheat kernels that have been steamed, dried, and crushed. You'll find that it has a nutty flavor and a nice crunch that we've played up a little more by adding chopped walnuts.

1 cup fine-grain bulghur wheat
4 large ripe tomatoes (about 3 pounds)
2 tablespoons fresh lemon juice
1 tablespoon extra-virgin olive oil
1 teaspoon salt
1/2 teaspoon ground coriander
1/2 teaspoon freshly ground black pepper
1/2 cup seeded and finely chopped cucumbers
1/2 cup chopped green onions (green and white parts)
1/2 cup minced fresh flat-leaf parsley
1/3 cup chopped walnuts
1/4 cup minced fresh mint

1. PUT the bulghur in a large bowl and stir in 2 cups boiling water. Cover tightly and let stand until the bulghur is tender and most of the water has been absorbed, 20 to 30 minutes.

2. DRAIN in a strainer, then pour the mixture onto a large kitchen towel and squeeze out any excess liquid. Return the bulghur to the bowl.

3. CUT off about 1/2 inch the top of each tomato. With your finger, poke the seed pockets and remove the seeds and juice. With a small sharp knife, cut out the inner pulp. Dice the pulp and discard the seeds.

4. WHISK the lemon juice, olive oil, salt, coriander, and black pepper in a large bowl and stir to blend. Add the chopped tomato pulp, cucumbers, green onions, parsley, walnuts, mint, and bulghur and mix well.

5. STUFF the tomato shells with the bulghur mixture. Serve at room temperature or chilled.

CELERY ROOT FRIES WITH CREOLE REMOULADE SAUCE

MAKES 4 SERVINGS

Celery root, also known as celeriac, is one ugly, knobby vegetable, but its sweet flavor, a cross between celery and parsley, belies its looks. A dear friend, the late chef Patrick Clark, turned me on to my first celery root fries. I prepared them on *Essence of Emeril* when we did a show on using everyday vegetables in creative ways. Matter of fact, they're so good that now I serve them as an accompaniment to roast lamb or chicken, or sometimes as an appetizer accompanied by remoulade sauce.

Vegetable oil for deep-frying
½ cup bleached all-purpose flour
1 tablespoon Emeril's Original Essence or Creole Seasoning (page 9)
1 large egg
½ cup fine dried bread crumbs
2 pounds celery root, peeled and cut into 3 × 1½-inch sticks
1 cup Creole Remoulade Sauce (page 103), optional

1. **POUR** enough oil into a large heavy pot or electric deep fryer to come halfway up the sides and heat to 360°F.

2. **COMBINE** the flour with 1 teaspoon of the Essence in a shallow bowl. Beat the egg with 2 teaspoons water in another shallow bowl. Combine the bread crumbs with 1 teaspoon of the Essence in another shallow bowl. One at a time, toss the celery root sticks in the flour, then dip in the egg wash and dredge in the bread crumbs to coat evenly. Shake to remove any excess and place on a baking sheet.

3. **IN** batches, without crowding, deep-fry the sticks until golden, about 2 minutes. Using a slotted spoon, transfer the sticks to a paper towel–lined baking sheet.

4. **SPRINKLE** the fries with the remaining 1 teaspoon Essence. Serve hot, with the remoulade sauce for dipping.

APPLE AND POTATO GRATIN

MAKES 6 SERVINGS

When Bernard Hine from Hine Cognac was a guest on *Emeril Live*, he and I practically drooled when we sampled this simple combination. The apples add a little sweetness. We agreed that it would serve as the perfect side dish to any great main course, whether chicken, beef, pork, or veal.

1. PREHEAT the oven to 400°F. Grease a 9 × 13-inch baking dish with the butter.

2. WHISK the cream, egg yolks, ½ teaspoon of the salt, ¼ teaspoon of the pepper, and the Essence in a mixing bowl.

3. LAYER one-third of the potatoes evenly in the bottom of the baking dish. Season lightly with the remaining salt and pepper. Sprinkle the cheese over the potatoes. Layer half of the apples over the cheese. Pour 1 cup of the cream mixture over the apples. Spread another layer of the potatoes over the apples, then firmly press down on the layers. Layer the remaining apples and potatoes, and pour the remaining cream mixture over all.

4. COVER the pan with foil. Bake for 30 minutes.

5. REMOVE the foil and continue to cook until the potatoes are tender and the top is bubbly and golden brown, 25 to 35 minutes. Let stand for 10 minutes before serving.

1 teaspoon unsalted butter
4 cups heavy cream
6 large egg yolks
1 teaspoon salt
½ teaspoon freshly ground white pepper
½ teaspoon Emeril's Original Essence or Creole Seasoning (page 9)
2 pounds Red Bliss potatoes, peeled and very thinly sliced
2 cups grated Gruyère (about 8 ounces)
2 pounds Rome or Winesap apples, peeled, cored, and very thinly sliced

CABBAGE AND POTATO BAKE

MAKES 6 SERVINGS

Instead of bacon, you can also use chopped pork sausage, cooking it until browned before adding it to the vegetables. This is a good accompaniment to Roasted Pork Loin (page 207), Spiced Baked Ham (page 206), corned beef, or even a big roast beef. We served it with lamb stew on a Saint Patrick's Day show.

1 head cabbage (2 to 2½ pounds), tough outer leaves removed
2 large Idaho potatoes (about 2½ pounds), peeled
¾ pound bacon, chopped
2 medium yellow onions, sliced thinly lengthwise
1 teaspoon salt
1 teaspoon freshly ground black pepper
2 cups Chicken Stock (page 2) or canned low-sodium chicken broth

1. **PREHEAT** the oven to 375°F.

2. **CUT** the cabbage into quarters and remove the hard core. Cut the cabbage quarters lengthwise in half. Peel the potatoes and cut crosswise in half. Cut the halves lengthwise into quarters. Arrange the cabbage and potatoes in alternating layers in a 9½ × 13½-inch roasting pan.

3. **FRY** the bacon in a large heavy skillet, stirring often, until just crisp, 6 to 8 minutes. Add the onions, salt, and pepper and cook until the onions are soft, about 5 minutes.

4. **DISTRIBUTE** the bacon mixture and pan drippings evenly over the vegetables. Add the chicken stock. Tightly cover the pan with aluminum foil. Bake until the potatoes are tender, about 1½ hours.

5. **LET** stand, covered, for 15 minutes before serving. Serve with the cooking juices.

SMASHED POTATO SALAD

MAKES 4 SERVINGS

Cowboys like this stuff. How do I know? Well, when we did a Wild, Wild West show on *Emeril Live* and paired this with a barbecued brisket, all we heard from the audience was "Yippee!" There are many variations on potato salad these days, but I love this smashed one. The technique of lightly smashing the potatoes in the bowl makes for a very unusual, tasty, tasty salad.

1. PLACE the potatoes in a large saucepan and add enough cold water to cover. Add 1 teaspoon of the salt. Bring to a boil over high heat. Reduce the heat to medium-low and simmer until fork-tender, about 10 minutes. Drain.

2. MASH the potatoes in a large mixing bowl with a hand-held masher or a heavy fork. They should still be lumpy. Mix in the onions, eggs, and garlic. Mix in ½ cup of the mayonnaise, the mustard, lemon juice, and brown sugar, stirring to dissolve the sugar. Add more mayonnaise if the salad is too dry. Season with the pepper sauce, Worcestershire, the remaining 1 teaspoon salt, and the pepper.

3. SERVE warm or chilled.

2 pounds new potatoes, scrubbed and cut into ½-inch pieces
2 teaspoons salt
½ cup minced yellow onions
3 Perfect Hard-Boiled Eggs (page 16), chopped
1 teaspoon minced garlic
½ to ¾ cup Mayonnaise (page 12) or store-bought mayonnaise
¼ cup Dijon mustard
2 tablespoons fresh lemon juice
1 tablespoon light brown sugar
½ teaspoon Emeril's Red Pepper Sauce or other hot pepper sauce
½ teaspoon Worcestershire sauce
1 teaspoon freshly ground black pepper

DRUNKEN HOMINY

Native Americans taught the colonists not only how to cultivate corn but also how to produce their many by-products, including hominy, grits, and cornmeal. After the hull and germ have been removed from the corn kernels, the kernels are dried to produce hominy. ■ When hominy is ground, it becomes grits, that great Southern dietary staple. Hominy is widely available, dried or canned, in supermarkets everywhere. Not many people think of serving hominy on its own—it's commonly seen as the Mexican soup Posole—but it really makes a great side dish or accompaniment to pork and chicken. This hominy has a definite Southwestern twist and is "drunken" from the tequila, which adds a nice little zip. Tasso is the heavily spiced cured pork that is popular in Cajun and Creole cuisines, and is a common ingredient in gumbos and stewed dishes. It definitely lends a kick to whatever you put it in but, if you like, substitute bacon or smoked ham, or leave out the meat altogether for a vegetarian offering.

2 tablespoons vegetable oil
1 cup finely chopped yellow onions
1 teaspoon salt
¼ teaspoon cayenne
½ pound Homemade Tasso (page 17) or ½ pound smoked ham, cut into ¼-inch cubes
¾ cup seeded and chopped tomatoes
2 teaspoons minced garlic
2 teaspoons minced jalapeños
Two 14½-ounce cans white hominy, rinsed and drained
1 tablespoon grated orange zest
½ cup tequila
½ cup fresh orange juice
2 teaspoons chili powder
1 teaspoon ground cumin
½ teaspoon ground coriander
¼ cup finely chopped green onions (green and white parts)
1 tablespoon minced fresh flat-leaf parsley
1 tablespoon minced fresh cilantro

1. HEAT the oil in a large heavy pot over medium-high heat. Add the onions, salt, and cayenne, and cook, stirring often, until the onions are softened, about 3 minutes. Add the tasso and cook until heated through, about 2 minutes. Add the tomatoes, garlic, and jalapeños. Cook, stirring often, until the tomatoes are heated through, about 1 minute. Add the hominy and orange zest and cook for 2 minutes longer.

2. ADD 1 cup water, the tequila, orange juice, chili powder, cumin, and coriander and bring to a simmer. Cook, uncovered, over medium heat until the liquid is slightly reduced, about 8 minutes.

3. STIR in the green onions, parsley, and cilantro. Serve hot.

TWICE-BAKED POTATOES WITH DUCK CONFIT

MAKES 12 SERVINGS

This king of baked potatoes was inspired by an *Emeril Live* comfort foods show. That day, we made duck confit and duck rillettes and stuffed the potatoes with the confit. When I made that dish, I realized that I really do love stuffed potatoes. You can substitute any of your favorite toppings; this just happens to be one of mine—as a meal in itself or an incredible, kicked-up side dish.

1. **PREHEAT** the oven to 350°F.

2. **RUB** the potatoes with the olive oil and season with ½ teaspoon of the salt and ⅛ teaspoon of the pepper. Put the potatoes on a heavy baking sheet and bake until fork-tender, about 1½ hours. Let cool until easy to handle (leave the oven on).

3. **CUT** each potato lengthwise in half. Scoop out the pulp with a melon baller or small spoon, leaving a ¼-inch border of potato pulp next to the skin, and put the pulp in a large mixing bowl. Return the potato shells to the baking sheet.

4. **MASH** the potato pulp with a fork. Add 1 cup of the cheese, the green onions, heavy cream, sour cream, butter, garlic, and truffle oil. Stir and mash until smooth. Fold in the confit and season with the remaining 1 teaspoon salt and ¼ teaspoon pepper. Add more cream if the mixture is too dry.

5. **STUFF** the potato shells with the potato mixture and sprinkle each with a few tablespoons of the remaining 1 cup cheese.

6. **BAKE** until the cheese on top is golden and bubbly, about 30 minutes. Serve immediately.

6 large Idaho potatoes, scrubbed
1 tablespoon olive oil
1½ teaspoons salt
3/8 teaspoon freshly ground black pepper
2 cups freshly grated extra-sharp white Cheddar (about 8 ounces)
¼ cup finely chopped green onions (green and white parts)
½ cup heavy cream or as needed
¼ cup sour cream
3 tablespoons unsalted butter
2 teaspoons finely chopped garlic
1½ teaspoons white truffle oil
2 cups Duck Confit (page 15) or cooked duck meat torn into bite-size pieces

EGGPLANT, TOMATO, AND FETA CHEESE NAPOLEONS

MAKES 4 SERVINGS

During the summer when eggplant and tomatoes are in season, I make these fabulous napoleons. They are a meal unto themselves! This makes plenty of pesto oil. Refrigerate the extra oil for one week, and use it on pasta or grilled shrimp.

PESTO OIL

2 cups loosely packed fresh basil leaves, washed and patted dry
2 teaspoons minced garlic
1 cup extra-virgin olive oil
1 teaspoon salt
½ teaspoon freshly ground black pepper

NAPOLEONS

1 medium eggplant
¼ cup plus 1 tablespoon extra-virgin olive oil
¼ cup balsamic vinegar
½ teaspoon salt
¼ teaspoon freshly ground black pepper
1 cup crumbled feta cheese or goat cheese (about 6 ounces)
2 tablespoons thinly sliced fresh basil leaves
2 large tomatoes, cored

1. **TO** make the pesto oil, pulse the basil and garlic in a food processor or blender until finely chopped. With the machine running, add the olive oil in a steady stream and process until well blended. Season with the salt and pepper. Transfer to a bowl and cover tightly.

2. **TO** make the napoleons, preheat the oven to 450°F.

3. **CUT** the eggplant crosswise into 12 slices about ¼ inch thick. Mix ¼ cup of the olive oil and the balsamic vinegar in a large bowl. Add the eggplant slices and toss to coat. Season with the salt and pepper.

4. **PLACE** the eggplant on a baking sheet in one layer and bake until soft, turning once, about 15 minutes. Let cool.

5. **IN** a small bowl, combine the cheese, basil, and the remaining 1 tablespoon of olive oil.

6. **SLICE** each tomato crosswise into 4 slices about ⅓ inch thick. Place 1 eggplant slice on a salad plate. Top with about 1 tablespoon of the cheese mixture, then a tomato slice. Drizzle 1 teaspoon of pesto oil over the tomato, then top with another tablespoon of cheese. Repeat with another eggplant slice, 1 tablespoon cheese, a tomato slice, and 1 teaspoon pesto oil. Finish with a final eggplant slice, another tablespoon of cheese, and a drizzle of pesto oil. Repeat with the remaining ingredients.

7. **SERVE** at room temperature, with pesto oil drizzled around each napoleon.

CAPONATA

Beware—this Sicilian-style eggplant relish is completely addictive! When I cooked it on an *Emeril Live* eggplant show, I accompanied it with grilled swordfish fillets that had simply been rubbed with a little olive oil, salt, and pepper before cooking. It's also a great match for grilled meats, and it makes a delicious hors d'oeuvre when spread on top of Croutons (page 258). Or toss it with some cooked pasta. While this recipe makes almost 5 cups, you'll find it goes quickly. If you've got any left over, just refrigerate it, tightly covered, for up to 1 week.

1. COMBINE the vinegar and sugar in a small saucepan over medium heat. Cook, stirring, until the sugar dissolves, about 2 minutes. Remove from the heat and let cool.

2. HEAT the oil in a large heavy saucepan over medium-high heat. Add the onions and cook, stirring occasionally, until softened, about 3 minutes. Add the garlic and stir until fragrant, about 30 seconds. Add the eggplant and salt and cook, stirring occasionally, until the eggplant is softened, about 6 minutes. Add the tomatoes and cook, stirring occasionally, until the caponata thickens, about 12 minutes.

3. ADD the olives and pine nuts. Stir in the vinegar mixture, a tablespoon at a time, until the desired flavor and consistency is reached (the caponata mixture should be sweet-and-sour and not too thin). Stir in the basil. Adjust the seasoning with salt if necessary, and serve warm or chilled.

1/3 cup red wine vinegar
1/3 cup sugar
1/4 cup olive oil
1/2 cup chopped yellow onions
1 tablespoon minced garlic
1 large eggplant (about 2 pounds), finely chopped
1/2 teaspoon salt, or more to taste
2 cups seeded and chopped tomatoes (about 4 large)
1 cup pitted and chopped green olives
1 cup toasted pine nuts
1/3 cup finely chopped fresh basil

ROASTED VEGETABLE AND GOAT CHEESE TERRINE WITH SUN-DRIED TOMATO SAUCE

This recipe is one we created for an *Essence of Emeril* terrines show. This dish makes an amazing presentation. The roasted eggplant encloses the vegetable and goat cheese layers, so that when you slice into this, you get great ribbons of color. The Sun-Dried Tomato Sauce is a burst of summer flavors that would also be great served with fish or chicken.

About ½ cup olive oil

One 1-pound eggplant, trimmed and cut lengthwise into ¼-inch slices

1 pound zucchini, trimmed and cut lengthwise into ¼-inch slices

1½ pounds yellow squash, trimmed and cut lengthwise into ¼-inch slices

1 teaspoon salt

¾ teaspoon freshly ground black pepper

10 ounces goat cheese

2 tablespoons minced fresh basil

2 tablespoons minced fresh flat-leaf parsley

2 tablespoons extra-virgin olive oil

2 large red bell peppers (about 1 pound), roasted, with cores, seeds, and skins removed

1 pound fresh spinach, washed and stems removed, blanched, and squeezed dry

2 large yellow bell peppers (about 1 pound), roasted, with cores, seeds, and skins removed

1. PREHEAT the oven to 425°F.

2. LINE 2 large baking sheets with aluminum foil and grease with ¼ cup of the olive oil.

3. COMBINE the eggplant, zucchini, and squash slices in a large bowl. Add ¾ teaspoon salt, ½ teaspoon pepper, and the remaining olive oil. Toss to coat evenly. Lay half of the vegetable mixture in a layer on the pans and bake until soft and just golden around the edges, 8 to 10 minutes. Remove from the oven and transfer to a plate to cool. Repeat with the remaining vegetable mixture.

4. COMBINE the goat cheese with the basil, parsley, and extra-virgin olive oil in a large bowl. Season with the remaining salt and pepper and mix well.

5. IN a 6-cup terrine (12 × 3 × 3 inches), arrange the eggplant slices across the bottom and over the sides, overlapping the slices to cover the terrine completely. Top with slices of red bell pepper, zucchini, squash, spinach, and yellow bell pepper. Crumble a layer of the goat cheese mixture on top of the yellow pepper, and repeat layering with the remaining vegetable slices. Wrap the overhanging eggplant over the bottom of the terrine. Wrap the terrine loosely in plastic wrap. Top with a terrine of equal size or a piece of cardboard wrapped in aluminum foil. Place a brick on top of the terrine and refrigerate at least 8 hours and up to 24 hours.

6. REMOVE from the refrigerator. Remove the weight and unwrap. Slice with a very sharp knife and serve one large or two thin slices per person with the Sun-Dried Tomato Sauce and toasted croutons.

Sun-Dried Tomato Sauce

1. COMBINE the sun-dried tomatoes, balsamic vinegar, garlic, salt, crushed red pepper flakes and black pepper in a food processor. Purée on high speed. With the motor running, gradually add the oil through the feed tube and process until well blended.

2. SET aside until ready to serve with the terrine.

1 cup tightly packed sun-dried tomatoes (not oil-packed), reconstituted in hot water and drained
1 teaspoon balsamic vinegar
4 garlic cloves, minced
1/4 teaspoon salt
1/4 teaspoon crushed red pepper flakes
1/8 teaspoon freshly ground black pepper
1 1/4 cups extra-virgin olive oil

the recipes

BREADS

Anyone can learn to make biscuits and corn bread. Once you have those quick breads under your belt, it's time to move onto yeast breads like the Oregano Flatbread and the Grape, Stilton, and Walnut Focaccia. Don't close the book when you see the word yeast! ▪ Kid-friendly breads include the Olive and Garlic Pretzels and the Spicy Sausage and Cheese Rolls. (And don't forget pizza.) Make bread baking a family event.

OLIVE AND GARLIC PRETZELS

MAKES 18 PRETZELS

Two of my favorite ingredients—garlic and olives—are included in this recipe. You know how I love street food, and what's better than pretzels? I made these on one of the shows about street food. This is a great item to make for a family project. Let the kids help you put the dough together, then shape the pretzels for a fun job. If the dough becomes too dry when you're rolling these out, first dampen your hands slightly and continue. When dipped in mustard, the pretzels are a terrific snack item for a cocktail party. Anchovies aren't your thing? Leave them out.

¾ cup pitted kalamata or other brine-cured black olives
2 anchovy fillets, drained
2 tablespoons olive oil
1 tablespoon chopped garlic
Pinch of freshly ground black pepper
One ¼-ounce envelope active dry yeast
2 tablespoons sugar
2 tablespoons vegetable oil
1½ cups warm (about 110°F) milk
4 to 4½ cups bleached all-purpose flour
1 teaspoon salt
1 tablespoon kosher salt
1 cup Creole or other spicy whole-grain mustard for dipping (optional)
1 large egg yolk, beaten with 1 tablespoon water, for glaze

1. COMBINE the olives, anchovies, 1 tablespoon of the olive oil, the garlic, and pepper in a food processor and pulse to make a thick paste.

2. COMBINE the yeast, sugar, and 1 tablespoon of the vegetable oil in the bowl of an electric mixer fitted with a dough hook. Add the milk and, with the mixer on low speed, mix for 4 minutes to dissolve the yeast. Add the flour, salt, and the olive paste and mix until the dough begins to come together. Increase the speed to medium and beat until the dough pulls away from the sides of the bowl and forms a tight ball, about 2 minutes. (Alternatively, dissolve the yeast, sugar, and 1 tablespoon of the olive oil in the warm milk in a large bowl. Let sit until foamy, about 5 minutes. Add the flour, salt, and the olive paste, stirring well with a wooden spoon to incorporate all the flour. Place dough on an unfloured surface and knead until smooth, 3 to 5 minutes.)

3. OIL a large mixing bowl with the remaining 1 tablespoon vegetable oil. Remove the dough from the mixer, place it in the bowl, and turn it to oil all sides. Cover with plastic wrap or a damp kitchen towel. Let stand in a warm, draft-free place until it doubles in size, about 2 hours.

4. PREHEAT the oven to 400°F. Grease two large baking sheets with the remaining 1 tablespoon olive oil.

5. TURN the dough out onto an unfloured surface. Roll it into a 12 × 10-inch rectangle. With a sharp knife, cut the dough into 18 pieces. One at a time, gently roll and pull each one into a long, thin rope about ½ inch in diameter and 14 inches long. To make the pretzel shape, bring the ends up to form a U-shape and twist to form a wreath, then bring the ends down and across the bottom of the wreath like a bow, pressing down to seal the ends, and place on an ungreased baking sheet.

6. BRUSH the pretzels with the egg glaze and sprinkle with the kosher salt.

7. ARRANGE the pretzels 1 inch apart on the prepared baking sheets. Bake, switching the position of the sheets from top to bottom halfway through baking, until golden brown, about 20 to 25 minutes.

8. SERVE warm with the mustard for dipping.

SPICY SAUSAGE AND CHEESE ROLLS

MAKES 24 ROLLS

Here's a prime example of why pork fat rules! Sausage and cheese are mixed into the dough to make dynamite dinner rolls. I prepared these on a show to demonstrate how easy it is to make good little breads. Be careful—everybody will be fighting over these, because no one is going to want to share!

½ pound andouille, kielbasa, or other smoked spicy sausage, removed from casing and coarsely chopped (about 2 cups)

1 cup minced yellow onions

1 tablespoon minced jalapeños

2 teaspoons minced garlic

One ¼-ounce envelope active dry yeast

2 tablespoons sugar

2 cups warm (about 110°F) water

2 tablespoons plus 1 teaspoon vegetable oil

5 to 5½ cups bleached all-purpose flour

¾ cup plus 1 tablespoon yellow cornmeal

2 teaspoons salt

2 cups grated white Cheddar (about 8 ounces)

1. **HEAT** a medium heavy nonstick skillet over medium-high heat. Add the sausage and cook, stirring, for 5 minutes. Add the onions and cook, stirring, until lightly golden, about 5 minutes. Add the jalapeños and garlic and cook, stirring often, for 2 minutes. Using a slotted spoon, transfer the mixture to paper towels to drain and cool.

2. **COMBINE** the yeast, sugar, water, and 2 tablespoons of the oil in a small bowl. Let stand for about 5 minutes, then whisk to dissolve the yeast and sugar.

3. **COMBINE** 5 cups of the flour, ¾ cup of the cornmeal, the salt, the Cheddar, the sausage-onion mixture, and the yeast mixture in the bowl of a large electric mixer fitted with a dough hook. Mix on low speed until the dough comes together and forms a ball, about 3 minutes. If the dough is too moist, add ¼ cup flour and mix to incorporate, about 1 minute. Check the dough consistency again, and add some or all of the remaining ¼ cup flour if needed. After the dough forms a ball, knead with the dough hook for 5 minutes longer.

4. **COAT** a large mixing bowl with the remaining 1 teaspoon vegetable oil. Remove the dough from the mixer, place it in the bowl, and turn it to oil all sides. Cover with plastic wrap or a clean damp towel. Let stand in a warm, draft-free place until it doubles in size, about 2 hours.

5. SPRINKLE the remaining 1 tablespoon cornmeal over two large baking sheets.

6. REMOVE the dough from the bowl and divide it into 3 equal portions. Roll each portion out under your hands on a lightly floured surface into a log about 24 inches long. Cut each log into 8 equal portions. One at a time, gently push down the dough while rolling it under your hand in a circular motion to form a smooth ball. Place the balls about 1½ inches apart on the prepared baking sheets.

7. SNIP the top center of each roll with kitchen shears to form an X. Cover the rolls with plastic wrap. Let stand in a warm, draft-free place, until they double in size, about 30 minutes.

8. MEANWHILE preheat the oven to 400°F.

9. REMOVE the plastic wrap. Bake the rolls, switching the positions of the sheets from top to bottom halfway through the baking time, until golden brown, about 20 minutes. Serve hot.

CHOCOLATE BREAD

Man, oh, man, is this bread ever good right out of the oven, spread with a little bit of butter! But it's equally good toasted for breakfast the next day. If you want to kick it up to notches unknown, make French toast out of this for an amazing brunch. This would also make an awesome bread pudding in place of regular bread.

1 tablespoon vegetable oil
One ¼-ounce envelope active dry yeast
2 tablespoons dark brown sugar
1½ cups warm (about 110°F) water
3½ to 4 cups bread flour
1 teaspoon salt
¼ cup unsweetened cocoa powder

1. LIGHTLY grease a 9 × 13-inch loaf pan with 2 teaspoons of the oil.

2. COMBINE the yeast, brown sugar, and water in a large mixing bowl. Stir with a wooden spoon to dissolve. Let stand for 5 minutes, or until the yeast looks creamy.

3. ADD 3½ cups of flour, the salt, and cocoa, stirring well to blend, adding more flour as needed to make a slightly sticky dough. Turn out onto a lightly floured surface. Knead until the dough comes together into a smooth, supple mass but is still slightly sticky, about 5 minutes.

4. LIGHTLY oil a large mixing bowl with the remaining 1 teaspoon oil. Put the dough in the bowl and turn it to oil all sides. Cover with plastic wrap or a clean damp kitchen towel. Let stand in a warm, draft-free place until it doubles in size, about 1½ hours.

5. TURN the dough out onto a lightly floured surface and pat into a rectangle about 1 inch thick. Fold one-third of the long end over toward the center, pressing down on the edge to seal. Fold the dough two more times toward the center, pressing and sealing both times, and pinching seams so they disappear into the dough. Roll the dough into a loaf shape and put in the greased loaf pan. Cover with plastic wrap and let rise until it doubles in size, about 30 minutes.

6. PREHEAT the oven to 400°F.

7. REMOVE the plastic. Bake until the bottom of the loaf makes a hollow sound when thumped with your fingers (take it out of the pan), about 30 minutes. Cool in the pan for 10 minutes, then turn out onto a wire rack and cool for at least 15 minutes before serving.

OREGANO FLATBREAD

MAKES 6 WEDGES

Flatbreads are fairly quick and easy, and they're also very versatile. Flavor yours with whatever herbs you have on hand, such as sage or basil. Holes may form when you're flattening the dough before baking it; don't worry about them, they just add character to the final bread.

1. COMBINE the yeast and water in a large bowl and let stand for 5 minutes, or until the yeast looks creamy. Stir to dissolve the yeast. Stir in 3 tablespoons of the olive oil, the oregano, and garlic. Add the flour and salt, and stir well until a smooth ball forms.

2. SPRINKLE the cornmeal over a large baking sheet and place the dough in the center. Cover with plastic wrap or a damp kitchen towel and put in a warm, draft-free place to rise until it doubles in size, about 50 minutes.

3. PREHEAT the oven to 400°F.

4. REMOVE the towel. Flatten the dough into a round with a rolling pin. Cut into 6 equal wedges. Flatten each wedge, pressing firmly with the palm of your hand, until very thin, about 1/8 inch. Transfer to ungreased baking sheets.

5. BAKE until golden brown, 10 to 12 minutes, switching the positions of the sheets from top to bottom halfway through the baking. Remove from the oven. Brush the wedges with the remaining 1 tablespoon olive oil and sprinkle with the kosher salt before serving.

1 teaspoon active dry yeast
3/4 cup warm (about 110°F) water
1/4 cup olive oil
2 tablespoons coarsely chopped fresh oregano
1 tablespoon minced garlic
2 cups bleached all-purpose flour
1/2 teaspoon salt
About 1/4 cup cornmeal for dusting
1 teaspoon kosher salt

HOMESTYLE ROLLS

MAKES 20 ROLLS

You're not going to believe how easy these rolls are. Yes, it will take you a bit of time to make them, but the process isn't difficult. Just make sure you set aside enough time for the first and second risings, and shape them into uniform-size balls.

2 cups warm (about 110°F) water
Two ¼-ounce envelopes active
  dry yeast
1 tablespoon plus 2 teaspoons
  sugar
2½ teaspoons salt
5 cups bleached all-purpose flour
2 teaspoons vegetable or
  olive oil
2 tablespoons yellow cornmeal
  for dusting
1 large egg yolk beaten with
  1 tablespoon water, for glaze

1. COMBINE the water, yeast, sugar, and salt in a large mixing bowl. Whisk with a fork until the yeast is dissolved. Mix in the flour ¼ cup at a time, stirring with a large wooden spoon, until the dough comes away from the sides of the bowl and forms a ball. (Alternatively, this can be done with a heavy-duty electric mixer fitted with a dough hook. Combine the water, yeast, and sugar in the bowl of the mixer. Add the salt and 4 cups of the flour and, with the mixer on low speed, beat until combined. Add the remaining 1 cup flour and, with the mixer on high, mix until the dough climbs up the hook, about 3 minutes.)

2. LIGHTLY oil a large bowl with the oil. Put the dough in the bowl and turn to oil on all sides. Cover the bowl with plastic wrap or a kitchen towel. Let stand in a warm, draft-free place until the dough doubles in size, 1½ to 2 hours.

3. SPRINKLE a large baking sheet with the cornmeal.

4. TURN the dough out onto a lightly floured surface and divide it into 20 pieces. One at a time, cup your hand over a piece of dough and gently push down on the dough while rolling it in a circular motion under your hand to form a smooth ball. Arrange the rolls about 1 inch apart on the prepared baking sheet. Cover with plastic wrap or a kitchen towel. Let stand in a warm, draft-free place until they double in size, about 30 minutes.

5. PREHEAT the oven to 400°F.

6. BRUSH the tops and sides of the rolls evenly with the egg glaze. Bake until golden brown, about 30 minutes. Cool for 10 minutes on the baking sheet, then serve warm.

CORN BREAD

MAKES ONE 9-INCH ROUND BREAD (ABOUT 6 SERVINGS)

Corn bread goes well with the Pecan-Crusted Chicken (page 175) or the Cornmeal-Crusted Redfish (page 116). Add some corn kernels or chopped jalapeños to the batter if you like. Or, if you're going to use it to make a dressing, like for Andouille-Stuffed Double-Cut Pork Chops (page 204), prepare the corn bread ahead of time and let it sit overnight to dry out slightly before using. My wife, Alden, wants me to remind you that true Southern corn bread never has sugar in it.

¼ cup plus 1 tablespoon vegetable oil
1 cup yellow cornmeal
1 cup bleached all-purpose flour
2 teaspoons baking powder
1 teaspoon salt
¼ teaspoon cayenne
1 cup buttermilk
1 large egg

1. PREHEAT the oven to 400°F.

2. PUT 1 tablespoon of the vegetable oil into a 9-inch round baking pan or cast-iron skillet. Put it in the oven to heat for at least 10 minutes.

3. STIR together the cornmeal, flour, baking powder, salt, and cayenne in a large mixing bowl. Add the buttermilk, the remaining 1/4 cup oil, and the egg and stir just to blend.

4. POUR the batter into the preheated pan. Bake until lightly golden brown, about 25 minutes. Let cool for 10 minutes before serving.

GRAPE, STILTON, AND WALNUT FOCACCIA

MAKES 6 SERVINGS

You might think of focaccia as a simple bread for dipping into olive oil. But it's really very adaptable, and you can make it with a variety of toppings, like the grapes and cheese I added on an *Essence of Emeril* "Savory Fruit" show. This is one of those simple but delicious things you can have before dinner with a glass of great red wine or after with some port. Or, if you're doing a cheese tasting, let this be your blue cheese contribution to the table.

1½ cups warm (about 110°F) water
1 tablespoon sugar
One ¼-ounce envelope active dry yeast
4 cups bleached all-purpose flour, or more as needed
2 teaspoons salt
¼ cup plus 2 teaspoons extra-virgin olive oil
1½ cups halved red seedless grapes
1 cup crumbled Stilton cheese
½ cup toasted walnut pieces

1. **COMBINE** the warm water and sugar in a small bowl and stir to dissolve the sugar. Sprinkle the yeast into the water and let stand for about 5 minutes, until creamy.

2. **COMBINE** 3½ cups of the flour, the salt, and the yeast mixture in the bowl of an electric mixer fitted with a paddle attachment. Mix on low speed with a dough hook until the dough comes together and forms a ball, 2 to 3 minutes. Increase the speed to medium and knead with the hook for 5 minutes. If the dough is still sticky, continue mixing and gradually add as much of the remaining ½ cup flour as needed.

3. **OIL** a large mixing bowl with 2 teaspoons of the oil. Put the dough in the bowl and turn to coat all sides with oil. Cover with plastic wrap or a damp kitchen towel. Let stand in a warm, draft-free place until the dough doubles in size, about 1½ hours.

4. **GREASE** a 9 × 13-inch baking sheet with 1 tablespoon of the olive oil. Turn the dough out onto the baking sheet and press it evenly over the bottom of the pan. Cover with plastic wrap and set in a warm, draft-free place until it rises to nearly 1 inch thick, about 30 minutes.

5. PREHEAT the oven to 400°F.

6. MAKE dimples in the dough at 3-inch intervals with your fingertips. Drizzle with 1 tablespoon of the olive oil and bake until just golden brown, 25 minutes.

7. REMOVE from the oven and drizzle with 1 tablespoon of the olive oil. Press the grapes into the dough. Return to the oven and bake until lightly golden brown, about 10 minutes. Remove from the oven and sprinkle with the cheese and walnuts. Bake until the cheese melts, about 5 minutes.

8. DRIZZLE the focaccia with the remaining 1 tablespoon olive oil. With a long spatula, transfer the bread to a rack and let cool slightly. Cut into squares and serve warm, or let cool to room temperature.

CROUTONS

Sure, it's easy to pick up crackers at the store, but there's nothing like having homemade croutons (or French bread toasts) to use with your spreads and dips. These have a fantastic crunch, and the freshness just can't be beat. And if you're one of those Caesar salad addicts who loves croutons in your salad, just rub these with a split garlic clove before toasting them, then cube them when they come out of the oven.

1 loaf French or Italian bread,
    cut into twenty ½-inch-thick
    slices
¼ cup olive oil
¼ teaspoon salt
⅛ teaspoon freshly ground black
    pepper

1. PREHEAT the oven to 400°F.

2. SPREAD the slices of bread on a large baking sheet. Brush the tops of the slices with the olive oil, then season with the salt and pepper. Bake until lightly golden brown, about 15 minutes. Cool completely.

BUTTERMILK BISCUITS

MAKES 12 BISCUITS

For breakfast, lunch, or dinner, buttermilk biscuits just can't be beat! Like most Southerners, I like to eat these in place of dinner rolls. You also could serve these with our Barbecued Oysters (page 94) or use instead of sliced bread for sandwiches. Now, I made these on an *Emeril Live* "Southern Secrets" show, and there is a secret to making great biscuits: don't overwork the dough! Mix it just until it comes together, and leave in those lumps.

2 cups bleached all-purpose flour
1 tablespoon baking powder
1 teaspoon salt
¼ teaspoon baking soda
6 tablespoons (¾ stick) chilled unsalted butter, plus more for serving
1 cup buttermilk

1. **PREHEAT** the oven to 425°F.

2. **SIFT** the flour, baking powder, salt, and baking soda into a large mixing bowl. Add the butter and work it in with your fingers or a fork until the mixture resembles coarse crumbs. Stir in the buttermilk just until the dough comes together, being very careful not to overwork the dough.

3. **LIGHTLY** dust a work surface with flour. Turn the dough out onto the work surface and pat into a ½-inch-thick round. Cut out the biscuits with a 2-inch cookie cutter, re-rolling the scraps. Place the biscuits about 1 inch apart on an ungreased baking sheet.

4. **BAKE** until golden on top and lightly brown on the bottom, about 12 minutes.

5. **SERVE** warm with butter.

the recipes

DESSERTS

Ah, desserts! I'm convinced that just about everyone has a sweet tooth that needs to be satisfied. I think our lineup in this chapter will please most palates. ▓ For the chocolate lovers, we have the Sour Cream Fudge Cake, the Mississippi Mud Cake, and Mr. Lou's Chocolate Praline Pie. ▓ For those of you with simpler tastes, I recommend the Berry Tiramisu and the Raspberry Sorbet. ▓ Sweet things, as far as I'm concerned, end the meal on a happy note. ▓ Sweets for the sweet!

MISSISSIPPI MUD CAKE

MAKES 1 CAKE

This Southern classic combines coffee, bourbon, and chocolate for a delicious crowd-pleaser. For you chocolate lovers who may have watched our show on chocolate, this is a very simple cake to make. Top yours with some homemade ice cream—vanilla's my favorite.

½ pound (2 sticks) plus
   2 teaspoons unsalted butter,
   cut into ½-inch pieces
1 tablespoon unsweetened cocoa
   powder
2 cups bleached all-purpose flour
1 teaspoon baking soda
⅛ teaspoon salt
½ cup bourbon
1½ cups strong brewed coffee,
   cooled
5 ounces unsweetened
   chocolate, chopped
1¾ cups sugar
1 teaspoon pure vanilla extract
2 large eggs, lightly beaten

1. **PREHEAT** the oven to 275°F.

2. **GREASE** a Bundt pan with 2 teaspoons of the butter, then lightly dust with the cocoa.

3. **SIFT** the flour with the baking soda and salt into a bowl, and set aside.

4. **WARM** the bourbon and coffee in the top of a double boiler or a stainless steel bowl set over a pan of simmering water for 5 minutes. Add the chocolate and remaining butter and cook, stirring, until melted and smooth, about 3 minutes. Remove from the heat. Add the sugar and stir to dissolve. Cool slightly.

5. **USING** a whisk or an electric mixer, stir the flour, ½ cup at a time, into the chocolate. Add the vanilla and eggs, whisking to mix well.

6. **POUR** the batter into the prepared pan and bake for 1 hour. (The cake will be slightly soft in the middle.)

7. **REMOVE** from the oven and let rest in the pan for 20 minutes, then turn out onto a cooling rack to cool for at least 30 minutes before serving.

SOUR CREAM FUDGE CAKE

MAKES 12 SERVINGS

For a show on comfort food on *Emeril Live*, we offered this simple cake for those days when you have the blues and feel down in the dumps, and only chocolate will do. Talk about food as medicine!

1. **TO** make the cake, preheat the oven to 350°F. Butter a 9 × 13 × 2-inch baking pan with 1 tablespoon of the butter and set aside.

2. **DISSOLVE** the coffee in the hot water and let cool. Sift together the flour, cornstarch, baking soda, and salt onto a large sheet of waxed paper.

3. **CREAM** the remaining 8 tablespoons butter and the sugar in a medium bowl with an electric mixer on high speed until light and fluffy, scraping down the sides as needed, about 3 minutes. Add the sour cream and mix well. In three additions, add the flour mixture, alternating with the eggs, beating well after each addition and scraping down the sides of the bowl as needed. Beat in the melted chocolate, dissolved coffee, and vanilla. Spread the batter in the prepared pan.

4. **BAKE** until a toothpick inserted in the center of the cake comes out clean, 40 to 45 minutes. Cool on a large wire rack for 10 minutes. Carefully run a knife around the edges of the cake, invert onto the rack, and cool completely.

5. **TO** make the icing, beat the butter in a large bowl with an electric mixer on high speed until fluffy, about 2 minutes. On low speed, beat in the sugar, about ¼ cup at a time, until smooth. Add the cooled chocolate and vanilla and mix well. If not using immediately, cover tightly with plastic wrap until ready to use.

6. **SLICE** the cake in half horizontally. Transfer the bottom, cut side up, to a platter. Spread half of the icing over the cake with a metal icing spatula. Top with the top half of the cake, cut side down. Spread the remaining icing over the top and sides of the cake. Sift the ¼ cup confectioners' sugar through a fine wire sieve to garnish, if desired. Serve at room temperature.

CAKE
- 8 tablespoons (1 stick) plus 1 tablespoon unsalted butter, at room temperature
- 2 teaspoons powdered instant coffee
- ⅓ cup hot water
- 1½ cups bleached all-purpose flour
- ½ cup cornstarch
- 1 teaspoon baking soda
- 1 teaspoon salt
- 1½ cups sugar
- 1 cup sour cream
- 2 large eggs
- 2 ounces unsweetened chocolate, melted
- 1 teaspoon pure vanilla extract

ICING
- ½ pound (2 sticks) unsalted butter, at room temperature
- 2 cups (about ½ pound) confectioners' sugar
- 6 ounces unsweetened chocolate, melted and cooled
- ½ teaspoon pure vanilla extract
- ¼ cup confectioners' sugar for garnish (optional)

PUMPKIN CHEESECAKE

MAKES 10 TO 12 SERVINGS

Looking for something other than pumpkin pie at Thanksgiving? I made this pumpkin cheesecake on *Good Morning America* for the holidays. But you don't have to wait for Turkey Day to make this, since I used canned solid-pack pumpkin purée, which is available year-round at well-stocked supermarkets.

1¾ cups graham cracker crumbs
¼ cup finely ground pecans
1 tablespoon light brown sugar
1 teaspoon ground cinnamon
8 tablespoons (1 stick) unsalted
 butter, melted
Three 8-ounce packages cream
 cheese, at room temperature
1½ cups sugar
2 tablespoons cornstarch
1 teaspoon pure vanilla extract
⅛ teaspoon freshly grated
 nutmeg
2 large eggs
2 large egg yolks
One 15-ounce can solid-pack
 pumpkin purée
¼ cup heavy cream

1. **PREHEAT** the oven to 350°F.

2. **COMBINE** the cracker crumbs, pecans, brown sugar, and ½ teaspoon of the cinnamon in a medium bowl. Mix in the melted butter. Press the mixture firmly and evenly into the bottom and about 1 inch up the sides of an ungreased 9-inch springform pan.

3. **BEAT** the cream cheese, sugar, cornstarch, vanilla, the remaining ½ teaspoon cinnamon, and the nutmeg in the bowl of an electric mixer on low speed until smooth and fluffy, scraping down the sides of the bowl as needed. Add the eggs and yolks and beat just until blended. Mix in the pumpkin and cream. Spread the batter in the pan, and place it on a baking sheet.

4. **BAKE** until the center is nearly set, 60 to 70 minutes. Cool on a wire rack for 15 minutes.

5. **CAREFULLY** run a sharp knife between the cake and the sides of the pan. Remove the sides of the pan. Cool completely on the rack before covering tightly with aluminum foil or plastic wrap. Refrigerate until well chilled before serving, at least 4 hours or up to 2 days.

MR. LOU'S CHOCOLATE PRALINE PIE

MAKES ONE 9-INCH PIE TO SERVE ABOUT 8

Mr. Lou Lynch has been the pastry chef at Emeril's in New Orleans since we opened. I am always amazed at his creativity with simple ingredients that he has in his pastry area. When we did a baker's pantry show for *Emeril Live*, I knew I had to include something from Mr. Lou. When we first put this recipe on the dessert menu at Emeril's, people went crazy! And is this ever rich! Mr. Lou uses Hawaiian Vintage Chocolate when he makes his pies, a superb chocolate grown and made in Hawaii, but feel free to substitute any semisweet chocolate you can get in your area. And, yes, go ahead and make the pralines yourself. Even though you only need 1 cup of crumbled pralines for this recipe, I'm sure you'll find a few friends and loved ones who'll enjoy helping you eat them!

1. **COMBINE** the cream, cornstarch, brown sugar, and cane syrup in a saucepan. Cook over medium-high heat, and whisk until a slightly thick custard forms, 10 to 12 minutes. Stir in the chocolate and mix well. Remove from the heat and place a piece of waxed paper directly on top of the custard to prevent a film from forming. Cool completely.

2. **FOLD** half of the crumbled pralines into the cooled custard, then pour the mixture into the prepared shell. Sprinkle the remaining pralines on top. Cover tightly with plastic wrap and refrigerate for at least 4 hours before serving.

2 cups heavy cream
¼ cup cornstarch
½ cup packed light brown sugar
½ cup Steen's 100% Pure Cane Syrup (see Source Guide, page 282)
1 cup semisweet chocolate, melted
1 cup crumbled Crunchy Pralines (page 267)
One 9-inch Chocolate Graham Cracker Crust (recipe follows), baked and chilled

Chocolate Graham Cracker Crust

1 cup graham cracker crumbs

¾ cup finely ground Oreo
  cookies (chocolate cookies
  only, cream stuffing removed)

4 tablespoons unsalted butter,
  melted

2 tablespoons sugar

1 egg white

1. PREHEAT the oven to 375°F.

2. COMBINE all the ingredients in a bowl and blend with a mixer or by hand. Transfer the mixture to a 9-inch pie pan, and press into the bottom and up the sides with your fingers. Place another 9-inch pie pan on top of the crust and press firmly to smooth and pack the crust. (Some of the crust may spill over the edges of the pan.)

3. BAKE until golden, 10 to 15 minutes. Remove from the oven and cool. Brush the crust with the egg white. Refrigerate, tightly covered, for one hour before using, or freeze for up to six weeks.

Crunchy Pralines

MAKES ABOUT 2 DOZEN

1. LINE a large baking sheet with wax paper.

2. COMBINE the brown sugar, butter, and water in a heavy saucepan over medium heat. Stir to dissolve the sugar. Continue to stir for 3 to 4 minutes. The mixture will begin to boil. Add the pecans and continue to stir for about 5 minutes.

3. REMOVE from the heat. Drop by the spoonful onto the wax paper. Let cool. Remove from the paper with a thin knife.

4. PRALINES may be store in an airtight container at room temperature for about two weeks.

1 pound light brown sugar
  (about 2½ packed cups)
2 tablespoons butter
¼ cup water
2 cups pecan pieces

BERRY TIRAMISU

MAKES 6 TO 8 SERVINGS

We made this three-berry dessert on an *Essence of Emeril* show. Don't confuse this with traditional tiramisu, a pudding-like dessert with layers of coffee-soaked ladyfingers, creamy mascarpone cheese, and other decadent ingredients. We use the mascarpone, but replace the ladyfingers with homemade pound cake and layer it with berries. You'll use just half of the pound cake, but I guarantee the rest won't go to waste. Slice and toast the leftover cake and spread it with a little butter for breakfast. Here's another idea: Make ice cream sandwiches with frozen cake slices.

1½ cups raspberries, rinsed and patted dry
1 cup blueberries, rinsed and patted dry
1 cup strawberries, rinsed, patted dry, hulled, and quartered
2 tablespoons granulated sugar
½ cup plus 3 tablespoons Chambord or other raspberry-flavored liqueur or ruby port
Raspberry Coulis (page 269)
2 cups heavy cream
½ cup confectioners' sugar
1 pound mascarpone
Eight ½-inch-thick slices Pound Cake (recipe follows), (about half of the cake)
Fresh mint sprigs, for garnish

1. **GENTLY** stir the raspberries, blueberries, and strawberries in a bowl with the granulated sugar, 2 tablespoons of the Chambord, and ½ cup of the raspberry coulis.

2. **WHIP** the heavy cream in a large bowl with an electric mixer on high speed or a whisk until it thickens and almost doubles in volume. Add ¼ cup of the confectioners' sugar and 1 tablespoon of the Chambord and whip until stiff peaks form.

3. **IN** a medium bowl, whip the mascarpone with the remaining ¼ cup confectioners' sugar with an electric mixer on low speed until smooth. Fold in half of the whipped cream.

4. **SPREAD** half the pound cake slices in the bottom of an 6 × 9-inch pan. Drizzle the remaining ¼ cup Chambord over the cake and cover with half of the berry mixture. Cover the berries with half of the mascarpone cream, gently spreading it into a smooth layer with a rubber spatula. Repeat with the remaining ingredients and top with a smooth layer of the remaining whipped cream. Cover tightly with plastic wrap. Refrigerate for at least 2 hours, and up to 1½ days.

5. **SPOON** into bowls and garnish with the mint sprigs. Serve with the remaining raspberry coulis spooned over each serving or passed on the side.

Pound Cake

MAKES 8 TO 10 SERVINGS

1. PREHEAT the oven to 325°F. Butter a 8½ × 4½ × 2½-inch loaf pan with the shortening and flour with 2 teaspoons of the flour, tapping out the excess.

2. SIFT the remaining 2 cups flour, the baking powder, and salt into a medium bowl.

3. CREAM the butter and sugar in a medium bowl with an electric mixer on high speed, scraping down the sides of the bowl as needed, until light and fluffy, about 3 minutes. On low speed, in three additions, beat in the flour, alternating with 1 egg at a time, scraping down the sides of the bowl as needed. Beat in the vanilla just until blended. Spread evenly in the prepared pan.

4. BAKE until the cake is golden brown and a cake tester or toothpick comes out clean, about 1 hour and 10 minutes. Cool on a wire cake rack for 10 minutes.

5. TURN the cake out onto the rack, turn right side up, and let cool for at least 30 minutes. Serve warm or at room temperature.

1 teaspoon vegetable shortening, for the pan
2 cups plus 2 teaspoons bleached all-purpose flour
1 teaspoon baking powder
¼ teaspoon salt
½ pound (2 sticks) unsalted butter, at room temperature
1 cup sugar
4 large eggs
1 teaspoon pure vanilla extract

Raspberry Coulis

MAKES 2 CUPS

1. BRING the raspberries, syrup, and lemon juice to a simmer in a heavy medium saucepan over low heat. Simmer, stirring occasionally, until the berries are very soft, about 10 minutes.

2. SPRINKLE the cornstarch over 2 teaspoons cold water and stir to dissolve. Pour into the simmering raspberry mixture. Cook, stirring occasionally, until the sauce thickens, about 3 minutes.

3. STRAIN through a fine-mesh wire sieve into a medium bowl; discard the seeds. Cool completely, then cover and refrigerate until ready to use. (Freeze any leftover coulis in a plastic container for up to one month.)

2 cups raspberries (about 12 ounces), rinsed
¾ cup Simple Syrup (recipe follows)
1½ tablespoons fresh lemon juice
½ tablespoon cornstarch

Simple Syrup

MAKES ABOUT 3 CUPS

2 cups sugar
2 cups water

Simple syrup is the base for a variety of dessert items, and sorbets in particular. Use it when making the Raspberry Sorbet (page 281) or the Raspberry Coulis (page 269). The syrup can be kept in an airtight container in the refrigerator for several weeks.

1. **BRING** the sugar and water to a boil in a heavy medium saucepan over high heat. Reduce the heat to medium-low. Simmer, stirring until the sugar is completely dissolved, 6 to 8 minutes. Let cool completely.

2. **TRANSFER** to an airtight container. Refrigerate until completely chilled, at least 4 hours.

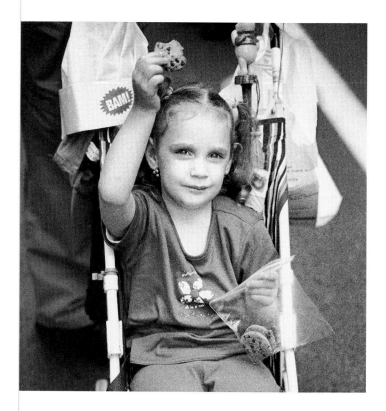

CHERRY AND WHITE CHOCOLATE BREAD PUDDING

MAKES 8 TO 10 SERVINGS

Bread pudding is one of New Orleans' most popular desserts. You and your guests will be blown away with this dried cherry and white chocolate combination.

1. **PREHEAT** the oven to 350°F. Butter a 10 × 14-inch baking dish with the room-temperature butter.

2. **WHISK** the eggs in a large bowl. Whisk in the cream, milk, brown sugar, vanilla, and cinnamon. Add the bread, chocolate, and dried cherries and stir well, then mix in the melted butter. Pour into the prepared dish.

3. **BAKE** until firm when pressed in the center, about 1 hour. Cool on a wire rack until just warm, about 20 minutes. Serve warm.

2 tablespoons (¼ stick) unsalted butter, at room temperature, plus 2 tablespoons, melted
4 large eggs
3 cups heavy cream
1 cup milk
1 cup packed light brown sugar
1 teaspoon pure vanilla extract
½ teaspoon ground cinnamon
6 cups ½-inch cubes day-old bread
6 ounces white chocolate, chopped
1 cup dried cherries

BENNE WAFER MILLE-FEUILLE WITH PINEAPPLE PASTRY CREAM AND BERRIES

MAKES 4 SERVINGS

On our "Spring Fling" show, we went wild! You're gonna go wild when you have this incredible dessert. The term *Mille-feuille* (literally, a thousand leaves in French) refers to the many-layered puff pastry used to create desserts such as Napoleons. Here benne wafers, thin, crisp cookies with sesame seeds, are used to the same effect. (*Benne* is an African word for sesame seeds; they were brought to America by slaves.) With layers of wafers, pineapple pastry cream, and a mix of berries, this is a dazzling dessert.

PASTRY CREAM

2 cups milk
¾ cup sugar
4 large egg yolks
¼ cup cornstarch
1 cup finely chopped fresh
    pineapple
1 tablespoon unsalted butter
1 teaspoon pure vanilla extract

BERRY FILLING

1 pint strawberries, rinsed,
    patted dry, hulled, and sliced
1 pint blueberries, rinsed, and
    patted dry
1 pint raspberries, rinsed and
    patted dry
½ cup sugar
2 tablespoons Grand Marnier

1. **TO** make the pastry cream, heat the milk to a boil in a heavy medium saucepan over medium heat, being careful not to scorch. Meanwhile, whisk the sugar, egg yolks, and cornstarch in a medium mixing bowl until smooth.

2. **WHISK** ½ cup of the hot milk into the egg mixture in a slow, steady stream. Then whisk the egg mixture into the saucepan of hot milk. Stir constantly over medium-low heat until the mixture thickens enough to coat the back of a spoon and reaches 170°F on an instant-read thermometer, about 5 minutes. Remove from the heat and stir in the pineapple, butter, and vanilla. Pour into a bowl.

3. **PRESS** a piece of plastic wrap directly onto the pastry cream to prevent a skin from forming. Let cool completely in the refrigerator.

4. **TO** make the berry filling, gently stir the strawberries, blueberries, raspberries, sugar, and Grand Marnier in a mixing bowl, being careful not to crush the berries. Cover and refrigerate until chilled, at least 1 hour.

5. **TO** make the wafers, in a dry medium skillet, cook the sesame seeds over medium heat, stirring often, until fragrant and golden, about 3 minutes. Immediately transfer to a plate and let cool completely.

6. **PREHEAT** the oven to 375°F. Line two baking sheets with parchment paper.

7. **COMBINE** the flour, sugar, and salt in a medium bowl. Add the butter and rub between your thumbs and fingertips until the mixture resembles coarse crumbs. Add the sesame seeds and yolks and mix to moisten. One tablespoon at a time, work in the ice water with your fingers just until the dough comes together, being careful not to overmix.

8. **ROLL** out the dough on a lightly floured work surface until ⅛ inch thick. With a 4-inch round cookie cutter or the bottom of a coffee can, cut the dough into 12 rounds. Arrange the rounds on the prepared baking sheets. Cover the wafers with another sheet of parchment paper.

9. **BAKE** until the wafers are lightly golden, about 15 minutes. Cool the wafers on the pans for a few minutes, then gently transfer the wafers to wire racks and let cool completely.

10. **WHIP** the heavy cream with the sugar in a chilled medium bowl until soft peaks form.

11. **SPREAD** 8 of the wafers with ¼ cup pastry cream each. Place 1 wafer, pastry cream side up, on each of four serving plates, and spoon ¼ cup of the fruit over each. Top each with another wafer, pastry cream side up, and spoon another ¼ cup of the fruit over each. Top each with a plain wafer, then with a generous spoonful of the whipped cream. Garnish each with a mint sprig and serve immediately.

BENNE WAFERS
½ cup sesame seeds
2 cups bleached all-purpose flour
½ cup sugar
⅛ teaspoon salt
6 tablespoons (¾ cup) unsalted butter, cut into ½-inch pieces and chilled
2 large egg yolks
3 to 4 tablespoons ice water

½ cup heavy cream
1 tablespoon sugar
4 sprigs fresh mint

BANANA BEIGNETS

MAKES 18 TO 24 BEIGNETS

Beignets—hot, deep-fried fritters of yeasty dough, are traditional breakfast fare in New Orleans, accompanied by cups of chicory coffee. I've been known to make savory beignets with crawfish, or shrimp and eggplant, but when you want a sweet treat, you'll like these. They're great for dessert or brunch. Or, hey, try them for a midnight snack when you've got a hankering for something sweet and ice cream just won't cut it. Serve these with a light dusting of confectioners' sugar. You could dip them in fresh sweetened whipped cream, or even warm chocolate sauce for something more indulgent!

2 large eggs
1 large ripe banana (about 6 ounces), sliced lengthwise in half and cut into ½-inch pieces
1½ cups bleached all-purpose flour
¾ cup milk
1 tablespoon sugar
1 teaspoon baking powder
¼ teaspoon salt
Vegetable oil for deep-frying
½ cup confectioners' sugar

1. **WHISK** the eggs in a large bowl. Add the banana, flour, milk, sugar, baking powder, and salt, and whisk well to make a smooth batter.

2. **POUR** enough oil to come halfway up the sides into a large deep pot or electric deep fryer and heat over high heat to 360°F.

3. **IN** batches, without crowding, drop heaping table-spoons of the batter into the hot oil (you can do 6 or 7 beignets at a time) and fry, turning them to brown evenly, about 2 minutes. Using a slotted spoon, transfer to paper towels to drain.

4. **SIFT** the confectioners' sugar through a sieve onto the beignets and serve warm.

SHOOFLY PIE

There are both dry-bottom and wet-bottom versions of this Pennsylvania Dutch specialty. The former is almost like a soft gingerbread in a crust, while the wet-bottom version, which we have here, is a tender molasses custard topped with crumbs. And, man, is this pie ever rich! Matter of fact, it's so sweet, I cut it with a little whipped cream or vanilla ice cream on the side. Let your sweet tooth decide how large the servings should be.

1 cup bleached all-purpose flour
3/4 cup packed light brown sugar
2 tablespoons unsalted butter
1/8 teaspoon salt
1 teaspoon baking soda
3/4 cup hot water
1 cup dark molasses
1 large egg
1/2 teaspoon pure vanilla extract
Basic Sweet Piecrust
   (page 277)
1 quart vanilla ice cream or
   2 cups sweetened, whipped
   cream for serving

1. COMBINE the flour, brown sugar, butter, and salt in a small bowl. Rub between your fingertips and thumbs until the mixture resembles coarse crumbs. Pour half of the mixture into a small bowl, and set aside for the topping.

2. DISSOLVE the baking soda in 1/4 cup of the hot water in a medium bowl. Add the molasses, egg, vanilla, and the remaining 1/2 cup hot water and whisk until smooth. Fold in the reserved crumb mixture (not the topping portion). Set aside.

3. PREHEAT the oven to 450°F.

4. ROLL out the dough on a lightly floured work surface into a 12-inch round about 1/8 inch thick. Transfer the dough to a 10-inch pie pan. Trim off any overhanging dough to make a 1/2-inch-wide overhang. Flute the edges of the dough with your fingertips. Pour the molasses filling into the pie shell. Sprinkle with the reserved crumb topping.

5. BAKE for 10 minutes. Reduce the heat to 375°F and continue baking until the filling is set, about 25 minutes. Cool on a wire rack for at least 30 minutes.

6. SERVE warm or cooled to room temperature, with a scoop of ice cream or dollop of whipped cream.

RHUBARB AND APPLE PIE WITH WALNUT CRUMB TOPPING

MAKES 8 SERVINGS

Rhubarb grew wild behind our house in Fall River. I love its bright, astringent flavor, and it makes such a great pie that I featured it on a Mother's Day show on *Emeril Live*.

Basic Sweet Piecrust (recipe follows)

2 pounds fresh rhubarb, trimmed and cut into 1-inch-thick pieces

2 pounds McIntosh apples (6 to 8 apples), cored, peeled, and each cut into 12 equal slices

1 cup granulated sugar

1 cup packed light brown sugar

¼ cup cornstarch

2 tablespoons fresh lemon juice

2 tablespoons Calvados, kirsch, or Cognac

1 cup bleached all-purpose flour

1 cup chopped walnuts

4 tablespoons (½ stick) unsalted butter, cut into ½-inch pieces and chilled

1 teaspoon ground cinnamon

Pinch of freshly grated nutmeg

1. **PREHEAT** the oven to 350°F.

2. **ROLL** out the dough on a lightly floured work surface into an 11-inch round about ⅛ inch thick. Transfer the dough to a 9-inch pie pan. Trim off any overhanging dough to make a ½-inch-wide overhang around the edge of the pan. Flute the edges of the dough with your fingertips.

3. **MIX** the rhubarb, apples, sugar, ½ cup of the brown sugar, the cornstarch, lemon juice, and Calvados in a large bowl and toss to coat the fruit evenly. Pour into the piecrust.

4. **COMBINE** the flour, walnuts, the remaining ½ cup brown sugar, the butter, cinnamon, and nutmeg in a medium bowl. Mix well with your fingertips until the mixture resembles coarse crumbs. Sprinkle evenly over the filling.

5. **BAKE** until the topping is golden brown and the juices are bubbling, 35 to 40 minutes. Cool on a wire rack for at least 15 minutes before serving.

6. **SERVE** warm or cooled to room temperature.

Basic Sweet Piecrust

1. SIFT the flour, sugar, and salt into a large bowl. Add the butter and shortening. Rub the fats between your fingertips and thumbs, or use a pastry blender, until the mixture resembles coarse crumbs. One tablespoon at a time, work in enough ice water just until the dough comes together, being careful not to overmix.

2. SHAPE into a smooth ball of dough, flatten into a disk, and wrap in plastic wrap. Refrigerate for at least 30 minutes, and up to two days.

- 1½ cups plus 2 tablespoons bleached all-purpose flour
- 1 tablespoon sugar
- ½ teaspoon salt
- 8 tablespoons (1 stick) unsalted butter, cut into ¼-inch pieces and chilled
- 2 tablespoons vegetable shortening, chilled
- 3 tablespoons ice water, or as needed

CHOCOLATE-HAZELNUT BISCOTTI

MAKES ABOUT 64 LARGE OR 96 SMALL COOKIES

Biscotti, which means twice-baked in Italian, are easy. These biscotti are sinful on their own, and when they're dipped in melted white chocolate, watch out! But if you want a kicked-up dessert, crumble the biscotti over Hazelnut Ice Cream (page 280). Once the white chocolate icing has cooled and hardened, these cookies will keep for up to 1 week in an airtight container at room temperature.

2⅔ cups bleached all-purpose flour

2 cups sugar

1 cup unsweetened cocoa powder

1½ tablespoons instant espresso powder or powdered instant coffee

1½ teaspoons baking soda

¼ teaspoon salt

1¾ cups toasted and peeled whole hazelnuts (see page 227)

⅔ cup semisweet chocolate chips

5 large eggs

1½ teaspoons pure vanilla extract

¾ pound white chocolate, finely chopped

1. **PREHEAT** the oven to 350°F. Line two large baking sheets with parchment paper.

2. **COMBINE** the flour, sugar, cocoa, espresso powder, baking soda, and salt in the bowl of an electric mixer. Mix for 30 seconds on low speed to combine. Add the hazelnuts and chocolate chips and mix well.

3. **IN** another bowl, lightly beat the eggs with the vanilla. On low speed, pour the eggs into the dry ingredients and mix just to form a soft dough.

4. **DIVIDE** the dough into 4 equal pieces. On a lightly floured work surface, roll each piece under your palms into a 14-inch cylinder about 2 inches in diameter. Transfer to the prepared baking sheets, placing 2 logs on each baking sheet, about 2 inches apart.

5. **BAKE** for about 30 minutes, until the logs are lightly browned and firm. Let cool completely on the baking sheets on wire racks. Reduce the oven temperature to 300°F.

6. **TRANSFER** one of the cooled logs to a cutting board. With a heavy sharp knife, cut the log into ¾-inch-thick slices. If sliced crosswise, each log will average 24 small cookies. If cut on an angle, each log will yield about 16 large pieces. Repeat with the remaining logs. Spread the cookies on the parchment-lined sheets.

7. BAKE the cookies for 30 minutes, turning halfway through baking, until crisp. Transfer the cookies to wire racks and cool completely.

8. PLACE the white chocolate in the top of a double boiler or metal bowl over simmering water and melt, stirring occasionally. Remove from the heat. Dip each cooled cookie halfway down into the melted chocolate, scraping off the excess chocolate against the rim of the bowl. Place the dipped cookies on a sheet of parchment or waxed paper and let cool until the chocolate sets.

HAZELNUT ICE CREAM

MAKES 1½ QUARTS

I am such a hazelnut fan that we devoted a whole nutty show to them on *Essence of Emeril*. Not only is this ice cream good on its own, it makes a really outstanding parfait. Just layer the ice cream in tall footed glasses with some favorite flavorings, like broken-up Chocolate-Hazelnut Biscotti (page 278), bits of Mississippi Mud Cake (page 262), pieces of Crunchy Pralines (page 267), chocolate sauce, and/or seasonal fresh fruit. Go ahead, just kick it up another notch!

1 cup hazelnuts
3 cups heavy cream
2 cups milk
1 vanilla bean, split lengthwise
12 large egg yolks
1 cup sugar
¼ cup hazelnut liqueur, such as Frangelico, or other nut-flavored liqueur, such as Nocello

1. **PREHEAT** the oven to 350°F.

2. **SPREAD** the hazelnuts on a baking sheet. Bake for about 10 minutes, stirring occasionally until the skins are cracked and the nuts (under the skins) are deeply golden brown. Place the nuts in a towel and rub them to remove most of the skins. Cool completely.

3. **COMBINE** the cream and 1 cup of the milk in a large heavy saucepan. Scrape the vanilla seeds into the cream mixture and add the bean and the hazelnuts. Bring to a gentle boil over medium heat.

4. **WHISK** the yolks and sugar in a medium bowl. In a slow, steady stream, whisk 1 cup of the hot cream mixture into the egg mixture. Gradually whisk the egg mixture back into the saucepan. Stir constantly over medium-low heat until the mixture thickens enough to coat the back of a spoon and reaches 170°F on an instant-read thermometer, about 5 minutes. Strain through a fine-mesh sieve into a heatproof medium bowl.

5. **DISCARD** the vanilla bean, and rinse the nuts in the strainer under cold running water; pat dry on paper towels. On a work surface, crush the nuts with a meat mallet or rolling pin, and stir into the custard. Stir in the remaining 1 cup milk and the liqueur. Cover with plastic wrap, pressing the wrap against the surface of the custard to prevent a skin from forming. Refrigerate until well chilled, at least 2 hours.

6. **POUR** the chilled custard into an ice cream machine. Churn according to the manufacturer's instructions. Pack into an airtight container and freeze until ready to serve.

RASPBERRY SORBET

You'll be surprised how easy this is to make. And if you don't want to use raspberries, make the sorbet with any berries you have on hand.

1. COMBINE the raspberries, syrup, and lemon juice into a bowl. Process, in two batches, in a food processor until smooth. Strain through a fine-mesh strainer into a medium bowl; discard the seeds. Refrigerate until well chilled, at least 2 hours.

2. POUR the purée into an ice cream machine and churn according to the manufacturer's instructions. Pack into an airtight container and freeze for at least 2 hours before serving.

3. TO serve, scoop into dessert bowls and drizzle with the raspberry coulis.

4½ cups raspberries (about 18 ounces), rinsed and drained
3 cups Simple Syrup (page 270)
3 tablespoons fresh lemon juice
Raspberry Coulis (page 269)

Michael's Provision Company

317 Lindsey Street
Fall River, MA 02720
Tel: 508/672–0982
Fax: 508/672–1307
WEBSITE:
www.michaelschourico.com
Portuguese food items, such as dried salt cod, dried fava beans, chorizo and linguiça sausages and patties

Emeril's Homebase

829 St. Charles Avenue
New Orleans, LA 70130
Tel:800/980–8474
Tel: 504/558–3940
WEBSITE: www.emerils.com
Emerilware cookware, cookbooks, specialty food products, chefware, and more

Steen's Syrup

119 North Main Street
Abbeville, LA 70510
Tel: 800/725–1654
Fax: 337/893–2478
WEBSITE: www.steensyrup.com
100% pure cane syrup, dark and light molasses

Hudson Valley Foie Gras

80 Brooks Road
Ferndale, NY 12734
Tel: 845/292–2500
Fax: 845/292–3009
WEBSITE: www.hudsonvalleyfoie gras.com
Duck products, including foie gras, fat, confit, mousse, magret, legs, and thighs

D'Artagnan

280 Wilson Avenue
Newark, NJ 07105
Tel: 800/327–8246
Fax: 973/465–1870
WEBSITE: www.dartagnan.com
Goose and duck foie gras, pâtés, sausages, smoked meats, and organic game and poultry (including venison, rabbit, quail, squab, and pheasant)

New Orleans Fish House

921 S. Dupre Street
New Orleans, LA 70125
Tel: 504/821–9700
Tel: 800/839–3474
Fax:504/821–9011
WEBSITE: www.nofh.com
Stone crabs, crawfish, alligator, and other products

Konriko Wild Pecan Rice

Conrad Rice Mill
307 Ann Street
New Iberia, LA 70560
Tel: 800/551–3245
Fax: 337/365–5806
WEBSITE: www.konriko.com

Zatarain's

82 First Street
New Orleans, LA 70053
Tel: 504/367–2950
Fax: 504/362–2004
WEBSITE: www.zatarain.com
Spices, crab and shrimp boil mixes, Creole mustard. Available at supermarkets nationwide

Emeril's Restaurants

Emeril's Restaurant
800 Tchoupitoulas Street
New Orleans, LA 70130
Tel: 504/528-9393

NOLA Restaurant
534 Rue St. Louis
New Orleans, LA 70130
Tel: 504/522-6652

Emeril's Delmonico Restaurant and Bar
1300 St. Charles Avenue
New Orleans, LA 70130
Tel: 504/525-4937

Emeril's New Orleans Fish House
3799 Las Vegas Boulevard South
Las Vegas, NV 89109
Tel: 702/891-7374

Delmonico Steakhouse
At the Venetian Resort Hotel Casino
3355 Las Vegas Boulevard South
Las Vegas, NV 89109
Tel: 702/414-3737

Emeril's Restaurant Orlando
6000 Universal Boulevard at Universal Studios City Walk
Orlando, FL 32819
Tel: 407/224-2424

Websites

Chef Emeril Lagasse
WEBSITE: www.emerils.com
The official website for everything Emeril. Here you will find listings for all his restaurants, shows, and merchandise, as well as in-depth background and insight into Emeril's culinary world, and a monthly online magazine and recipes. Bam!

All-Clad Cookware
WEBSITE: www.emerilware.com
The cookware that Chef Emeril believes in. Here you will find all the selections of Emerilware by All-Clad—from skillets to sauté pans.

B&G Foods
WEBSITE: www.bgfoods.com
If you want to kick up your kitchen a notch, look for Emeril's Original spice blends, salad dressings, marinades, hot sauces, and pasta sauces. Created by Chef Emeril and distributed by B&G Foods.

Food Network
WEBSITE: www.foodtv.com
Log on to the Food Network's site for all recipes and scheduling information for *Emeril Live* and the *Essence of Emeril* shows, and ticket information for *Emeril Live*.

HarperCollins
WEBSITE: www.harpercollins.com
This informative site offers background and chapter excerpts of all of Chef Emeril's best-selling cookbooks.

NBC Network
WEBSITE: www.nbc.com
From dinnertime to prime time: Find recipes and information on Chef Emeril's sitcom *Emeril* on the NBC website.

Index